COMMUNITY POLICING

Community
Policing
RHETORIC OR REALITY

EDITED BY

Jack R. Greene

AND

Stephen D. Mastrofski

PRAEGER

New York
Westport, Connecticut
London

Copyright Acknowledgments

The authors and the publisher gratefully acknowledge
permission to use the following copyrighted materials:

Extracts, reprinted with permission of The Free Press, a
Division of Macmillan, Inc. from *New Blue Line: Police
Innovation in Six American Cities* by Jerome H. Skolnick and
David H. Bayley. Copyright © 1986 by Jerome H. Skolnick and
David H. Bayley.

Tables 1 and 2 from *Reducing Fear of Crime in Houston and
Newark: A Summary Report* by A. M. Pate, W. G. Skogan, M. A.
Wycoff, and L. W. Sherman. Washington, D.C.: Police
Foundation, 1986.

Library of Congress Cataloging-in-Publications Data

Community policing: rhetoric or reality / edited by Jack R. Greene
  and Stephen D. Mastrofski.
    p. cm.
  Bibliography: p.
  Includes index.
  ISBN 0-275-92952-3 (alk. paper)
  ISBN 0-275-94063-2 (pbk. : alk. paper)
    1. Police—United States—Public relations. I. Greene, Jack R.
II. Mastrofski, Stephen D.
HV7936.P8C658 1988
659.2′93632′0973—dc19   88-15559

Library of Congress Catalog Card Number: 88-15559
ISBN: 0-275-92952-3
        0-275-94063-2 (pbk.)

First published in 1988
Paperback edition 1991

Praeger Publishers, One Madison Avenue, New York, NY 10010
An imprint of Greenwood Publishing Group, Inc.

Printed in the United States of America

The paper used in this book complies with the
Permanent Paper Standard issued by the National
Information Standards Organization (Z39.48-1984).

10 9 8 7 6 5 4 3

CONTENTS

PREFACE

Every several years the police, as a social and political institution, are reformed. Current trends in police reform stress a contextual role for the police, one that emphasizes greater interaction with the community toward the resolution of persistent community problems supposed to lead to crime and social disorder. This newest in a long tradition of reform has many implications for police role definitions, strategic and tactical operations, and understanding about the limits of formal and informal social control—including the institutions charged with producing social order.

Critics of past police reform efforts suggest that the police have lost their "community context," they are estranged from the people they police. The legacy of administrative police reform is said to have made the police bureaucratic, indifferent to their clientele, organized into a passive and reactive response to community disorder and crime, and encumbered by administrative rules and regulations that exclude the police and the public from the policy-making process. Furthermore, the narrow, almost singular, definition of police work as "thief taking" emphasizes those circumstances least encountered by the police themselves, often to the exclusion of other and equally important (certainly more frequently enacted) police roles.

Collectively, bureaucratic, routinized crime control policing is said to have failed. From its ashes, a communal version of policing has arisen. Cloaked in the symbols of consensus, community empowerment, and public safety, community policing programs have sprung up throughout the United States and in several other Western countries. These programs take many forms. Some apply old police techniques like foot patrol to the newer problems of community decay, most particularly in large, urban areas. Others stress an effective communication between the police and those policed in setting the agenda for police activity locally.

While many programs are currently under way, there has yet to be a systematic look at the new police strategies and tactics. Many questions remain unanswered. Is this a new form of policing, or is it "old wine in new bottles?" Is this reform substantive or rhetorical? Such questions occupy much of this book.

"Community policing" has been used to refer to a wide range of programs and activities. In a recent essay, Herman Goldstein (1987) identified several conceptual elements common to a variety of programs all bearing the name community policing. Central to these elements is the broadening of the police mission to extend traditional law enforcement and order maintenance definitions of the police role, and to include the idea that the police are integral to promoting the common welfare. The police are also to become proactive in resolving community problems according to this line of reasoning. Here the concern is to free the police from their traditional response-driven method of handling incidents or complaints, and to replace this tactic with a problem-driven and preventive approach, emphasizing the underlying causal forces associated with crime and disorder.

Linked closely to this problem focus, rank-and-file police officers are to be given wider latitude in decision making to facilitate problem identification and to generate solutions to community problems. All of this occurs in a social environment where the police and the community are encouraged to work in closer harmony, both in defining problems and solutions.

The community is viewed as an active agent in social change, and the police are, in part, responsible to activate the community in its own self-protection. Finally, justification of the police and what they do is now cast in terms of their responsiveness to the community and their contribution to "civility"—the level of social and physical disorder, fear of crime, and ultimately crime itself.

The tactics of community policing are many and varied. Common elements, according to Goldstein (1987), include (1) increased police-citizen accessibility; (2) use of problem-oriented approaches to policing; (3) aggressive and/or punitive order maintenance strategies requiring police intervention without a specific complaint; (4) increasing contact between the police and community organizations, and supporting the development of community organization in those neighborhoods where it does not exist; (5) strengthening community cohesion, including perceptions of community order and citizen willingness to "retake the streets"; and (6) encouraging and sponsoring community crime prevention activities. Elements of these programs can be found in the programs outlined in this book.

It should be emphasized that community policing means many things to many people. It is at once an ideology, an organizing framework for many police activities, and a set of individual programs. Community policing can be seen as a convergence of several police reform efforts of the past. There are elements of community relations in these programs, with their emphasis on increased harmony between the police and the community. These programs have operationally benefited from a research literature that has squarely tackled the myths of law enforcement—full versus selective enforcement, preventive patrol, rapid response, and follow-up criminal investigations.

These programs have also incorporated a concern for the workers in police organizations—the police themselves. Liberalizing influences associated with a lessening of the military bureaucracy so characteristic of police agencies have resulted in increased emphasis on police officer involvement in policy making. Giving police officers a legitimate role in problem definition, and providing solutions for community problems, is directly attached to the philosophy and practice of community policing efforts. Collectively, these strains of police reform and research have merged to provide a foundation for the community-oriented policing efforts of today.

Yet there is still a great deal to be learned in watching this reform movement. Most community policing programs are still primitive in design, implementation, and assessment. They must make many assumptions about the role of the police in a democratic society, about how police services should (and can) be delivered, and about the public's willingness to become an active partner in producing public order. The chapters presented here help to frame the major issues confronting the community policing movement, and they point out the rhetoric and reality associated with this important institutional change.

As is the case with any written document, many individuals contributed to the development and preparation of this book. We extend our appreciation to the authors who have contributed to this effort. Their front-line efforts in implementing and evaluating this, the newest of police reform, provide the opportunity to capture the richness of this concept while it is still evolving.

The College of Arts and Sciences at Temple University through Dean Lois S. Cronholm and the Department of Criminal Justice, chaired then by Dr. Alan Harland, provided the supporting intellectual and social environment for this collection. In May 1987, Temple University sponsored the International Symposium of Community Policing, to which many of the authors in this volume were invited. The symposium had as its goal to bring together many of the scholars and practitioners actively engaged in community policing efforts for the purpose of sharing information on program and evaluation development. An oftentimes spirited three-day debate about the problems, prospects, and pitfalls of community police ensued, and this collection is richer for that debate.

We would also like to acknowledge the support of Ms. Tama Mansfield-Kahn for her proofreading assistance and Ms. Karen Eckstein for her library research assistance. Ms. LaSaundra Scott typed what must have seemed like an endless manuscript, complete with several revisions. More than anything, we thank the spirit of innovation that has gripped the police in recent years.

PART I
THE CONTEXT OF COMMUNITY POLICING

The chapters in Part I help us place community policing in context. They offer varying perspectives and viewpoints that can be arrayed across at least four dimensions. First, each piece offers an explanation of the emergence of community policing. George Kelling and Mark Moore suggest that policing in the United States has advanced historically through different stages or eras, each characterized by the "organizational strategies" espoused by the ascendant reformers of the time. Since the nineteenth century, organizational strategies have evolved through three stages: political, reform, and community. Shifts from one stage to the next have been stimulated by the revealed failures of the established approach and the inability of old ways to meet the demands of a changing environment. Peter Manning interprets community policing as a major dramatic device designed to control how people think and feel about their police. It has arisen because the police and their reformers feel the need to address obvious social, cultural, and economic schisms in a heterogeneous society that no longer readily accepts a melting pot ideal. Stephen Mastrofski understands community policing as a reform that must wrestle with the same fundamental and largely insoluble problems that have always faced U.S. police: defining the police role, establishing mechanisms for effective control of officer discretion, and securing the bases of occupational legitimacy.

A second dimension addressed by these chapters is the nature of the community policing message. Each chapter addresses the rhetorical meaning of community policing and suggests what its relationship to reality might be. Kelling and Moore imply a relatively close coupling, as contemporary reformers attempt to alter program strategies to meet environmental demands. Manning and Mastrofski argue that there is or may be a considerable gulf between what is claimed and assumed by the movement's advocates and what is known or can reasonably be expected.

A third dimension revealed in these chapters is the internal coherence of community policing's framework and theory. Kelling and Moore suggest that the strategic elements of community policing cohere rather well around a number of closely related issues—that the new program elements are mutually reinforcing and offer a well-integrated approach to policing. Both Manning and Mastrofski suggest that the appeal of this coherence is deceptive, since there are a number of underlying inconsistencies in the model that are impossible or unlikely to be resolved.

Finally, the chapters can be arrayed roughly according to their optimism about community policing's prospects. All three offer—to a greater or lesser extent—positive assessments of the vitality of the rhetorical elements of the movement: Police seem to be warming to the idea. However, the chapters differ markedly in their assessment of the consequences of this trend. Kelling and Moore see it in a very positive light; community policing takes the best from the strategies of earlier eras and discards that which is bad or no longer effective. Manning, while acknowledging potential benefits to policing as an occupational and organizational enterprise, concludes that community policing strategies cannot accomplish their ostensible objectives. Mastrofski, though sharing Manning's skepticism, suggests ways in which the reform might itself be reformed to deal more realistically with the dilemmas police face.

Taken as a whole, Part I addresses major philosophical and theoretical issues about the police occupation's identity—past, present, and future. These chapters extend our understanding of where community policing might take us and how it might get us there. The contributors, all scholars with extensive field experience observing police, offer provocative studies that should stimulate debate in both the academic and law enforcement communities. The authors' differing viewpoints are testimony to the need for a continuing discussion of the fundamental principles that structure and justify police work.

1

FROM POLITICAL TO REFORM TO COMMUNITY: THE EVOLVING STRATEGY OF POLICE

GEORGE L. KELLING AND MARK H. MOORE

INTRODUCTION

Policing in the United States is changing. In what directions, how rapidly, how profoundly, how permanently, and whether this change is evolutionary or revolutionary is the source of some debate (Kelling, 1985; Klockars, 1985). Because, as Soren Kierkegaard has noted, life is lived forward but understood backward, understanding historical patterns of police is required to more fully comprehend current patterns of change. Note that we used the term "patterns" when referring both to the history and current circumstances of police. To identify patterns, we have chosen to analyze U.S. police history and its current movement using the concept of organizational strategy.[1]

STRATEGY

Our concept of strategy is one that is largely derived from the private-sector concept of corporate strategy. Corporate strategy is

the pattern of major objectives, purposes, or goals and essential policies and plans for achieving those goals ... stated in such a way as to define what business the company is in or is to be in and the kind of company it is or is to be (Chandler, 1962:13).

Note that this definition includes two key elements: the determination of long-term goals, and the adoption of courses of action and allocation of resources to obtain them.

The popularity of this concept in the private sector came about largely as a consequence of the convulsions U.S. businesses experienced during the 1960s and 1970s. During this era, rapidly changing technology, global competition, slower growth, the information explosion, deregulation, political instability, profound value changes, and other discontinuities put many companies and industries into a spin. Even companies deemed as "excellent" have suffered the consequences of such change (Peters and Waterman, 1983). The demise of People's Express airline and the current scramble of IBM to maintain its dominance in the computer field are two outstanding examples.

The world of public-sector service organizations has been no less tumultuous than that of private corporations. Many of the same events have had important consequences for public organizations: rapidly changing technology, slower economic growth, the information explosion, political instability, and profound value changes. Other changes have had their impact as well: growing disparities in income, the changing age structure of the population, gentrification of some areas of cities and continued deterioration of others, the increase in low-paying service jobs and the decrease in higher paying positions in industry and manufacturing, as well as other discontinuities.

In response to these changes, public-sector organizations have had to rethink their missions as well. During the 1950s and 1960s, police thought they were law enforcement agencies primarily fighting crime; many prison administrators believed they were in the business of rehabilitating prisoners; and, likewise, many parole agents believed they were caseworkers, akin to psychotherapists, providing therapeutic services. These conceptions have been challenged. As a consequence, some of these agencies are moving vigorously to rethink their values and missions. Some are being pushed into reconsideration of the basic mission as a result of diminishing public support or emerging private-sector competition. Others are vigorously resisting change and holding tight to their current strategy.

In such changing circumstances, the concept of corporate strategy has been important both for *organizational* analysts and agency administrators. Adapted as organizational strategy, the concept of strategy is useful for public-sector organizations to understand their historical and current strategies, as well as develop strategies for the future. Organizational strategy, similar to corporate strategy, consists of the following elements:

1. *Authorization*. Authorization, akin to capital in the private sector, refers to the sources of authority that provide the mandate and resources for public agencies to operate. Sources of authority include law, legislative intent, politics, ongoing financial support (annual appropriations), professional expertise, and tradition.

2. *Function.* Function refers to the values, missions, and goals of an organization. Values in the case of parole, for example, could include respect for the individual, civil rights, protection of the community, concern for victims, the enhancement of an individual's potentialities, protection of life, and others. Missions and goals could include crime reduction, retribution, psychological growth of clients, increased levels of education, rehabilitation, and others.

3. *Organization.* Organization refers to the structure, human resources, management processes, and culture of agencies. Agencies can be structured in a variety of ways: by function or geography, centralized or decentralized, professionally, militarily or quasi-militarily, by division, in matrixes, as quasi-holding companies, and in other ways. Human resources refers to the portfolio of skills, experiences, abilities, and capabilities an organization must have if it is to accomplish its goals. Management processes include planning, programming, rewarding and disciplining, and accounting and budgeting systems of the organization. Culture refers to the myths and beliefs of an organization, its informal patterns of communications and expected roles, personal values, attitudes and beliefs about why things happen, and how decisions are made.

4. *Demand.* Demand for an agency's services can come from a variety of sources. In the case of parole, to use that example again, it can come from prisoners, their families and friends, prisons, judges, victims, politicians, and others.

5. *Environment.* Environment refers to the pattern of external conditions that affect the organization. Most often environmental influences are technological, economic, social, and political in kind. Technology has to do with the discoveries of new means of producing products or services; economics refers to the consequences of economic trends on financial resources available to the organization, on other relevant organizations, on staff, and on clients (or the pool of potential clients). Social developments include influential forces such as civil rights, women's rights, changing patterns of work and leisure, the emergence and spread of AIDS, rising crime, changing mores, and the aging of the population. Political factors refer to election of officeholders, the relationship between levels of government, the politicization of social movements or issues (crime, AIDS, race), and other processes and issues.

6. *Tactics.* Tactics are the methodologies that organizations use to obtain their goals. (Other descriptive words are activities or outputs.) These activities can be at the level of an individual worker, combinations of workers, or units in the organization.

7. *Outcomes.* Outcomes are the results of an organization's activities, anticipated or unanticipated, desirable or undesirable.

At least three problems attend the use of this framework to analyze police strategies historically. First, in attempting to identify the changes that have taken place over time, the continuities in police history tend to be ignored. Second, police in the United States are not a homogenous group or organization; there are at least 17,000 police agencies. Characterizing dominant realities or ideologies tends to wash out this pluralism. Finally, police organizations themselves are pluralistic. In every police agency, one will find differing knowledge, values, and skills driving practice. We concede these problems. Nevertheless, we believe that dominant strategies exist; they shape how occupations and professions view themselves and present themselves to consumers, policy makers and politicians, and other occupations; and that they change over time.

THE CHANGING ORGANIZATIONAL STRATEGY OF POLICE

The strategic history of policing in the United States can be divided into three eras: political, reform, and community. The political era, so named because of the close ties between police and politics, dated from the introduction of police into municipalities during the 1840s, continued through the Progressive period, and ended during the early 1900s. The reform strategy developed in reaction to the political. It took hold during the 1930s, thrived during the 1950s and 1960s, began to erode during the late 1970s, and, arguably, gave way to the community strategy during the early and mid-1980s.

The reform strategy that dominated policing from the 1920s to the 1970s was a remarkable construction—internally consistent, rigorous, and based on the most advanced organizational and tactical thinking of the time. It created a set of symbols around which U.S. police could rally and was policing's first internally generated professional *raison d'être*. At times, this strategy was explicit and incorporated into written documents; at other times, the strategy was implicit and had to be deduced from what police managers and reformers did. Many police managers adhered to this strategy because they shared the vision of its primary architect, O. W. Wilson. Some adhered to it because for them it was cast in stone—there simply was no other way they could think about the business of policing.

STRATEGIC ERAS OF POLICING

The Political Era

Historians (Fogelson, 1977; Walker, 1977) have described the characteristics of early policing in the United States, especially the struggles between various interest groups to govern the police. Elsewhere, the authors of this chapter analyzed a portion of the history in terms of its organizational strategy (Moore and Kelling, 1983). The following discussion of elements of the police organizational strategy during the political era is an expansion of that exploratory effort.

Authorization. Early U.S. police were authorized locally by municipalities. Unlike their English counterparts, police had no central authority such as the crown providing a unifying core mandate for their existence or activities. Although responsive to law, U.S. police derived both their authorization and resources from local political leaders, often ward politicians. Their link to neighborhoods and local politicians was so tight that both Jordan (1972) and Fogelson (1977) refer to the early police as adjuncts to local political machines. The relationship was often reciprocal: political machines recruited and maintained police in office and on the beat, while police helped ward political leaders maintain their political offices by encouraging citizens to vote for certain candidates, discouraging them from voting for others, and, at times, by assisting in rigging elections.

Definition of function. Police provided a wide array of services to citizens during the political era. Certainly police departments were involved in crime prevention, control, and order maintenance, but they were public social service agencies as well. Police ran soup lines; district or precinct stations were designed to provide brief lodging for immigrant workers when they arrived in cities (Monkkonen, 1981); police assisted ward leaders in finding work for immigrants, both in police and other forms of work; and police provided a wide variety of other services.

Organizational design. Although ostensibly organized quasi-militarily, police organizations were nevertheless decentralized. Cities were divided into precincts, and precinct-level managers often, in concert with the ward leaders, ran precincts as small-scale departments—hiring, firing, managing, and assigning personnel as they deemed appropriate. In addition, decentralization combined with primitive communications and transportation gave police officers considerable discretion in handling their individual beats. At best, during the later stages of this era, officer contact with central command was maintained through the call box.

Police relationship to their environment. Police were intimately connected to the social and political world of the ward. Police officers often resided in the neighborhoods they patrolled and were of the same ethnic stock as the dominant political groups in the localities. They may not have been intimately linked to all or even a majority of citizens in a neighborhood or ward, but more often than not they were linked to the dominant local group.

Demand or market for police service. Demand for police services came primarily from two sources: Ward politicians making demands on the organization and citizens making demands directly on beat officers.

Decentralization and political authorization encouraged the former source of demand; foot patrol, lack of other means of transportation, and poor communications structured the latter. Basically, the demands for police services were received, interpreted, and responded to at the precinct and street level.

Tactics and technology. The primary tactic of police during the political era was foot patrol. Detective divisions existed, but without the prestige of current detective bureaus. Operating from a caseload of "persons" rather than offenses (Eck, 1983), detectives relied on their caseload to inform on other criminals. The "third degree" was a common means of interrogating criminals. Detectives were often especially valuable to local politicians for gathering information on individuals for political or personal rather than offense-related purposes. The technological apparatuses available to police were limited. However, with the availability of call boxes, police administrators used them for supervisory and managerial purposes; and, when early automobiles became available, police used them to transport officers from one beat to another. The new technology thereby increased the range, rather than changing the mode, of patrol officers.

Outcomes. The expected outcomes of police work included crime and riot control, maintenance of order, and relief from many of the other problems of an industrializing society (hunger and temporary homelessness, for example). Consistent with their political mandate, police emphasized maintaining citizen and political satisfaction, with police service as an important goal of police departments.

In sum, the organizational strategy of the political era of policing included the following elements:

- Authorization—politics and law
- Function—broad social services
- Organizational design—decentralize
- Relationship to environment—intimate
- Demand—decentralized, to patrol and politicians
- Tactics and technology—foot patrol
- Outcome—citizen political satisfaction

The political strategy of early U.S. policing had strengths. First, police were integrated into neighborhoods and enjoyed the support of citizens— at least the support of the dominant and political interests of an area. Second, and probably as a result of the first, the strategy provided useful services to communities. There is evidence that it helped contain disorder, especially riots; many citizens believed that police prevented crime or solved crimes when they occurred (Reppetto, 1978); police assisted immigrants in establishing themselves in communities and finding jobs; and police provided other social and emergency services.

The political strategy also had weaknesses. First, intimacy with community, closeness to political leaders, and a decentralized organizational structure with its inability to provide supervision of officers gave rise to police corruption. Officers were often required to enforce unpopular laws foisted on immigrant ethnic neighborhoods by crusading reformers (primarily of English and Dutch background) who objected to ethnic values. Because of their intimacy with the community, the officers were vulnerable to being bribed in return for non- or slack enforcement of laws. Moreover, police closeness to politicians created such forms of political corruption as patronage and police interference of elections. Even those few departments that managed to avoid serious financial or political corruption during the late nineteenth and early twentieth centuries (Boston for example) succumbed to large-scale corruption during and after Prohibition.

Second, close identification of police with neighborhoods and neighborhood norms often resulted in discrimination against strangers and others who violated those norms, especially minority, ethnic, and racial groups. Often ruling their beats with the "ends of their nightsticks" (Kelling, 1987b), police regularly targeted outsiders and strangers for rousting and "curbstone justice."

Finally, the lack of organizational control over officers resulting from both decentralization and the political nature of many appointments to police positions caused inefficiencies and disorganization. The image of "Keystone Cops"—police as clumsy bunglers—was widespread and often descriptive of realities in U.S. policing.

The Reform Era

Control over police by local politicians, conflict between urban reformers and local ward leaders over the enforcement of laws regulating the morality of urban migrants, and abuses (corruption, for example) that resulted from the intimacy between police, political leaders, and citizens produced a continuous struggle for control over police during the late nineteenth and early twentieth centuries (Walker, 1977; Fogleson, 1977). Nineteenth-century attempts by civilians to reform police organizations by applying external pressures largely failed; twentieth-century attempts at reform, originating from both internal and external forces, shaped contemporary policing as we knew it through the 1970s (Fogelson, 1977).

Although it was Oakland, California's police chief, August Vollmer, who rallied police executives around the idea of reform during the 1920s and early 1930s, it was his protégé, O. W. Wilson, who emerged as the principal architect of the reform organizational strategy. Vollmer's vision of policing was the trumpet call: police in the postflapper generation were to remind U.S. citizens and institutions of the moral vision that made the United States great and of their responsibilities to maintain that vision. Wilson, however, departed from Vollmer's vision. Wilson's efforts paralleled J. Edgar Hoover's moves to transform the corrupt and discredited Bureau of Investigation into the honest and prestigious Federal Bureau of Investigation (FBI). (For more detailed discussions of this process, see Walker, 1977; Moore and Kelling, 1983; Kelling, 1987a.)

Hoover's moves were brilliant. He centralized organizational control over and tightened supervision of agents; narrowed the FBI's functioning mainly to crimes that did not require investigation and, thereby, corrupting undercover activities; limited investigation of crimes to those that were relatively easy to solve and that brought favorable publicity to the FBI (kidnapping and bank robbery); established special task forces that concentrated on criminals of particular notoriety (John Dillinger, for example); and developed public relations programs that presented the FBI and its agents in the most favorable light. (For those of us who remember the 1940s, for example, one of the most popular radio phrases was, "The FBI in peace and war"—the introductory line in a radio program that portrayed a vigilant FBI protecting us from foreign enemies, as well as villains on the "10 Most Wanted" list, another Hoover/FBI invention.)

Struggling as they were with corruption, inequities, inefficiency, and a very bad press, municipal police reformers found Hoover's model attractive. Instructed by O. W. Wilson's texts on police administration, they began to shape an organizational strategy for urban police that was similar to the FBI's. The elements of the strategy follow.

Authorization. Reformers rejected politics as a form of authorization for policing. If anything, political involvement was *the* problem in U.S. policing. Police reformers therefore allied themselves with Progressives. They moved to end the close ties between local political leaders and police. In some states, control over police was usurped by state government. Civil service eliminated patronage and ward influences in hiring and firing policing officers. In some cities (Los Angeles and Cincinnati, for example), even the position of chief of police became a civil service position to be attained through examination. In others (such as Milwaukee), chiefs were given lifetime tenure by a police commission, to be removed from office only for cause. In yet others (Boston, for example), contracts for chief were staggered so as not to coincide with the mayor's tenure. Concern for separation of police from politics did not focus only on chiefs, however. In some cities such as Philadelphia, it became illegal for patrol officers to live in the beats they patrolled. The purpose of all these changes was to isolate police from political influences.

Law, especially criminal law, and police professionalism were posited as the sources of police authority. When police were asked why they performed as they did, the most common answer was that they enforced the law. When they chose not to enforce the law—for instance, in a riot when police isolated an area rather than arrested looters—police justification for such action was found in their claim to esoteric professional knowledge, skills, and values that uniquely qualified them to make such tactical decisions. Even in riot situations, police rejected the idea that political leaders should make tactical decisions; that was a police responsibility.

So persuasive was the argument of reformers to remove political influences from policing that police departments became one of the most autonomous public organizations in urban government (Goldstein, 1977). Under such circumstances, policing a city became a legal and technical matter to be left to the discretion of professional police executives under the guidance of law. Political influence of any kind on a police department came to be seen as a failure of police leadership and as corruption in policing.

Definition of function. Using the focus on criminal law as a basic source of police legitimacy, police moved to narrow their functioning to crime control and criminal apprehension. Police agencies became law enforcement agencies, and activities identified as "social work" became the object of derision. A common line in police circles during the 1950s and 1960s was: "If only we didn't have to do social work, we could really do something about crime." Police retreated from providing emergency services as well—ambulance and emergency medical services were transferred to medical, private, or firefighting organizations. The 1967 President's Commission on Law Enforcement and Administration of Justice ratified this orientation: heretofore, police had been conceptualized as an agency of urban government; the President's Commission reconceptualized them as part of the criminal justice system.

Organizational design. Reformers moved to centralize command and control of police activities. Although many precincts or districts remained in place, functional control of patrol and detectives was centralized. The organizational form adopted by police reformers generally resembled the scientific or classical theory of administration advocated by Frederick W. Taylor during the early twentieth century. At least two assumptions attended classical theory: Workers are inherently uninterested in work and, if left to their own devices, are prone to avoiding it; and, since workers have little or no interest in the substance of their work, the sole common interest between workers and management is found in economic incentives for workers. Thus both workers and management benefit economically when management arranges work in ways that increase workers' productivity and link productivity to economic rewards.

Two central principles followed from these assumptions: division of labor and unity of control. The former posited that if tasks can be broken into components, workers can become more skilled in the particular components and thus more efficient in carrying out the tasks. The latter posited that the workers' activities are best managed by a pyramid of control, with all authority finally resting in one central office. Using this classical theory, police leaders moved to routinize and standardize police work, especially patrol work. Police work became a form of crime fighting in which police enforced the law and arrested criminals if the opportunity to do so presented itself. Attempts were made to limit discretion in patrol work: A generation of police officers was raised with the idea that they merely enforced the law.

If special problems arose, the typical response was to create special units (e.g., vice, juvenile, drugs, tactical) rather than to assign them to patrol. The creation of these special units, under central rather than precinct command, served to further centralize command and control and weaken precinct commanders (Fogelson, 1977). Moreover, police organizations emphasized control over workers through bureaucratic means of control: supervision, limited span of control, flow of instructions downward and information upward in the organization, establishment of elaborate record-keeping systems requiring additional layers of middle managers, and coordination of activities between various production units (e.g., patrol and detectives), which also required additional middle managers.

Police relationship to their environment. Police leaders in the reform era redefined the nature of a proper relationship between police officers and both politicians and citizens. We have discussed efforts to sever police from political controls and influence. Likewise, police would be impartial law enforcers who related to citizens in professionally neutral and distant terms. No better characterization of this model can be found than television's Sergeant Friday, whose response, "Just the facts, ma'am," typified the idea: impersonal or oriented toward crime solving rather than responsive to the emotional crisis of a victim.

The professional model also shaped the police view of the role of citizens in crime control. Police redefined the citizen role during an era when there was heady confidence about the ability of professionals to manage physical and social problems. Physicians would care for health problems, dentists for dental problems, teachers for educational problems, social workers for social adjustment problems, and police for crime problems. The proper role of citizens in crime control was to be relatively passive recipients of professional crime control services. Citizens' action on their own behalf to defend themselves or their communities came to be seen as inappropriate, smacking of vigilantism. Citizens met their responsibilities when a crime occurred by calling police, deferring to police actions, and being good witnesses if called upon to give evidence. The metaphor that expressed this orientation to the community was that of the police as the "thin blue line." This metaphor connotes the existence of dangerous external threats to communities, portrays police as standing between that danger and good citizens, and implies both police heroism and loneliness.

Demand or market for police service. Learning from Hoover, police reformers vigorously set out to sell their brand of urban policing. They too performed on radio talk shows, consulted with media representatives about how to present police, engaged in public relations campaigns, and in other ways presented an image of police as crime fighters. In a sense, they began with an organizational capacity—anticrime police tactics—and intensively promoted it. This approach was more like selling than marketing. Marketing refers to the process of carefully identifying consumer needs and then developing goods and/or services that meet those needs; selling refers to having a stock of products or goods on hand irrespective of need and selling them. The reform strategy had as its starting point a set of police tactics (services) that police promulgated as much for the purpose of establishing internal control of police officers and enhancing the status of urban police as for responding to community needs or market demands.[2] The community "need" for rapid response to calls for service, for instance, was largely the consequence of police selling the service as efficacious in crime control rather than a direct demand from citizens.

Consistent with this attempt to sell particular tactics, police worked to shape and control demand for police services. Foot patrol when demanded by citizens was rejected as an outmoded, expensive frill. Social and emergency services were terminated or given to other agencies. When citizens persisted in their demands for those other services, police explained that citizens had to learn that police were not social workers and that police could deal with crime effectively only if they were not perceived of as such: social agencies did social work and police did law enforcement. Moreover, receipt of demand for police services was centralized. No longer were citizens encouraged to go to "their" neighborhood police officers or districts; all calls went to a central communications facility. When 911 systems were installed, police aggressively sold 911 and rapid response to calls for service as effective police service. If citizens continued to use district or precinct telephone numbers, some police departments disconnected those telephones and/or got new telephone numbers.[3]

Tactics and technology. The primary tactics of the reform strategy were preventive patrol by automobile and rapid response to calls for service. Foot patrol, characterized as outmoded and inefficient, was abandoned as rapidly as police administrators could obtain cars. The initial tactical reasons for putting police in cars were to increase the size of the areas police officers could patrol and to take the advantage away from criminals who began to use automobiles.

O. W. Wilson later developed the theory of preventive patrol by automobile as an anticrime tactic. He theorized that if police drove conspicuously marked cars randomly through city streets and gave special attention to certain "hazards" (bars and schools, for example), a feeling of police omnipresence would be developed. In turn, that sense of omnipresence would both deter criminals and reassure good citizens. Moreover, it was hypothesized that vigilant patrol officers moving rapidly through city streets would happen upon criminals in action and be able to apprehend them.

As telephones and radios became ubiquitous, the availability of cruising police came to be seen as even more valuable: If citizens could be encouraged to call the police via telephone as soon as problems developed, police could respond rapidly to calls and establish control over situations, identify wrongdoers, and make arrests. To this end, 911 systems and computer-aided dispatch were developed throughout the country.

In addition and consistent with classical theories of organization, a number of specialized units were developed during this era: juvenile, tactical, vice, traffic, and others. As problems developed, drugs for example, it was not unusual for police departments to create additional special units, usually operating out of central headquarters, to deal with them rather than depend upon routine (and routinized) preventive patrol. Detective units continued although with some modifications. The "person" approach ended and was replaced by the "case" approach. As with other special units, most investigative units were directed by central headquarters.

Outcomes. The primary desired outcomes of the reform strategy were crime control and criminal apprehension. To measure achievement of these outcomes, August Vollmer, working through the newly vitalized International Association of Chiefs of Police, developed and implemented a uniform system of crime classification and reporting. Later the system was taken over and administered by the FBI and became the primary standard by which police organizations measured their effectiveness—the Uniform Crime Reports. Individual officers' effectiveness in dealing with crime was judged primarily by the number of arrests they made. Other measures of police effectiveness included response time—the time it takes for a police car to arrive at the location of a call for service—and "number of passings"—the number of times a police car passes a given point on a city street. Regardless of all other indicators, however, the primary measure of police effectiveness was the crime rate as measured by the Uniform Crime Reports.

In sum, the reform organizational strategy contained the following elements:

- Authorization—law and professionalism

- Function—crime control

- Organizational design—centralized, classical

- Relationship to environment—professionally remote
- Demand—centralized
- Tactics and technology—preventive patrol and rapid response to calls for service
- Outcome—crime control

In retrospect, the reform strategy was impressive. It successfully integrated its strategic elements into a coherent paradigm that was internally consistent and logically appealing. Narrowing police functions to crime fighting made sense. If police could concentrate their efforts on prevention of crime and apprehension of criminals, it followed that they could be more effective than if they dissipated their efforts on other problems. The model of police as impartial, professional law enforcers was attractive because it minimized the discretionary excesses that developed during the political era. Preventive patrol and rapid response to calls for service were intuitively appealing tactics, as well as means to both control officers and shape and control citizen demands for service. Also, the strategy provided a comprehensive, yet simple, vision of policing around which police leaders could rally. The metaphor of the thin blue line reinforced their need to create isolated independence and autonomy in terms that were acceptable to the public. The patrol car became the symbol of policing during the 1930s and 1940s; when equipped with a radio, it was at the limits of technology. It represented mobility, power, conspicuous presence, control of officers, and professional distance from citizens.

During the late 1960s and 1970s, however, the reform strategy ran into difficulty. First, regardless of how police effectiveness in dealing with crime was measured, police failed to improve their record substantially. During the 1960s, crime began to rise. Despite large increases in the size of police departments and in expenditures for new forms of equipment (911 systems, computer-aided dispatch, etc.), police failed to meet their own or public expectations about their capacity to control crime or prevent its increase. Moreover, research conducted during the 1970s on preventive patrol and rapid response to calls for service suggested that neither was an effective crime control or apprehension tactic.

Second, fear rose rapidly during this era. The consequences of this fear were dramatic for cities. Citizens abandoned parks, public transportation, neighborhood shopping centers, churches, as well as entire neighborhoods. What puzzled police and researchers was that levels of fear and crime did not always correlate: crime levels were low in some areas, but fear was high; conversely, in other areas, levels of crime were high, but fear was low. Not until the early 1980s did researchers discover that fear is more closely correlated with disorder than with crime (Police Foundation, 1981; Skogan and Maxfield, 1981; Trojanowicz, 1987). Ironically, order maintenance was one of those functions that police had been downplaying over the years. They collected no data on it, provided no training to officers in order maintenance activities, and did not reward officers for successfully conducting order maintenance tasks.

Third, despite attempts by police departments to create equitable police allocation systems and to provide impartial policing to all citizens, many minority citizens, especially blacks during the 1960s and 1970s, did not perceive their treatment as equitable or adequate. They protested not only police mistreatment, but lack of treatment—inadequate or insufficient services—as well.

Fourth, the civil rights and antiwar movements challenged police. This challenge took several forms. The legitimacy of police was questioned: students resisted police, minorities rioted against them, and the public observing police via live television for the first time questioned their tactics. Moreover, despite police attempts to upgrade personnel through improved recruitment, training, and supervision, minorities and then women insisted that they had to be adequately represented in policing if police were to be legitimate.

Fifth, some of the myths that undergirded the reform strategy—police officers use little or no discretion and the primary activity of police is law enforcement—simply proved to be too far from reality to be sustained. Again and again research showed that use of discretion characterized policing at all levels and that law enforcement comprised but a small portion of police officers' activities (Wycoff, 1982; Goldstein, 1977).

Sixth, although the reform ideology could rally police chiefs and executives, it failed to rally line police officers. During the reform era, police executives had moved to professionalize their ranks. Line officers, however, were managed in ways that were antithetical to professionalization. Despite pious testimony from police executives that "patrol is the backbone of policing," police executives behaved in ways that were consistent with classical organizational theory: patrol officers were low status, their work was treated as if it was routinized and standardized, and petty rules governed issues such as hair length and off-duty behavior. Meanwhile, line officers received little guidance in use of discretion and were given few, if any, opportunities to make suggestions about their work. Under such circumstances, the increasing "grumpiness" of officers in many cities is not surprising, nor is the rise of militant unionism.

Seventh, police lost a significant portion of their financial support, which had been increasing or at least constant over the years, as cities found themselves in fiscal difficulties. In city after city, police departments were reduced in size. In some cities, New York City for example, financial cutbacks resulted in losses of up to one-third of departmental personnel. Some, noting that crime did not increase more rapidly or arrests decrease during the cutbacks, suggested that New York City had been overpoliced when at maximum strength. For those concerned about levels of disorder and fear in New York City, not to mention other problems, that came as a dismaying conclusion. Yet it emphasizes the erosion of confidence that citizens, politicians, and academicians had in urban police—an erosion that was translated into lack of political and financial support.

Finally, the urban police departments began to lose to their competition: private security and the community crime control movement. Despite the inherent value of these developments, the fact that businesses, industries, and private citizens began to search for alternative means of protecting their property and persons suggests a decreasing confidence in either the capability or the intent of the police to provide the services that citizens want.

In retrospect, the police reform strategy has characteristics similar to those that Snow and Miles (1978) ascribe to a defensive strategy in the private sector. Some of the characteristics of an organization with a defensive strategy are (with specific characteristics of reform policing added in parentheses): its market is stable and narrow (crime victims); its success is dependent on maintaining dominance in a narrow, chosen market (crime control); it tends to ignore developments outside its domain (isolation); it tends to establish a single core technology (patrol); new technology is used to improve its current product or service rather than to expand its product or service line (use of computers to enhance patrol); its management is centralized (command and control); promotions generally are from within (with the exception of chiefs, virtually all promotions are from within); and there is a tendency toward a functional structure with high degrees of specialization and formalization. A defensive strategy is successful for an organization when market conditions remain stable and few competitors enter the field. Such strategies are vulnerable, however, in unstable market conditions and when competitors are aggressive.

The reform strategy was a successful strategy for police during the relatively stable period of the 1940s and 1950s. Police were able to sell a relatively narrow service line and maintain dominance in the crime control market. The social changes of the 1960s and 1970s, however, created unstable conditions. Some of the more significant changes included: the civil rights movement; migration of minorities into cities; the changing age of the population (more youths and teenagers); increases in crime and fear; increased oversight of police actions by courts; and the decriminalization and deinstitutionalization movements. Whether or not the private-sector defensive strategy properly applies to police, it is clear that the reform strategy was unable to adjust to the changing social circumstances of the 1960s and 1970s.

The Community Era

All was not negative for police during the late 1970s and early 1980s; however, police were scoring victories of which they were barely cognizant. Foot patrol remained popular, and in many cities, citizen and political demands for it intensified. In New Jersey, the state funded the Safe and Clean Neighborhoods Program, which funded foot patrol in cities, often over the opposition of local chiefs of police. In Boston, foot patrol was so popular with citizens that when neighborhoods were selected for foot patrol, politicians often made the announcements, especially during election years. Flint, Michigan, became the first city in memory to return to foot patrol on a citywide basis. It proved so popular there that citizens twice voted to increase their taxes to fund foot patrol—most recently by a two-thirds majority. Political and citizen demands for foot patrol continued to expand in cities throughout the United States. Research into foot patrol suggested it was more than just politically popular, it contributed to city life: it reduced fear, increased citizen satisfaction with police, improved police attitudes toward citizens, and increased the morale and job satisfaction of police (Police Foundation, 1981; Trojanowicz, 1983).

Additionally, research conducted during the 1970s suggested that one factor could help police improve their record in dealing with crime: information. If information about crimes and criminals could be obtained from citizens by police, primarily patrol officers, and could be properly managed by police departments, investigative and other units could significantly increase their effect on crime (Pate, Bowers, and Parks, 1976; Eck, 1983).

Moreover, research into foot patrol suggested that at least part of the fear-reduction potential was linked to the order maintenance activities of foot patrol officers (Kelling, 1981; Trojanowicz, 1983; Wilson and Kelling, 1982). Subsequent work in Houston and Newark, New Jersey, indicated that tactics other than foot patrol that, like foot patrol, emphasized increasing the quantity and improving the quality of police-citizen interactions had outcomes similar to foot patrol (fear reduction, etc.) (Pate et al., 1986). Meanwhile, many other cities were developing programs, though not evaluated, similar to those in the foot patrol, Flint, and fear-reduction experiments (Skolnick and Bayley, 1986; Reiss, 1985a).

The findings of foot patrol and fear-reduction experiments, when coupled with research on the relationship between fear and disorder, created new opportunities for police to understand the increasing concerns of citizens' groups about disorder (gangs, prostitutes, etc.) and to work with citizens to do something about it. Police discovered that when they honestly asked citizens about their priorities, citizens appreciated the inquiry and also provided useful information—often about problems that beat officers might have been aware of, but about which departments had little or no official data (e.g., disorder). Moreover, given the ambiguities that surround both the definitions of disorder and the authority of police to do something about it, police learned that they had to seek authorization from local citizens to intervene in disorderly situations.

Simultaneously, Goldstein's (1979) problem-oriented approach to policing was being tested in several communities: Madison, Wisconsin; Baltimore County, Maryland; and Newport News, Virginia. Problem-oriented policing rejected the atomistic approach in which police dealt with each incident, whether citizen- or police-initiated, as if it had neither history nor future—both the incident and the police response to it were viewed as isolated events. Pierce's (1987) findings about calls for service illustrate Goldstein's point: 60 percent of the calls for service in any given year in Boston originated from 10 percent of the households calling the police. Furthermore, Goldstein and his colleagues in Madison, Newport News, and Baltimore County discovered the following: police officers enjoy operating with a holistic approach to their work; they have the capacity to do it successfully; they can work with citizens and other agencies to solve problems; and citizens seem to appreciate working with police—findings similar to those of the foot patrol experiment (in Newark and Flint) and the fear-reduction experiments (in Houston and Newark) (Pate et al., 1986).

The problem confronting police, policy makers, and academicians is that these trends and findings seem to contradict many of the tenets that dominated police thinking for a generation. Foot patrol creates new intimacy between citizens and police. Problem solving is hardly the routinized and standardized patrol modality that reformers thought was necessary to maintain control of police and limit their discretion. Indeed, use of discretion is the sine qua non of problem-solving policing. Relying on citizen endorsement of order maintenance activities to justify police action acknowledges a continued or new reliance on political authorization for police work in general. Moreover, accepting the quality of urban life as an outcome of good police service serves to emphasize a wider definition of the police function and the desired effects of police work.

These changes in policing are not merely new police tactics, however. Rather, they represent a new organizational strategy. The elements of this strategy are:

Authorization. Renewed emphasis is placed on community or political authorization for many police tasks. Certainly, law continues to be a major source of justification, but it is not sufficient to authorize police actions to maintain order, negotiate conflicts, and solve problems. Neighborhood or community support and involvement are required to accomplish those tasks. Professional bureaucratic authority, especially that which tends to isolate police and insulate them from neighborhood influences, is lessened as citizens contribute more to definitions of problems and identification of solutions. Although in some respects similar to the authorization of policing's political era, community authorization exists in a different political context. The civil service movement, the political centralization that grew out of the Progressive era, and the bureaucratization, professionalization, and unionization of police stand as counterbalances to the possible recurrence of the corrupting influences of ward politics that existed prior to the reform movement.

Definition of function. As indicated above, the definition of police function broadens in the community strategy. It includes order maintenance, conflict resolution, provision of services through problem solving as well as other activities. Crime control remains an important function with an important difference, however. The reform strategy attempted to control crime directly through preventive patrol and rapid response to calls for service. The community strategy emphasizes crime control as an indirect result of or an equal partner to the other activities.

Organizational design. Community policing operates from organizational assumptions different from those of reform policing. The idea that workers have no legitimate, substantive interest in their work is untenable when programs such as those in Flint, Houston, Los Angeles, New York City, Baltimore County, Newport News, and others are examined. Consulting with community groups, problem solving, maintaining order, and other such activities are antithetical to the reform ideal of eliminating officer discretion through routinization and standardization of police activities. Moreover, organizational decentralization is inherent in community policing: the involvement of police officers in diagnosing and responding to neighborhood and community problems necessarily pushes operational and tactical decision making to the lower levels of the organization. The creation of neighborhood police stations (storefronts, for example), reopening of precinct stations, and establishment of beat officers (in schools, churches, etc.) are concrete examples of such decentralization.

Decentralization of tactical decision making to precinct or beat level does not imply abdication of executive obligations and functions, however. Developing, articulating, and monitoring organizational strategy remains the responsibility of management. Within this strategy, operational and tactical decision making is decentralized. This implies what may at first appear to be a paradox: While the number of managerial levels may decrease, the number of managers may increase. Sergeants in a decentralized regime, for example, have managerial responsibilities that exceed those they had in a centralized organization.

At least two other elements attend these decentralizations: increased participative management and increased involvement of top police executives in planning and implementation. Chiefs have discovered that programs are easier to conceive and implement if officers themselves are involved in their development through task forces, temporary matrix-like organizational units, and other organizational innovations that tap the wisdom and experience of sergeants and patrol officers. Additionally, police executives have learned that good ideas do not translate themselves into successful programs without extensive involvement of the chief executive and his close agents in every stage of planning and implementation, a lesson learned in the private sector as well (Gardner et al., 1986).

One consequence of decentralized decision making, participative planning and management, along with executive involvement in planning, is that fewer levels of authority are required to administer police organizations. Some police organizations, including the London Metropolitan Police (Scotland Yard), have begun to reduce the number of middle-management layers, while others are contemplating doing so. Moreover, as in the private sector, as computerized information-gathering systems reach their potential in police departments, the need for middle managers whose primary function is data collection will be further reduced.

Police relationship to their environment. Community policing relies on an intimate relationship between police and citizens. This is accomplished in a variety of ways: permanent assignment of officers to beats, programs that emphasize familiarity between citizens and police (police knocking on doors, consultations, crime control meetings for police and citizens, assignment to officers of "caseloads" of households with ongoing problems, problem solving, etc.), revitalization or development of Police Athletic League programs, educational programs in schools, and other programs. Moreover, police are encouraged to respond to the feelings and fears of citizens that result from a variety of social problems or from victimization.

Further, the police are restructuring their relationship with neighborhood groups and institutions. Earlier, during the reform era, police had claimed a monopolistic responsibility for crime control in cities, communities, neighborhoods; now they recognize serious competitors in the "industry" of crime control, especially private security and the community crime control movement. Whereas in the past, police had dismissed these sources of competition or, as in the case of community crime control, had attempted to co-opt the movement for their own purposes (Kelling, 1987a), now police in many cities (Boston, New York, Houston, and Los Angeles, to name a few) are moving to structure working relationships or strategic alliances with neighborhood and community crime control groups. Although there is less evidence of attempts to develop alliances with the private security industry, a recent proposal to the National Institute of Justice envisioned an experimental alliance between the Fort Lauderdale (Florida) Police Department and the Wackenhut Corporation in which the two organizations would share responses to calls for service.

Demand or market for police services. In the community strategy, a major portion of demand is received on a decentralized basis with citizens encouraged to bring problems directly to beat officers or precinct officers. Use of 911 is discouraged, except for dire emergencies. Whether tactics include aggressive foot patrol such as in Flint or problem solving as in Newport News, the emphasis is on police officers' interacting with citizens to determine the types of problems they are confronting and to devise solutions to those problems. In contrast to reform policing with its selling orientation, this approach is more like marketing: customer preferences are sought, and satisfying customer needs and wants rather than selling a previously packaged product or service is emphasized. In the case of police, they gather information about citizens' wants, diagnose the nature of the problem, devise possible solutions, and then determine which segments of the community they can best serve and which can be best served by other agencies and institutions that provide services, including crime control.

Additionally, many cities are involved in the development of demarketing programs (Compton and Lamb, 1986). The most noteworthy example of demarketing is in the area of rapid response to calls for service. Whether through the development of alternatives to calls for service, educational programs designed to discourage citizens from using the 911 system, or, as in a few cities, simply not responding to many calls for service, police actively attempt to demarket a program that had been actively sold earlier. Often demarketing 911 is thought of as a negative process, but it need not be so. It is an attempt by police to change social, political, and fiscal circumstances to bring consumers' wants in line with police resources and to accumulate evidence about the value of particular police tactics.

Tactics and technology. Community policing tactics include foot patrol, problem solving, information gathering, victim counseling and services, community organizing and consultation, education, walk and ride, and knock-on-door programs, as well as regular patrol, specialized forms of patrol, and rapid response to emergency calls for service. Emphasis is placed on information sharing between patrol and detectives to increase the possibility of crime solution and clearance.

Outcomes. The measures of success in the community strategy are broad: quality of life in neighborhoods, problem solutions, reduction of fear, increased order, citizen satisfaction with police services, as well as crime control. In sum, the elements of the community strategy include:

- Authorization—community support (political), law, professionalism
- Function—broad, provision of service
- Organizational design—decentralized, task forces, matrices

- Relationship to environment—intimate
- Demand—decentralized
- Tactics and technology—foot patrol, problem solving, etc.
- Outcomes—quality of life and citizen satisfaction

CONCLUSION

We have argued that there were two stages of policing in the past, political and reform, and that we are now moving into a third, the community era. To carefully examine the dimensions of policing during each of these eras, we have used the concept of organizational strategy. We believe that this concept can be used not only to describe the different styles of policing in the past and the present, but also to sharpen the understanding of police policy makers of the future.

For example, the concept helps explain policing's perplexing experience with team policing during the 1960s and 1970s. Despite the popularity of team policing with officers involved in it and with citizens, which was often believed to be effective, it generally did not remain in police departments for very long. It was usually planned and implemented with enthusiasm and maintained for several years. Then, with little fanfare, it would vanish—with everyone associated with it saying regretfully that for some reason it just did not work as a police tactic. However, a close examination of team policing reveals that it was a strategy that innovators mistakenly approached as a tactic. It had implications for authorization (police turned to neighborhoods for support), organizational design (tactical decisions were made at lower levels of the organization), definition of function (police broadened their service role), relationship to environment (permanent team members responded to the needs of small geographical areas), demand (wants and needs came to team members directly from citizens), tactics (consultation with citizens, etc.), and outcomes (citizen satisfaction, etc.). What becomes clear, though, is that team policing was a competing strategy with different assumptions about every element of police business. It was no wonder that it expired under such circumstances. Team and reform policing were strategically incompatible—one did not fit into the other. A police department could have a small team policing unit or conduct a team policing experiment, but business as usual was reform policing.

Likewise, although foot patrol symbolizes the new strategy for many citizens, it is a mistake to equate the two. Foot patrol is a tactic, a way of delivering police services. In Flint, its inauguration has been accompanied by implementation of most of the elements of a community strategy that has become business as usual. In most places, foot patrol is not accompanied by the other elements. It is outside the mainstream of "real" policing and often provided only as a sop to citizens and politicians who are demanding the development of different policing styles. This certainly was the case in New Jersey when foot patrol was evaluated by the Police Foundation (1981). Another example is in Milwaukee where two police budgets are passed: the first is the police budget, the second, a supplementary budget for modest levels of foot patrol. In both cases, foot patrol is outside the mainstream of police activities and conducted primarily as a result of external pressures placed on departments.

It is also a mistake to equate problem solving or increased order maintenance activities with the new strategy. Both are tactics. They can be implemented either as part of a new organizational strategy, as foot patrol was in Flint, or as an "add-on," as foot patrol was in most of the cities in New Jersey. Drawing a distinction between organizational add-ons and a change in strategy is not an academic quibble; it gets to the heart of the current situation in policing. We are arguing that policing is in a period of transition from a reform strategy to what we call a community strategy. The change involves more than making tactical or organizational adjustments and accommodations; just as policing went through a change in its basic business when it moved from the political to the reform strategy, it is now going through a similar change. If elements of the emerging organizational strategy and the policing institutional strategy are identified, and the policing institution is guided through the change rather than left blindly thrashing about, we expect that the public will be better served, policy makers and police administrators more effective, and the profession of policing revitalized.

A final point: The classical theory of organization that continues to dominate police administration in most U.S. cities is alien to most of the elements of the new strategy. The new strategy will not accommodate to the classical theory: The latter denies too much of the real nature of police work, promulgates unsustainable myths about the nature and quality of police supervision, and creates too much cynicism in officers attempting to do creative problem solving. Its assumptions about workers are simply wrong. Organizational theory has developed well beyond the stage where it was during the early 1900s, and policing does have organizational options that are consistent with the newly developing organizational strategy.

Arguably, policing that was moribund during the 1970s is beginning a resurgence. It is overthrowing a strategy that was remarkable in its time, but that could not adjust to the changes of recent decades. Risks attend the new strategy and its implementation. The risks, however, for the community and the profession of policing are not as great as attempting to maintain a strategy that failed on its own terms during the 1960s and 1970s.

NOTES

1. As will be clear in this chapter, we will be using the term *organizational strategy* to refer to the three police strategies that have dominated police thinking and actions throughout this country. Although it might be more appropriate to refer to this intercity strategy as an industrial, or perhaps "institutional," strategy, for the sake of consistency we will refer to it as an organizational strategy.

2. For a detailed discussion of the differences between selling and marketing public-sector services, see Compton and Lamb (1986).

3. Commissioner Francis "Mickey" Roache of Boston has said that when the 911 system was instituted there, citizens in neighborhoods persisted in calling "their" police—the district station. To circumvent this preference, district telephone numbers were changed so that citizens would be inconvenienced if they dialed the old number.

2

COMMUNITY POLICING AS A DRAMA OF CONTROL

PETER K. MANNING

INTRODUCTION

The image of community policing is a dramatic one. This rich and evocative imagery sets the police in context, defining them as an essential part of a well-integrated communal whole. In the past, police in the United States have distanced themselves from communities by an emphasis upon rational crime fighting and "professionalism," and by maintaining an aloof attitude to problems of local communities that were not, strictly speaking, matters of crime (Manning, 1977). As Fogelson (1977) has noted, this positioning was in part an attempt to create an apolitical force that might better withstand local pressures for corruption, and in part an attempt by senior members of the occupation to arrogate greater respect and deference to the occupation and its practitioners. With the appearance of the work of August Vollmer and O. W. Wilson in the late 1930s scientifically based crime fighting and administration became thematic of modern professional policing (see Stead, 1977 for a review of this transformation).

Although there is no perceptible diminution of these themes in modern policing, the rise of large minority populations in urban areas and their exclusion from many opportunities changed the problems of urban social integration and crime into the more serious issue of politically managing a rising underclass demanding wider access to all forms of community service. Meanwhile, policing styles changed little, and minority pop-

This chapter is drawn from remarks prepared for the International Conference on Community Policing, Temple University, Philadelphia, May 11-13, 1987.

ulations continued to be policed closely with resultant high rates of arrest. Urban police could less easily segregate audiences and appeal to majority sentiments with a crime control strategy, while seeking to appeal to minority and lower class groups with a service strategy. Although identification with the police for many groups reproduces the response that identification with a community can produce, this became increasingly problematic. Police could expect fewer people to benefit from their association with symbols of community integration and appeals to commitment to the moral order. Public support of the police was more and more patterned by race, class, and age. Recent events, especially the riots of the 1960s and the growing number of large cities with black politicians in positions of authority, reduced the viability of conventional police strategies. Urban diversity is now sought and politically acceptable.

Policing, one of the most traditional of modern secular occupations, began to change in subtle ways that were not fully understood. Police experts, prior to the publication in 1974 of the Kansas City Patrol Study (Kelling, Dieckman, and Brown, 1974), did not question visible patrol as the primary basis for community service and protection. Patrol is being questioned, and innovations in directed patrol, computer-assisted dispatching, differential response strategies, and problem-oriented policing are discussed and used in a few departments.

While community identification and the symbolic authority of the police and other U.S. institutions is declining, a new ideological theme has been emerging in police rhetoric in the last five to ten years: community policing. Rather than being a new strategy that replaces the crime control professionalism strategy that produced social distance, it is a contrapuntal theme: harmony for the old melody. It now seeks control of the public by a reduction in social distance, a merging of communal and police interests, and a service and crime control isomorphism. Clearly, as in the past, the symbols created, organized, and displayed by police are ways of shaping thinking, focusing attention, and defining the meaning of situations. The community policing strategy, which is both a rhetoric and an operational strategy taking many tactical forms, is a new tool in the drama of control. Perhaps a brief outline of the concept, the drama of control, might be worthwhile at this point.

DRAMA OF CONTROL

When using the term, "the drama of control," one refers to the selective display of symbols that serve to draw the bounds of the permissible, the possible, and the deviant (see Burke, 1962; Goffman, 1959; Gusfield, 1981). Symbols organize experience; they serve dramaturgical ends. In arguing that symbols serve the dramaturgical purposes of the police, it is claimed that by their displays of symbols such as the flag; slogans invoking duty, honor, and service; and the tools of authority and violence in the form of guns, nightsticks, and ammunition, the police indicate their connection with social order. Insofar as the police become a part of the on-going sense of community life and evoke that sense of mutual shared fate with community members to strengthen and make vibrant their position in the community, the police will maintain power and authority. The continued deference of citizens to police authority in the absence of specific demands, commands, or laws designed to produce compliance or punish its absence is the source of police power. The aim of the selective display of symbols, what can be considered a drama, is to maintain the appearance of control. The police are at best able to sustain aspects of social integration, for the informal and traditional sources of social control are determinants of patterns of social integration (Black, 1976). Nevertheless, symbolic sources of power are essential to agencies of formal social control such as the police, as they claim to act neutrally as third parties on behalf of the state. The power and legitimacy of the police are integral to their survival as an organization, and thus they stand ready to adapt new tools of persuasion as weapons when required (Selznick, 1952).

The rhetoric of community policing, a new appeal to the community and an additional basis for claimed legitimacy, whatever else it might be, is a tool for shaping public opinion. Since public opinion is divided on the approval of police practices, many unanticipated and negative consequences result from the appeal to audiences on different grounds and the use of complementary strategies of community control. It is important to ask what role community policing plays in the drama of control as well as the claims that have been made for it.

In order to examine the concept of community policing, one has to appreciate initially that the concept is loosely associated with a series of ideological assumptions. These assumptions link the police to the community and the community to the police in the minds of police administrators. Police administrators have long been wed to the notion of a rational-bureaucratic policing that would permit both greater control over discretion and new sources of internal control, evaluation, supervision, and promotion. They espouse the idea of community policing. They are inclined to justify the idea with reference to assumptions about the needs of the community rather than administrative needs. Those posited assumptions about community needs are not written, found in police rules and regulations, or implied by the operational objectives attached to programs. They are, like social life itself, rather unclear, unfolding, indeterminate, and subject to redefinition. Nevertheless, such ideas are quite powerful in shaping police community programs.

Several key assumptions lie behind the community policing facade. Some of these assumptions have been previously outlined (Manning, 1984:212-213), and are elaborated below.[1] It should be noted that these assumptions spring from the ameliorative drives and excesses associated with the community police movement. They are rather factious and dubious in empirical validity. They are summarized rather loosely in the following paragraphs.

One of the key notions is the assumption that the public (undefined) yearns for order and that the police should and will quench this nostalgic thirst by means of community policing. This thirst is further characterized by a set of emotive-cognitive attitudes and beliefs that surround the core idea. The concept of order in some sense implies a crime-free environment, although several urban ethnographies have described the extent to which many urban areas are crime-dependent, and that order is in fact integrally related to criminal activities (see Suttles, 1968; Horowitz, 1984). This imagined order is seen as created or at least facilitated by police actions with, for, and by communities (also undefined). The envisioned community police are efficient, courteous, and accessible, and combine, within current budget limitations, both specialist and generalist functions. The crime control theme of policing in the United States remains; community policing enacts the ever viable continuing fantasy that seeks a form of policing with the above elements that is capable of controlling urban crime.

Police administrators and politicians also entertain, perhaps necessarily, assumptions about the nature of public demand, and the public needs to which they are responding. Some of these were previously noted (Manning, 1984), and they serve as a tacit justification or rationale for "selling the community police package." These include the notion that the public is currently dissatisfied with present police practices, and that previous police approaches are seen as failed or have been demonstrated to have failed. Yet the core function of the police patrol is used to label the new solution; community policing and its central idea of foot patrol. It is still assumed that there is a public consensus about what is desirable and good in society and that notions like "order" and "disorder" share agreed upon referents.

A further set of assumptions bear on the role of the police. The presumed decline or erosion of the binding power of informal bases of social control in communities can be restored by police action to renew and reinforce these eroded patterns. The role of the police is central to the renewal of the quality of urban life, and, therefore, people wish to see and be in routine personal contact with police officers in their neighborhoods and places of business. The police are responsible for defining, shaping, and pursuing community good, order, and quality of life. The more police are seen, the more satisfaction there is with policing. Evidence of the success can be adduced from aggregated public opinion data, which in turn provide a valid picture of the social organization of a community. Community policing best meets the above needs, or responds to these posited limits or failures of previous approaches. Oddly enough, the basic organizational tenets are unchanged; the organizational context of policing remains, adding credence to the claim that community policing is cosmetic and dramaturgical in nature. Let us now briefly examine the organizational contexts of policing.

ORGANIZATIONAL CONTEXTS

Two distinct types of policing are envisioned by the several publics in question, police and police researchers. These two types deserve some discussion because each is a dramaturgical "face" or aspect of the selective police display of symbols and meanings. They retain life in part because police research has often uncritically amplified elements of such faces and contributed to their epistemological status as social realities. They remain in tension within police organizations. Both are ideal types and do not exist empirically. They are conceptual fictions used to explain aspects of police behavior and structure. Using such types highlights the need for research using the ideal types to focus inquiries. There is much to be discovered yet about the types and kinds of policing practices in the urban United States, and much of this work should be historical, if not historical and comparative-cross-cultural. Exploration of organizational types, as well as studies of strategies and tactics across organizations, should be attempted.[2]

The first type is the *bureaucratic type* characterized by invisible, indirectly available, impersonal, specialist officers. They are focused on crime as a legal infraction and are disinterested in "community work" as not truly "police work." Bureaucratic police are hierarchically and strategically organized to produce a rational and appropriate response to the scale, severity, and potential for development of a given problem. They are centrally commanded and owe allegiance to the commander and carry out orders that originate above. Although dispersed ecologically, they are allocated and directed from a central communications center that stands as a surrogate for the orders of the chief. Certain tensions exist as a result and are resolved by working agreements that generate apparent consensus and the commonsense reality of policing (see Manning, 1977; Jermeir and Berkes, 1979).

The second type serves as something of a contrast conception to the first crime fighting rationally administered type. It contains an implicit critique of the rational-bureaucratic model of policing because it claims to be a solution to problems of police morale and divided internal efforts as well as better suited to controlling and serving communities. It might be called a democratic or *community policing type*. The community policing type is peopled by visible, available, and personal officers. The officers, often located in a neighborhood school, storefront, or ministation when not out serving the public on foot, represent a form of dedifferentiated social control. They are members of the community and are expected to act as moralists-in-residence. The officer represents a kind of symbol for the community and stands in contrast to the stereotypic crime-focused specialist. The organization serves general community needs. It is focused on disorder of a miscellaneous character and upon the quality of life. There are intimations that such a force will also be more democratic and concerned with the quality of the officers' lives. It will increase morale and loyalty to the organization and its mission. The community will provide the hypothecated focus and source of information, reward, and satisfaction. Community policing models will provide a solution to integrated crime fighting as well as the maintenance of community well-being.

These types of policing represent the divided or paradoxical nature of police claims. The police strive to increase morale and bureaucratic administration while better serving the community, yet they have quite different conceptions of the nature of the police mandate and of police function. There are similarities lying beneath the surface. In many respects, the community model relies on patrol as does the bureaucratic model. It is the functional difference and the focus of patrol that is emphasized. The officer is on foot rather than in a vehicle, and is guided and directed by programmatic interests toward certain tasks and duties. Thus both types address the unsolved question of how to guide and constrain discretion in patrol and to increase the degree of administrative guidance of patrol officers' activities. The relatively unchanged nature of the underlying paradigm of policing and an organizational form that is essentially unchanged (the rational-bureaucratic model) suggest that any effects of the community policing package would be revealed in the impact(s) it might have on the community. This was examined by experiments done in the early 1980s by the Police Foundation in Newark (1981).

Unfortunately, the evidence available to authors of early critical reviews of studies of community policing (see Chapters 3, 11, and 13 in this volume by Mastrofski, Greene and Taylor, and Klockars, respectively) was limited. Later it was possible to consider the raw data and full technical reports. Untested and unproved assumptions were made about the impact and consequences of community policing programs. The assumptions listed above and the ideologies invoked to rationalize community policing programs (however defined, see Manning, 1984:207-211) were tacit and unexplicated. Furthermore, the links between the assumptions, ideologies, and programs, operational tactics, and strategies were even more opaque. Evidence bearing directly upon assumptions, promised outcomes, or programs was uneven and difficult to interpret. The existing evidence is not convincing and to a rather surprising degree supports neither the assumptions made about the desires and needs of the public nor the posited effects of the policing programs. Since late 1981 when evaluations of community policing programs were beginning to appear, additional research and evaluations have been published.

Some of the most telling problems resulted in early evaluations as well as in later works because key concepts are neither theoretically deduced or derived nor operationally defined. Five key concepts are briefly reviewed: community, authority, training, fear of crime, and definitions of success. Let us review these conceptual matters.

CONCEPTUAL DISARRAY

The history of the concept on *community* in sociology suggests that it has been a gloss for the notions of integration and moral solidarity. Although sociologists have valiantly sought to define community operationally or empirically, it remains well-embedded in commonsensical ideas that make it a symbol for vast, undifferentiated, and vague notions. "Community" represents a sense of integration that people wish, hope, and envision as being a central part of their collective lives. The concept is used as if it had a clear and generally accepted meaning and that police somehow both stand for its presence and its absence (but potential hoped-for arrival). The most important and telling research suggests that the equation of safety with police presence and a public wish for visible police is not sustained (see Greene and Taylor, Chapter 11 in this volume). Furthermore, the class, race, and neighborhood context of such ideas as order, fear, good policing, and the like, previously shown by the work of Ostrom and associates (1973), is overlooked in generalizations about the merits of community policing. The resultant picture is not impressive for advocates of "policing by consent" as it is called in England.[3]

Questions concerning the sources and consequences of police authority are raised by the rationales offered for community policing. There are at least two quite different *models of authority* within the police, and community policing serves to illustrate the resulting tension. Authority can be based upon an office, the domains of which are spatial and temporal. This is the traditional authority of the patrol officer. A second form of authority is expert-based and inheres in specialist groups and units such as juvenile bureau, detective division, and tactical squads (see Gouldner, 1954). These two forms of bureaucratic authority conflict in many organizations. The result of this tension is that patrol and specialized units cooperate when necessary to maintain autonomy and control. Community policing programs do not fit either of these forms of authority, for they derive theirs from "the community" and seek their legitimation in community satisfaction. This makes the community police officer something like the "quack" within the medical profession—a person who is somewhat overly sensitive to the assessments and opinions of the client (Hughes, 1958). There is an irony here, since as long as the police exercise authority and violence in the name of the state, they will be feared and loathed by some segments of the community and will represent this violence potential to all segments of the community. The fact is, police will exercise violence and periodically will be unpopular, the target of protest, and viewed ambivalently. Traditionally, of course, since the introduction of the police in London in 1829, the public has had little use for the police unless they are in trouble (Reith, 1938; Miller, 1977). Police presence is not reassuring unless one wants reassurance. Public attitudes to police remain ambivalent, and doubtlessly will continued to do so, given their powers and potential. It is not surprising that the ambivalence of police to public admiration and respect and the reduced social distance that results is reflected in officers' evaluations of foot patrol as an example of community policing (see Trojanowicz and Banas, 1985a,b).

The issue of *training* of community police officers has been almost completely overlooked (however, see Trojanowicz and Belknap, 1986). The actual duties and obligations of community patrol officers, with the exception of the Flint research, is not specified. What do these people do for the hours they are meant to be "patrolling?" There is little mention in evaluation reports of such basic matters as training, rewards, motivation, promotion opportunities, and the like. Unless these basic organizational matters are studied and structural changes made to reflect these realities, the ideational nature of community policing will remain.

One of the most vexing issues is what is the role of *fear of crime* in a community? Does increased fear tighten social integration, polish the norms, and renew social values? Or is fear an erosive force that depletes a community's moral reserve (see Trojanowicz, 1987)? Since it is defined as an individual property rather than a property of a community, it is difficult to assess the importance of reported data on the reduction in fear in Houston, for example. Since it is assumed to be a negative force and the concept itself is not articulated with social relations, generally the sociological question of the functions of fear cannot be answered. In large, it would appear that the old and the most frightened are those with the least contact with crime and violence. The role of the media in creating and amplifying fear requires further investigation.

What is to be defined and measured as an indication of *success* in the community policing field? Since the ideas and assumptions noted above are largely myths about an imagined and idealized urban life, urban policing, and informal social control, they are difficult to define operationally and to evaluate systematically. The police on the whole use the ideas as a means to promote their programs. They are political statements, ideologies. Ideologies are formalizations, in verbal or written form, of political programs that are nevertheless unexplicated. Thus, to urge that a community be crime-free, or that the public is dissatisfied with current practices, does not provide an alternative program; it simply states a justification for the current state of affairs or new programs (e.g., community policing). Or, to put it yet another way, community policing is a solution in search of a problem.

The community police/foot patrol/involvement ideology in its various programmatic forms and guises has not proven a more effective, less costly source of increasing community satisfaction. As previously argued, the ideology argues for increased crime control as well as community satisfaction. Both are to be achieved simultaneously and at a lower cost than previous programs. The program possesses the advantage of a dual legitimation in cost-saving and in crime control. These rhetorics that link programs and ideologies are an important aspect of police dramaturgical action. The research has not shown this to be the case.

RECENT DEVELOPMENTS

The strategic aims of community policing have been stated recently by Kelling (1987a), by Wilson (in the context of the Houston/Newark experiments, 1986), and by Trojanowicz et al. (1986) in a series of publications summarizing a three-year evaluation of community policing in Flint, Michigan. Trojanowicz also draws upon some anecdotal evidence from New York City and Boston. Kelling, in summary remarks written for the Mott Foundation's *Annual Report* (1987a: 15-16) about its programs, claims: "We already know how to reduce fear of crime, we know how to increase citizen participation and we know what citizens want." He further asserts, rather flatly, that the aims of community policing are to increase the quality and quantity of police-citizen contact as well as to improve mechanisms for citizen input. This "input" is to be used to develop plans to address identified problems. Community policing expands the abilities of communities to develop self-defense capacities and serves to decentralize police decision making. Kelling is also concerned about enhancing the role and rewards of the community officer. Some important and yet modest qualifications have been introduced (see Mott, 1987a; Trojanowicz, 1987; Wilson and Williams in Pate et al., 1985). These strategic aims, it is perhaps worthwhile to note, are restatements at a lower level of generality of the broader ideological assumptions and claims found in previous reviews of research claims. They focus on what people are presumed to want or *need:*

1. People desire more information, in particular, about their own cases, wherever the case may be located in the criminal justice system, about victimization in their own "community," and about the quality of life within their community.
2. People view dirt and disorder (undefined) as "signs of crime." Removing or altering these will decrease perceptions of fear.

There are some claims made about the *consequences of police activities:*

1. Police activities in the community (various programs are included in this generalization) increase police job satisfaction.
2. Police actions—positive, proactive, or initiatory—in the community promote community integration and satisfaction.
3. Community policing reduces posited psychological distance between the police and the public.
4. Community policing provides reassurance to citizens.
5. Increased visibility of foot officers increases citizen satisfaction.
6. Increased access to police and "personal" contact with police increases citizen satisfaction.
7. The police foot officer is a surrogate for the community at large, functioning as communal eyes and ears, and acting as a moral and political force on behalf of the community.
8. Community policing reduces the fear of crime.
9. Community policing reduces physical disorder (dirt, abandoned cars, etc.)
10. Community policing increases the security of target groups (the aged, women and children).

Claims are also made about the *internal effects* of community policing on the police and police organization:

1. Community policing increases the psychological involvement of officers in the community.
2. Community policing officers develop new skills and roles; for example, they serve as mediators of disputes, as well as being channels through which citizens can contact schools, local social services, and government.
3. Community policing reduces demand upon police time as indicated by changes in the number of calls made to the police.
4. Community policing facilitates police information-gathering.

There are a series of stated *goals* as well as assumptions about the nature and impact of policing on communities:

1. Community policing programs aim to increase citizens' perception of their personal safety.
2. Community policing programs aim to decrease the amount of actual or perceived criminal activity.

3. Community policing programs aim to create community awareness of crime problems, and methods of increasing law enforcement's ability to deal with actual or potential criminal activity effectively.

4. Community policing seeks to develop citizen volunteer actions aimed at various target crimes in support of and under the direction of the police department.

5. Community policing aims to eliminate citizen apathy about reporting crimes to the police.

SOME QUERIES

Within the space limitations of this chapter and given the reviews found elsewhere in this volume, each of these points cannot be carefully assessed. Some queries do arise given this overview of claims. The assumptions of community policing are general and entail *posited*, unmeasured, or assessed community "needs," requirements, or wants.

When data gathered on these assumptions are analyzed, the findings are rather ambiguous. The first problem is that the community contexts within which such programs are mounted is sociologically diverse, the scale and size vary widely. Theory derived from Durkheim (1933) would suggest that the degree of social integration of these communities varies with size. Size in turn is related to community needs. Programs have been organized in cities ranging from 125,000 with declining population, parts or most of Boston, and in a few precincts in New York City. Major coordinated programs have been launched and evaluated in Newark, New Jersey, and Houston, Texas, by the Police Foundation, and in Flint by Michigan State University's School of Criminal Justice with support from the Mott Foundation.

The second problem is that major evaluations, themselves presented in very widely diverse fashion in publications, are scarce (see Weatheritt, in Weatheritt, forthcoming; Trojanowicz, n.d.). With the exception of the well-designed and -crafted Flint studies, none of these studies is time-based such that the "halo effect" argument could be rejected when positive findings are reported. Conversely, the Flint studies do reveal drops in virtually all the measures of satisfaction from 1981 to 1985 (the period of the study). Reported crime did decrease 8.7 percent in 1979-81, the first year of the study, and calls to the police from the areas patrolled decreased by about 43 percent.

In almost every case, the findings are ambiguous as to their meaning in part because of the complexity of the relationships measured and/or investigated and in part because the "independent" or treatment variable, "community policing," varies from city to city and program to program. The perspective within which they are viewed shifts constantly in the reports, in the press releases, and in the police public statements. Two examples may suffice. Assertions of the efficacy and worth of community policing continue to be made in spite of empirically measured decline in level of satisfaction, reported visibility, effectiveness, and preference for motorized as opposed to foot patrol officers (Trojanowicz et al., 1986). The programs called community policing or fear reduction are very diverse, including some seven major programs and several subprograms in Houston and Newark. Kelling (1984) claims that increased community capacity to look after itself is a general aim of community policing in Boston. When in the Newark studies people said they had taken more steps to arm themselves, this was viewed as a positive effect or experimental effect of the independent variable that was a community policing scheme (Police Foundation, 1981). In what sense, one might ask, is an armed public a sign of police trust, confidence, and improved social integration? Does this suggest anything about the trust in the police and the promise that police will reduce the fear of crime?

In both the Kelling report (1984) on changes in the Boston Police Department and the various Trojanowicz studies, reduced calls to the police were cited as evidence of the effectiveness of police. In the Flint Study, Trojanowicz infers that this takes place because the foot officers are now able to handle matters themselves rather than waiting merely to respond to a situation. Kelling notes that demand as measured by telephone calls to the central number fell off sharply in Boston, and that crime clearance rates also increased in Boston during that same period. It is claimed that since most calls to the police are service and order calls, reducing the level of such calls should (1) permit police more opportunities for engaging in real crime work; (2) reduce work load within the communications center, freeing officers for other duties; and (3) increase the citizens tendency to contact officers directly, thus serving the other general aim of reducing impersonal contact between the police and the public. Research carried out in a very large Midwestern urban police department and an English provincial constabulary suggests some points relevant to these two arguments (Manning, forthcoming).

The number of calls and demand in general are related to size and number of telephones per capita in the city. Demand is further shaped by social factors and political and policy decisions within the police. Social factors that affect decisions that lie beyond the control of the police, such as when and whom to call about a problem, vary from neighborhood to neighborhood and from community to community (Spelman and Brown, 1981). The social organization of call processing is critically important in organizing a police response to calls. One might take, for example, decisions about how calls defined as rape or family disturbance calls will be processed. The degree of centralization of dispatch, whether calls are received and processed at one or several centers, and whether they are then sent to secondary distribution points such as precincts rather than directly to officers, significantly alters the capacity of the central police administration to control the allocation and response to calls. The greater the differentiation of the organization of call response, the lower the control from the center of the nature, level, and quality of the police response.

Second, work load figures are easily manipulated by departmental procedures and definitions. What counts as a call, for example? One should bear in mind that most calls are internal communication between segments of the police organization and account for as much as 50 percent of the phone traffic. Many calls—such as wrong numbers terminated, or incomplete calls where caller or operator hangs up, or calls that merely request information—do not require police action beyond an answer. As Thompson (1967) would suggest, slack resources are maintained to respond to high fluctuations in demand and diversity in the nature of the calls. More importantly, what is processed is in part a function of the technology of call-processing and monitoring, and in part based on habits, practices, and interpretations of operators. Call classification systems vary widely and there is no assurance of their internal validity or reliability. Such simple matters as the number of operators on duty during given shifts will pattern inputs as well as outputs. Policies of the department and rules governing operators' behavior can reduce or increase the number of calls received, processed, and responded to by officers. Studies of calls to the police have examined only the *input* of calls at the operator level. They do not measure or note the calls lost, terminated, or closed at the operator level. Furthermore, officers can affect calls by instructing citizens not to call the central number, but to call them at a local station, at home, or at some other location where they can collect their messages. Officers can also control output by controlling the number of calls that they intend to accept and do accept in a given turn of duty. Fieldwork in Midwest City suggests that officers work to a set number of calls to which they respond, something around three calls an hour, or about 20-25 a shift. The assignment of calls to officers is patterned not only by their work load, but by their mobility. Assignments made by dispatchers to foot officers are carefully selected and rarely involve crime. There are problems in associating calls, addresses, and location of problems since calls are made from other than the location of the problem, and locations to which the officer is sent may be a hospital or simply the place where a report is to be taken. Overall, commercial establishments are the source of the largest number of calls to the police (see Sherman et al., 1987). Thus, variations in the level of calls cannot be taken to indicate characteristics of the city, of the callers, or even the nature of the events in the city. Certainly, one should be cautious in comparing the level of demand, known or estimated, without the results of very careful ethnographic work in communications centers.

COMMUNITY POLICING AS A DRAMA:
FURTHER OBSERVATIONS

Several dramatic themes integrate the strands woven into the community policing idea. They seem to be built upon the key idea that officers walking in an assigned area for at least some time during their tour of duty will increase the quality and quantity of contact between the police and public. This contact, in turn, will have the anticipated consequences with respect to fear of crime, and so on. This is a kind of police-cast drama or rhetoric in which they produce the script, the players, the roles, and also judge the performance as critics. The police play a role in larger political dramas as well (see Wagner-Pacifici, 1986), but they are the primary source of definitions of crime and deviance in the community.

The police with some increasing skill have been engaged in the management of impressions of their power, efficacy, and impact for the last 30 years. The police seek to produce the impression of control by means of a set of strategies. These may be rhetorical, such as the emphasis upon community policing and its value; operational, such as allocating more officers to foot patrol; or merely tactical, such as putting more officers on patrol on Halloween. The police attempt to control information about crime and disorder. They seek to reduce information that will damage this sense of order and control and to amplify information that enhances this sense. To display a unity of purpose in their actions is essential to the dramaturgical task. They work to cultivate, identify, and maintain the sense that there is an isomorphism between the state, the police, law, and morality (even at the neighborhood level). They are nominally in charge of protection of the moral order maintained by the state through law, even in the face of repeated evidence of the independence of these ideas. Police aim to produce the appearance of similarity of aims of the police and the society through the use of the rhetoric of community policing. Community policing is no different from other police strategies aimed at shaping and manipulating public opinion.

These strategies work best when they work least; when they are invisible, played out to segregated audiences so that potential contradictions are not apparent, and when other strategies are also employed. Is there a relationship between dramaturgical strategies and results? In previous work, it was argued that the police resorted to strategies of information control and manipulation of symbols when they took on a *mandate*—that is, the eradication of crime, a goal that is and was patently impossible (Manning, 1977). There are different means by which dramatic purposes are achieved in varieties of police work. With respect to more specialized work, such as that of detectives and vice/drug work, the job of dramaturgical presentation is more complex and subtle. It is also community or context-specific to a marked degree. The less the public knows about day-to-day operations, the better; major events, such as "busts" of large numbers of "dealers" and seizures of drugs, are highly publicized. Routine figures on arrests are issued, but most of these are made by patrol officers, and (varying from city-to-city) many cases are never brought to trial because the arrestee is "turned" to make cases on other users/dealers. If one looks at the dramaturgical potential of detective work, one sees quickly that detectives are not Sherlock Holmes in modern dress, but are clerks. They are, in fact, primarily "paper pushers" who take advantage of whatever information is available rather than creating new information or following up leads. When they do make an arrest, it is often with information obtained from witnesses at the scene by patrol officers (see Greenwood, Chaiken, and Petersilia, 1977). Much of their important work is "cooling out the mark," explaining to the public why it is impossible for overworked detectives to make an arrest and why the victim or complainant should consider their case unsolvable. Again, detectives elevate the rare arrest of a famous case or a solution based on diligent pursuit of evidence and witnesses, and depress the tiresome, boring, and unrewarding task of simply filing the vast majority of crime complaints for which no witness or forensic evidence is available (see Waegel, 1981).

PARADOXES OF THE COMMUNITY POLICING MOVEMENT

Setting aside for the moment the empirical and research questions that admittedly cry out for further examination, there are a number of questions that might be asked about the implicit, unintended consequences of community policing, whether seen as ideology, program, tactic, or passing historical moment. These issues include such matters as the increasing dependence of the community upon the police for ordering social relations and the increasing use of the media to influence public opinion. The politicization of the police that is the growing notion that the police defend and advance their own interests, which may or may not coincide with the hypothetical "greatest good" argument, even with the apparent decline of the police unionization movement, remains apparent. A continuing issue is the potential that more sophisticated, electronically equipped police with greater legal and social power of surveillance have for even further penetrating private spheres (see Stinchcombe, 1964; Ericson and Shearing, 1986). What are some other paradoxes of the community police movement?

1. Will community policing further *weaken community ties* and insidiously encourage further dependence upon the police? The claim is that the police should now create, maintain, and nurture community values and programs, and dramatize and amplify the community's sense

of itself. (See Wilson and Kelling, 1982). Police are engaging now in a new form of community organization, much like the social workers, blue-stocking upper-class women, and community workers tried after World War I in Chicago, and at the turn of the century in New York City. Police constables in Birmingham, England, created a sports club and had a large fund to support community activities. They are engaged in shaping community values. Where do these imputed values come from? Is there not danger, further, that the police may use this power base for their own ends?

2. Will police use of the media serve to *undermine the capacity of the community for community self-study and self-knowledge?* Media are now used by the police to heighten their own power and control over the definitions and consequences of deviance. The works of Beare (1987) and Ericson, Baranek, and Chan (1987) demonstrate conclusively that in Canada at least the police—by use of police public relations officers, press releases, and press conferences—maintain control of crime-related information, and therefore of the social construction of the events. The media rarely pursue sources other than the official sources they routinely contact. Rather than the media controlling the police, as police often feel, a fine transactional balance is maintained between the police and media. The more apparently open the officials with the media, the more the media are dependent upon them and reproduce their versions of complex events. The police are more effective with the media than other segments of the criminal justice system because they provide more information. The police are adept, in spite of their own frustrations, at transforming real events into media events, which are then reproduced as the social reality of the viewer. The use of newsletters, victim surveys, public opinion polls, and such media announcements unifies the media and the police in producing mutually acceptable images.

3. Is community policing a new form of *invisible social control?* It seeks to enable the community to achieve what police aim to display as an accomplishment (Cohen, 1985). By penetrating social relations and organizing communities on their own behalf, police using the community policing ideology beg the question of "whose order?" and "whose disorder?" By creating neighborhood organization as was attempted in Houston, the police presume to know and to reproduce some sense of order, social values, and community sense that is typically absent in sprawling, rapidly growing urban areas. It is the very open, developing, and noncontrolling ambience that urbanites seek by moving to cities like Houston from Newark, Detroit, Pittsburgh, and other urban areas. Surely there is an irony here insofar as the police create the community order they are responsible for protecting. For example, police in a community program in Maryland used police vans to transport citizens to meetings so that they could express their needs to the police at a police-community meeting.

4. Does community policing produce further *inequity* within police organizations? There is a serious problem inherent in the notion of encouraging foot patrol and community officers to choose their assignments, while denying the choice of assignment within patrol under usual circumstances to other patrol officers. This pattern of self-selection also affects the outcomes of studies of morale of foot patrol officers when compared to those in motorized patrol (as other authors in this volume have pointed out). As all studies since the Police Foundation study of team policing (Sherman, Milton, and Kelly, 1973) discovered, program innovations have little consequence if no permanent resources are allocated and few new rewards are provided to program participants. This point is linked with the previous one about the need for training and supervision, and they suggest, taken together, that many community policing programs have been merely cosmetic or rhetorical strategies in the on-going dramatic struggle with crime and disorder. If community policing succeeds in altering rewards, promotional opportunities, and morale among community police officers, then it will have been successful where other reform movements have failed. But it is too early to draw such a conclusion yet—we are in the first phase of the on-going reform of the urban police.

5. Are the police becoming more *political* in their aims and programs? The police have always been a political force in life in the United States and have used various strategies to achieve power and authority (Reppetto, 1978). Thus concerns that police may give unequal service or become more corrupt or political seem unfounded: The police have mastered the urban service game by claiming uniformity and controlling access to service on their own terms. There is no reason to think that community policing as a tactic is any less or more political than any of the other tactics such as "wars on drugs," "crime control strategies," federally funded task forces for the pursuit of "career criminals," or computer-assisted command and control systems. Because corruption is always a matter of definition, it is difficult to know whether the service provided in the Houston or Newark programs provided opportunities for corruption. It is not certain how political decisions affect the future of foot patrol. It is not clear, for example, whether the foot patrol program in Flint, Michigan, sponsored by a chief who was fired by the outgoing mayor failing to control crime will survive the recent election of a young incumbent (November 1987).

6. Is community policing *more democratic* than conventional policing? It is claimed that community policing is democratic because it increases the public's capacity to influence policing. Decentralized decision making, absence of a national police force, local control over funding, resources and their allocation have always been characteristic of U.S. policing. The nature, source, and kinds of democratic influence people have

with respect to policing remain open questions. On the one hand, police control, allocation of services, and almost unfettered discretion remain at the bottom of the organizational hierarchy. On the other hand, the command structure and the modern (post–O. W. Wilson) tradition of policing reinforce the pattern of even allocation of officers (and roughly therefore of service) across neighborhoods. Equalization of service delivery is a general rule in urban forces; this suggests that police administrative practices determine allocation more than does the "demand" or the environment (see, for example, Slovak, 1987; Manning, 1980, 1982). This observation points to yet another democratic paradox: One cannot coerce, enforce, punish, and maintain formal social control while maintaining equally high ratings with all population segments. Police administrators seek the image of greater responsibility and accountability to the public. At the same time, police administrators have increasing technological means to escalate their own power and control over officers.

COMMENTS

To argue that the police engage the world dramatically merely extends to the analysis of policing a perspective relevant for the analysis of all collective actions. The drama of policing, however, takes many forms, uses changing symbols, tactics, and rhetorics; and is flexible to meet emerging needs. It works with essentially dramatic stuff—the rise and fall of reputations, of good and evil, of individual morality. It possesses abundant traditions and conventions and participates in important community celebrations. The moral drama and the police role in it remain a vibrant and engaging spectacle, and each new mask is greeted with anticipation and has emotional potential. Police rhetoric remains a flexible and innovative tool, and recently community policing is an idea whose rhetorical time has come.

Community policing is a dramaturgical strategy that seeks to reduce the costs of policing, increase the crime-control capacity of policing, renew and restore the morality and integrity of communities, reduce morale and turnover within police organizations, reduce the fear of crime as well as the actual level of crime, and restore urban government to its proper role in maintaining community well-being. It is certain to fail in doing these things. The goals may be mutually exclusive or conflicting. They are one facet of the very cumbersome and awkward machinery of local government on the one hand, and an even smaller part of the apparatus of social control.

The question does arise concerning the impact that community policing might have upon policing as an occupation and organization, and here the possibility is quite promising. Through the development and execution of large operations, shifting resources, mounting evaluations, and engaging in political dialogue, the police may begin to see themselves in a new light. They may continue to examine the nature of their role, the rewards associated with it, the limits of the crime-fighting rhetoric, and the challenges of urban diversity.

It is impossible to examine the claims and aims of community policing, as Mastrofski (Chapter 3 in this volume) notes, outside the context of the police reform movement. It is not surprising that the major resource work has been funded by reform-oriented foundations such as the Mott Foundation and the Police Foundation and its progeny, the Police Executive Research Forum. Community policing should be seen as part of an ongoing reform movement that includes various foundations, educational institutions, urban politicians in non-machine cities, and criminal justice educators. It cannot be seen independently of other movements that stress the unity of life, the wholeness of experience, and other rather loose ideologies of the modern age. In the same way that health spas, exercise videos, and natural foods advocates urge better health for the person, community policing supporters urge, as does Jane Fonda, better communal health through a form of dedifferentiated social control (Merelman, 1984).

NOTES

1. These are gathered from the publications listed in this bibliography, especially the works of Kelling, Trojanowicz, and the authors of the articles of the special issue of *Crime and Delinquency* 33(1) 1987.

2. It is perhaps likely that a number of types of social integration and command authority exist in urban departments. (This is a theme in Wilson's *Varieties of Police Behavior* (1968), but see also Bordua and Reiss, 1987; Reppetto, 1978). Rubinstein's work (1973) is a limited picture, despite its detail because it omits discussion of police authority and decisions above the level of the street. Ethnographies based solely upon observation of discretion by uniformed patrol officers are an inadequate basis for generalization about policing. Interactional studies are valuable and among those the careful and comprehensive works of Brent and Sykes (1983) and Michael Brown (1981) stands out. Brown's work is important because it details policy differences and attempts comparative analysis of patterns of discretion among patrol officers in several Southern California cites. Issues arising from the comparative study of policing are well illustrated by the work of David Bayley, especially his internationally focused *Patterns of Policing* (1985).

3. There is some sense in which the idea of community policing in Britain has been developed as a rhetorical device to combat criticism of policing, especially in London, and to produce organizational disequilibration as a prelude to reform and reorganization. This was certainly one theme in the organizational reforms undertaken by the previous commissioner of the police, Sir Kenneth Newman.

3

COMMUNITY POLICING AS REFORM: A CAUTIONARY TALE

STEPHEN D. MASTROFSKI

American society has always faced three fundamental problems with its police: defining their role, devising effective controls over their discretion, and establishing the bases of their legitimacy. Community policing is a recent manifestation of this Sisyphean effort. Reacting to the failures of previous reform eras, community policing advocates propose a significant departure from the ways in which issues of role, control, and legitimacy are addressed. Order maintenance replaces law enforcement as the police mission; legalistic constraints on officer discretion are reduced, while direct linkages to the community are increased; and policies and actions are justified less in terms of their impact on the objective risks of criminal victimization and more in terms of the sense of peace, order, and security they impart to the public.

Manning (1984; Chapter 2, this volume) suggests that community policing has appeal because it evokes powerful metaphors that play to contemporary cultural themes. It responds to an affection for less conflict and greater personalized treatment of an imagined past. In a broader sense, community policing taps a nostalgia for the U.S. democratic grass-roots tradition of citizen initiative and melds it with impatience with an unresponsive law and cumbersome government bureaucracy. It offers instead a government that acts to enhance the "natural" mechanisms of social control peculiar to a locale rather than imposing an inflexible alien order. Through community policing government offers succor to the deserving poor and disadvantaged, and to the middle classes it promises a comprehensive approach to diverse social problems that trouble both the urban and suburban United States.

To develop momentum for these changes, reform proponents sometimes sell its appealing objectives while ignoring or downplaying contradictions and complexities in its underlying assumptions. Police reform in the United States has traditionally required the hard sell. Agonizing self-doubt over its potential weaknesses is not the way to get leaders in a fragmented and tradition-reverent industry to change. Yet failure to consider these problems carefully will inevitably relegate the best-intentioned efforts to the ash heap of discarded fads that litter the history of U.S. police reform. This chapter is thus an exercise in skepticism. While there is much in community policing that offers refreshing alternatives to traditional approaches, its rhetoric shrouds complex realities that must be addressed. In an extraordinarily probing essay by an advocate of community policing, Herman Goldstein (1987) suggests that we must lift that shroud and explore some tough fundamental questions. By discussing several of the reform's tenets regarding role, control, and legitimacy, I hope to explore some difficulties in moving this reform from rhetoric to reality.

THE PROBLEMS OF ROLE TRANSFORMATION

Police role may be defined in terms of both ends and means (Bittner, 1970), and community policing promises to transform both. The key to the change in mission is captured by the implications of the concept of "community." Similarly, the reform carries a number of strategic and tactical elements presumed to be instrumental to community objectives. The following discussion highlights complications, dilemmas, and paradoxes that derive from the reformulation of police role embodied in the community policing reform.

Community

Advocates of community policing justify the shift in mission from serious crime to order maintenance in two ways. First, the reduction of minor disorders may ultimately lead to a reduction in serious crime by disrupting the hypothesized escalatory cycle of community decay thought to produce rampant serious crime. Second, order maintenance is justifiable in its own right in that it contributes to the establishment of a civil, livable environment in which citizens may, without fear, exercise their right to pursue their livelihood, commerce, self-expression, entertainment, and so on. It is in particular the need to respond to this moral mandate for civilized order that makes the role transformation compelling to proponents of community policing (Sykes, 1986:505). Where the law is vague in matters of distinguishing order from disorder (and this is typical), the basis for police intervention becomes the "political will of the community" (Kelling, 1987a). Clearly, establishing community is important for this reform in terms of the policeman's legitimacy and effectiveness.

To make this line of argument feasible, proponents of the reform posit a series of assumptions about the nature of community in the urban United States. First, there is a broad popular concern about the quality of urban life—one that crosses ethnic and social class boundaries—and a widely shared desire to see order restored, established, or maintained. Second, there are different views of how order should be defined, some being extreme and unacceptable, based for example, on bigotry. The unacceptable extremes are easy to identify, however, so that, third, the police can be responsive to legitimate variations in views of social order and disorder that occur between separate and homogeneous neighborhood-communities (Scheingold, 1984:207, 214).

Public opinion polls show that Americans have for some time expressed concern about disorders, large and small, in the urban cities. Whether or not that reflects in the abstract a widespread mandate for order, it is in the specific and particular that police must come to grips with these issues, and it is here that the notions of community, consensus, and mandate face difficulties. Many urban neighborhoods do not manifest a political will about order. Some are silent and others cacophonous.

At the core of the reform's problem is the need to define community and establish its existence as the basis for order maintenance policing. Greene (1985) has noted the need for greater specificity in defining community in programs, proposals, and evaluations. On a conceptual level, the community policing model would seem to require the following as a minimum standard. A basis for police action requires a demonstration that a group of people—say a neighborhood—shares a definition of what constitutes right order, threats to it, and appropriate methods for maintaining it. To the extent that community implies a basis for citizens to work collectively with police to restore and preserve order, it also requires a sense of group identity or attachment—a "we-ness" derived from shared experience and interaction. There are undoubtedly neighborhoods that possess to a high degree this value homogeneity and group attachment, but it is precisely in the most afflicted areas that community is problematic in the sense required by the reform.

Greenberg and Rohe (1986:85) review a body of research that shows the absence of shared norms about order in heterogeneous low-income neighborhoods. This is also supported by recent survey research in two Toronto neighborhoods where fewer than one-third of the resident samples agreed that *any* of a variety of crimes and disorders constituted a "big" problem (Murphy and de Verteuil, 1986:19).

Some neighborhoods that *appear* to share a common perspective on order are found upon closer examination not to do so. Horowitz's (1983) ethnography of an inner-city Chicano neighborhood in Chicago shows how easily one might be deceived by the appearance of a common heritage and shared customs. Her study details a complex tension between the subcultural values of "honor" (acquiring respect) and the "American dream" (occupational mobility and material success). How individuals in this neighborhood resolve this tension varies considerably. Neighborhood residents come to hold diverse and sometimes self-contradictory views on such matters as gang membership and disorderly activities, womanhood and sexual promiscuity, and obtaining an education or job. To assume that the people of this small urban area—relatively homogeneous as to income and ethnicity—share anything resembling an unambiguous consensus on these issues would be a grave error. In neighborhoods that *do* develop strong informal social control systems, the existence of these systems may not reflect value consensus, but only the political or cultural dominance of one group over others less well organized or connected. Even apparently homogeneous white middle-class neighborhoods may not have the level of consensus about order presumed by community policing advocates. Crenson's (1983) study of Baltimore neighborhoods shows that such areas (even with the highest levels of attachment and participation) develop their infrastructure out of social conflict and distrust directed at neighbors. Even in these kinds of neighborhoods, the rate of participation is typically a small minority of households (Rosenbaum, 1987).

The difficulty of using police to reinforce informal community norms is probably most severe when a "defended" neighborhood is threatened by intrusion. Rieder's (1985) depiction of Canarsie in the 1970s and 1980s shows how Italian and Jewish residents of this white working- and lower-middle-class Brooklyn neighborhood reacted vehemently to the threat of black incursion. Ultimately, tensions between white Canarsians and blacks erupted into confrontations: arson, racist sloganeering, vigilantism, school riots, block associations and crime patrols designed to make blacks feel watched and unwanted, civil disobedience against busing, and private listing of real estate sales to facilitate recruitment of white buyers (Rieder, 1985:172, 186). Considering this context, the solidarity of Jews and Italians created a sense of community consensus and informal control that—should the police have reinforced them—made them party to bigotry, something advocates of community policing do *not* support (Wilson and Kelling, 1982:35; Goldstein, 1987:25).

But herein is an unresolved dilemma for community police, for their claims to serve as supporters and advocates of neighborhood norms would be revealed as only transparent rhetoric should officers fail to follow through with active support. To uphold the law actively—which would mean bringing *all* law breakers to justice, including the white homeowners—would cost the support of the group whose interests they have vowed to uphold. Or they can forsake the protection of individual rights and reinforce the racist and illegal acts of the residents—something that runs counter to notions of equity, traditional professional values, and risks stimulating outside involvement by elected representatives, state and federal agencies, and the courts.

Neither approach seems palatable to the police, but a middle course is scarcely more preferable. They might studiously avoid "ass-kicking," harassment, and other forms of punitive policing while also overlooking the violent, illegal self-help efforts of local vigilantes. The tacit and sometimes explicit police "licensing" of informal justice *did* occur to some extent in Canarsie as a police coping mechanism (Rieder 1985:111). Although this did *not* occur under the auspices of a community policing program, it would seem more, not less, likely to foster such a response.

The problems of the defended neighborhood may represent the extreme instance of the community conflict problem, but virtually every major metropolitan area has at least one such area. Even in smaller cities and older suburbs, economic and demographic changes bring groups with sharply divergent life-styles in sufficient proximity to create friction. The theoretical and programmatic literature on community policing finesses the community problem, and the empirical evaluations virtually ignore it; the officers who work the streets cannot, however.

To claim to know the will of the community, police require some observable manifestation to guide and justify a course of action. The law admirably served this function for earlier reformers, but in deemphasizing laws, rules, and regulations as a basis for action, community policing must identify other institutions. The values of a community's "informal" systems of social control are thought to be embedded in neighborhood associations, businesses, industry, churches, and civic groups. Where these organizations do not exist, community policing programs endeavor to create them, as they provide a democratic guide beacon to police action in the neighborhood. They articulate the nuances of the locale's moral mandate and serve as mediating structures between the members of the community and the police agency.

In fact, these mediating institutions are not microcosms of the neighborhoods they are alleged to represent (Bohm, 1984:451). They, like all social institutions, are heavily influenced by the distribution of power, status, and wealth within their domain. Even in these voluntary associations where membership rules are not restrictive, participation is skewed to those of higher socioeconomic status, married, and homeowners with children (Rosenbaum, 1987:108). The experiences of a Hartford pilot program are instructive. A large proportion of the experimental neighborhood's population was minority, yet, despite the creation and growth of citizen organizations as part of a neighborhood-oriented police program, there was little minority participation in formal community organizations (Fowler and Mangione, 1982: Ch. 6). Even more important, research suggests that the perceptions of those active in neighborhood organizations do not correlate to any significant extent with the perceptions of the neighborhood at large regarding what are problems for their neighborhood (Rich, 1986).

If neighborhood groups are not representative, a principled basis for acting on their view of order is the claim of their substantive "rightness." Shifting to this line of argument takes one down a slippery slope, however, since it forces the police to justify often controversial actions without the benefit of an explicit democratic process as an expression of the people's will. In reality, this is usually handled by simply failing to acknowledge the merit of opposing views that may arise. An example from the author's research experience in a predominantly black neighborhood policed by a large, highly regarded professional department is illustrative. The police chief tended to identify the sources of right order with the neighborhood's leaders who expressed values acceptable to him: ministers, business people, minor government officials, and the NAACP (National Association for the Advancement of Colored People). He regarded as disorderly and aberrant a cadre of younger residents who, displeased with the moderation and "inactivity" of the established neighborhood leadership, had formed an activist group that had successfully mobilized some large protests alleging police misuse of force and violation of constitutional rights. This group clearly tapped a sensitive source of neighborhood concern, but—in addition to being discounted by the chief as a significant expression of neighborhood sentiment—it became the object of police surveillance and enforcement efforts.

A more subtle approach to the problem of unacceptable expressions of the neighborhood's view of order is to channel the perception and activities of neighborhood groups into a framework palatable to the police. Anyone who has observed a variety of community crime prevention programs readily ascertains that the bulk of the communication is *from* the police *to* the citizen, explaining and selling prepackaged strategies devised without the particular neighborhood and its residents' preferences in mind. Several evaluations of these programs show that they emphasize organizing to *do* crime prevention, not to stimulate the neighborhood to voice its demands in matters of police business (Lindsay and McGillis, 1986; Schneider, 1986; Fowler and Mangione, 1986; Rosenbaum, Lewis, and Grant, 1986).

The multifaceted Houston and Newark fear-reduction programs appear to be designed to maximize neighborhood responsiveness to police. Although the program description speaks of collaboration and police not imposing themselves on the neighborhood, the police are in control of the information-gathering and dissemination regarding crime, disorder, and police work and also play the main role in identifying community groups with which to collaborate (Police Foundation, 1983). Newsletters are supposed to provide residents and businesses with a more accurate picture of crime in the neighborhood, balancing the bad news with the good (Lavrakas, 1986). It is difficult to imagine what criteria one might apply to determine what an accurate picture of crime requires, but it is not difficult to envision a police department shaping the picture of crime in the neighborhood to suit its objectives for that neighborhood, no matter how honorable. In Newark before police undertook an intensified aggressive public order enforcement campaign, they contacted citizen groups "to inform them of the purpose of such actions and to convince them that they are in the community's self-interest" (Police Foundation, 1983:29). This and the door-to-door selling of community participation programs by patrol officers appear to be designed more to persuade than respond. These programs seem to *enlarge* the capacity of the police bureaucracy to impose its formulation of order on the neighborhoods and encourage citizens to focus their efforts in ways that conform to the department's notion of useful police-community interaction. That such programs have been hard to sustain over time in neighborhood associations may reflect in part their tendency to tell more than listen.

This does not preclude the possibility that neighborhood organizations can and do exert influence over police policy and practices. Fowler and Mangione (1982:51) report that a Hartford neighborhood Police Advisory Committee was able to persuade police to focus on certain forms of disorder that police had traditionally ignored and were also able to lobby effectively for more resources. However, outside of a narrow range of acceptable demands, the conditions under which lobbying becomes more effective are when the organization enjoys resources and political connections independent of the police department, as was the case in Hartford.

Police Tactics and Strategies

Community policing proposals and programs are quite diverse in the emphasis they place on how to do police work. The community policing umbrella covers what J. Q. Wilson (1983) has termed "crime attack" and "community service" strategies. This section discusses thorny problems for the application of the crime attack (aggressive order maintenance) and community service strategies associated with community policing.

Aggressive Order Maintenance

Aggressive order maintenance (Kelling, 1987a), street justice (Sykes, 1986), soft crime law enforcement (Reiss, 1985a), and ass-kicking (Wilson and Kelling, 1982) all refer to the proactive application of formal and informal sanctions to the presumed proximate causes of public disorder on the beat: winos, panhandlers, prostitutes, drug violators, rowdy juveniles, and other street people. Aggressive order maintenance strategies include rousting or arresting people thought to cause public disorder, field interrogations and roadblock checks, surveillance of suspicious people, vigorous enforcement of public order and nuisance laws, and, in general, much greater attention to the minor crimes and disturbances thought to disrupt and displease the civil public. These strategies are not new to policing, but the frequency and intensity of their use have fluctuated with changes in local pressure and the prevailing legal doctrine about the appropriateness of such methods. Now some community policing advocates seek to justify them as a routine response to or preventive of disorder. Several problems attach to this approach.

First, aggressive order maintenance has been offered as a sort of all-purpose curative for neighborhood disorders, but there are both empirical and theoretical reasons making its effectiveness highly suspect. Greene and Taylor (Chapter 11, this volume) outline the difficulty of drawing meaningful conclusions from the available empirical assessments of community policing. One of the most recent attempts to assess the impact of aggressive order maintenance indicated that it contributed to increased criminal victimization and citizen dissatisfaction, while fear of crime and residents' perceptions of disorder remained unaffected (Sherman, 1986a: 369; Williams and Pate, 1987; Skogan, 1987). From a theoretical perspective, the proposition that proactive policing contributes to urban disorder needs to be explored. Under some circumstances, it may actually disrupt what limited, informal social control mechanisms are currently operating to provide: at least *some* level of order and safety. An example is given in New York City's Operation Pressure Point (OPP), an attempt to run drug dealers off the streets of the Lower East Side of Manhattan. Videotaped surveillance shows that street dealing was abundant and blatant before OPP, yet those same films show streets full of people going about their daily business. Amidst these busy streets were queues for drug transactions more orderly than those found by many licensed liquor stores. The benefits of OPP seem particularly dubious when, as many have acknowledged, such programs only run drug abusers into more secluded places where violence is more likely—precisely because transactions are less visible to the public.

Second, aggressive order maintenance tactics seem decidedly inappropriate for dealing over the long term with many of the social disorders that plague urban neighborhoods. The "broken windows" argument assumes that the main causes of neighborhood disorder are imported or somehow alien to the area, a plague visited upon the indigenous population. Yet many forms of disorder derive from the sorts of racial, cultural, and economic tensions that arise among those who legitimately live, work, and recreate in a given area. The severe disorders born of racial tensions in the Howard Beach area of New York City, for example, cannot be solved by running a few troublemakers off the streets or out of the area. The imposition of curfews and other aspects of martial law may be necessary to handle crisis conditions, but they hardly offer much promise for reducing the underlying tensions that feed chronic interracial strife. Under such conditions, attempting to harness aggressive order maintenance to the strengthening of informal social control mechanisms of the locale will only inflame the tensions and delegitimate police efforts for, at least, one side of the dispute. The experience of the Royal Ulster Constabulary in policing the highly polarized society of Northern Ireland is a case in point (Weitzer, 1985).

Third, prescribing aggressive order maintenance as a general policy response to the host of disorders that plague urban neighborhoods shows remarkable disregard for the need for and capacity of officers to craft their actions on the street to best fit particular circumstances. Aggressive order maintenance as a general policy does *not* increase the range of an officer's discretion but actually constrains it by requiring officers to rely exclusively on their coercive powers for handling street disorders. Doing so is like requiring physicians to use penicillin to treat all infections.

Muir (1977) discusses in detail the consequences of a police style that relies principally on coercion: moral depletion, danger, an alienated community, and long-term ineffectiveness in establishing order. What is missing from the discussion of community policing as aggressive order maintenance is a delineation of the noncoercive tools of the trade. Muir suggests that even in the most blighted skid row areas, police cannot rely solely on coercion to govern those who might be inclined to rebellion. Even the most dispossessed, detached, and irrational may be civilized by fair, consistent treatment. Muir's professional police officer does not see the law as an obstacle to effective governance and community development; he seeks ways to use it to demonstrate its ennobling qualities.

What makes strengthening the will to coerce particularly troubling is that most public disorders arise from complex circumstances where the assignment of right and wrong is no easy matter. Selecting a course of action should not depend only upon the officer's will to use force and his or her understanding of the community's standards, but also upon developing sophisticated skills of observation, the capacity to make judgments, and an integrated understanding of people's life circumstances (Muir, 1977: Ch. 10). An example proffered by George Kelling (1985:302) may help to illustrate the point.

Two officers on foot patrol intervene in a disturbance involving a man and a pregnant woman with a child who are waiting for a bus. The man, apparently intoxicated, appears to be harassing the woman. After inquiring of the woman whether she knows the man—and she says she does not—the officers forcefully instruct the man to depart. He protests but is warned that if he persists, he will go to jail. Ultimately, he does not heed the officers and is arrested.

Without actually observing such an incident, it is difficult to judge whether it was policing at its best. We are not told the original cause of the fracas, nor are we given an indication that the officers were interested in learning it. The officers—after immediately intervening to stop any potential harm to the woman and her child—might have inquired as to the source of the problem, hearing both the man's and woman's side and, if necessary, the testimony of bystanders. Kelling would have us believe that the man was doing something wrong, if not illegal, and indeed that may have been the case. But the man may also have had a legitimate beef. Whether or not that was the case here, the officers' decisive action without further investigation may have unnecessarily aggravated the man to rebel to save face before his colleagues. The experience would not seem likely to imbue him with respect for the form of street justice he received, and one wonders how he will behave in the future. It is possible, then, to construe this incident—and many others like it—not as an exemplar, but as what Muir would call a botched experiment. Greater attention to developing officers' skills in reducing misjudgments, a risk for even the best, would go a long way toward increasing confidence that the police are in possession of the requisite tools to maintain order, protect individual rights, and develop respect.

Community Service

The problems associated with the community service strategies of the reform are more subtle as they focus on the traditionally overlooked "velvet glove" aspect of police work: newsletters, block watch, foot patrol, friendly getting-to-know-you police-citizen encounters, victim follow-up, and so on. Although it is difficult to deny the appeal of the police officer's helping hand, we need to explore more assiduously how it is actually done, what it accomplishes, and who benefits.

A key element of the community service strategy is the notion that to accomplish safer, more orderly communities, police must acknowledge that they share that responsibility with the citizenry—that indeed without close cooperation these objectives can never be realized. This notion of police-community reciprocity or coproduction (Skolnick and Bayley, 1986:213) has the ring of a coequal partnership between police and public, but in practice its programs manifest a markedly asymmetrical relationship. Coproduction in practice means citizens doing what police think is best. The police offer an array of police-developed crime-prevention programs to a neighborhood beset with crime and disorder. In many cases, citizens are more than ready to defer to police expertise, only too happy to be getting any attention at all. Where citizens do articulate demands that fall outside the organization's routine programmatic response mechanisms, those demands usually tax departmental resources, disrupt administration, violate the law, or have only a meager prospect of success according to current professional wisdom. In these circumstances, the police would scarcely seem more likely to share decision making with the public than professors are on pedagogy and course content with their students.

More problematic than the rhetorical obfuscation of police-community reciprocity is the prospect of program success for community service activities. A certain level of police-citizen cooperation is, of course, essential to make most crime control and order maintenance strategies function, but the real issue is whether these new coproduction programs add significantly to existing levels of public safety. In many urban areas, police already enjoy high levels of respect and cooperation from citizens. In these areas, new coproduction programs may approach a level of diminishing returns in controlling crime and disorder. In areas where police-community relations are not good, programs designed to increase citizen participation are unlikely to address the things about police that really dissatisfy citizens, discouraging them from doing those coproductive acts that might contribute to program success. The extant empirical evaluations of coproductive programs fall considerably short of a ringing confirmation of success. If one takes the methodologically conservative view of Greene and Taylor (Chapter 11, this volume), there is little that can be concluded from these studies, one way or the other. If one takes a less demanding position, the results are at best mixed. A recent collection of assessments of residential crime prevention programs shows that of the six evaluated with victimization data, two encouraged the evaluators to render positive-effect conclusions with little or no qualification (Lindsay and McGillis, 1986; Schneider, 1986), one offered mixed results (Fowler and Mangione, 1986), two reported no effects (Pate, 1986; Skogan and Wycoff, 1986), and one found pointedly negative effects in three of four sites (Rosenbaum et al., 1986). Clearly, at this stage, there is little that *is* clear about what contribution community service programs can make to community safety.

Whether community service strategies reduce crime and disorder, they are important ways of demonstrating that the police are *trying* to protect and care for the public. However, these programs can work to justify the bifurcation of the police clientele into those who merit special police protection and personalized service and those who do not. Indeed, the community service component of this reform is designed to mobilize some citizens in a campaign against others, presumably the sources of disorder. The programs urge the respectable clientele to serve as the department's eyes and ears, and some attempt to convince them to accept more aggressive police interventions in their neighborhood (Weisburd, McElroy, and Hardyman, n.d.:9). They create community by, as Durkheim (1983) suggests, focusing people's awareness and energies on identifying, controlling, or expelling an outgroup held responsible for the area's ills. It is thus that Skolnick and Bayley (1986:214) can suggest that crime might be an antidote to anomie. These programs may have value for those who receive their services, but if they create a sense of community, they do so at the cost of ignoring those with some of the toughest problems. In fairness, some community policing programs have focused specifically upon improving the lot of those at the lower social and economic margin, yet a number of studies also suggest that the distribution of these services appears to be skewed to whites and the middle class (Yin, 1986; Wycoff, Chapter 6, this volume).

THE PROBLEM OF CONTROL

Controlling police discretion has always been as difficult as defining the police role. Community policing attempts to maximize order maintenance effectiveness by loosening bureaucratic and legalistic restrictions on the rank and file to allow them to practice their craft or experiment with even more effective ways of problem solving. The trick, of course, is to maximize this sort of effectiveness without increasing police misbehavior, abuse of authority, and bad judgment. This requires more attention than it has received thus far.

Conceptual arguments for the reform generally acknowledge the risk of police abuse but propose to handle the problem in a variety of ways. At one end of the spectrum, Sykes (1986) argues that the risks of street justice are far outweighed by the benefits of freedom from criminal oppression it bestows, especially on the poor, minorities, women, and children and others least capable of self-protection. But allowing the need for some restraints, he suggests that the political process (presumably he means those things influencing the executive and legislative branches) is a more efficacious alternative than the courts for handling police oppression. Although procedural due process is a far-from-perfect instrument of justice, Sykes' exercise in *realpolitik* underestimates the impact of due process reforms on police practices over the years. As a practical matter, it is hard to imagine that a mentally competent defendant with a case to make on police abuse would spend his money on a political solution rather than the services of a combative attorney. Indeed, it has long been the function of our courts to protect powerless and unpopular minorities from the excesses of those who manage to exercise political dominance. That they have not done it as well as we would wish—or that they have done it *too* well—is not sufficient reason to cast due process protections to the wind.

Occupying a middle ground on the matter of controlling police abuses, Wilson and Kelling (1982:35) express hope "that by their selection, training, and supervision the police will be inculcated with a clear sense of the outer limit of their discretionary authority." Elsewhere Kelling (1985:305-306) expresses faith that "bureaucratization, unionization, and professionalization that characterize contemporary policing seem more than ample bulwarks against the inappropriate influence of any single neighborhood or interest." That is, the very unresponsive institutions for which community policing is a remedy are the essential mechanisms to restrain the reform's excesses. The real argument being made here is that both the urban environment of policing and the police themselves have changed sufficiently to make it safe to grant and legitimate greater decision-making autonomy for the street officer (Moore and Kelling, 1983). Klockars (1986) argues that it is the very cumbersome and punitive nature of existing structures that limits the police use of extralegal tactics on citizens. While most police historians would stipulate that officer corruption and misbehavior are less frequent nowadays, we have no reliable basis for knowing just how extensive those problems are. They may well be far more common than we would like to admit.

Regardless of the current state of police integrity, there is little or no evidence to support the claim that professionalism and bureaucracy are effective restraints on police abuses. The impact of recruitment, education, and training on officer adherence to performance and proper standards of behavior simply has not been established and remains an article of professional and academic faith (Sherman, 1980; Mastrofski, 1987). Most of the potential effects of education and training appear to be overwhelmed by the police socialization experience (Rubinstein, 1973; Van Maanen, 1974). Police field supervision in most departments appears to remain a rather crude device for ensuring compliance with standards of right conduct (Allen, 1982; Allen and Maxfield, 1983; Rubinstein, 1973; Van Maanen, 1983). In general, bureaucratic mechanisms in departments of any size have proven not insignificant but nonetheless modest bulwarks against police misbehavior. Where they have constrained police deviance, they have also fostered a proclivity to avoid involvement or decisive action in ambiguous situations. These are, unfortunately, the very situations that call for police initiative under community policing. Ultimately, this line of argument comes hard against the dilemma of having one's cake and eating it too. To the extent that police organizations retain the bureaucratic features essential to control abuses, they cannot be expected to provide officers the scope of discretion necessary to accomplish order maintenance objectives. Goldstein (1977: Chs. 7 and 8) offers a detailed analysis of this dilemma and suggests ways in which administrators might walk the tightrope between too much and too little control. However, his sensible prescriptions are not easy to implement; we do not know if they can prosper alongside community policing arrangements; and we lack rigorous empirical assessments of those cases where they have been tried.

Some are beginning to suggest ways in which traditional bureaucratic methods might be altered to resolve the control dilemma under community policing. Wycoff (Chapter 6, this volume) suggests that the appropriate supervisory practice allows officers to exercise initiative, deemphasizes the old rule-suffused supervision, but intensifies on-scene monitoring of officers and obtaining community feedback on police behavior. This is, in fact, what observers report as routine practice in one of the few empirical studies of supervision under community policing arrangements

(Weisburd et al., n.d.). Bayley (Chapter 12, this volume) outlines some of the potential hazards of this approach. In addition, this form of supervision calls not only for a shift in the *quality* of supervision, but also in the *quantity*. Intensive observation of officers and community feedback contacts takes time. Administrators will find it difficult to obtain the resources necessary to fulfill the demanding requirements of this approach to supervision. Although its effectiveness has yet to be evaluated, realistic expectations of its capacity to control police abuses must remain modest at best. The fundamental structure of the supervisor-to-officer relationship remains unchanged. Officers are sent into the community to do their work where it remains hard to know precisely what they are doing and how they are doing it.

Herman Goldstein (1987:21) offers the most restrained resolution to the dilemma of controlling community police: "[A] police administrator may be able to implement community policing only in those departments in which integrity and conformity with established legal requirements are the rule; where one can, with reasonable assurance, depend on self-discipline." The first problem is, of course, knowing which departments can reasonably depend upon self-discipline. Scandals about police corruption and brutality surface periodically in big city departments—even those that have been reputedly cleaned up. Even in some of the suburbs where police enjoy strong professional reputations, the public is occasionally shocked and disbelieving when such scandals are aired (see, for example, Bowman, 1987). Assuming that one can with justifiable confidence identify departments where officers exercise the requisite level of self-control, there are still many for whom the latest and hottest police reform is quite inappropriate. Yet the community and professional pressure to stay in vogue can be considerable. Under these circumstances, it would seem unlikely that the police chief would react by acknowledging that his officers were insufficiently trustworthy to make the program work. More likely, the chief will either implement the reform or make superficial changes and declare that the department is on the community policing bandwagon.

It may be virtually impossible to learn the extent to which community policing fosters officer misbehavior because reliable data are exceedingly difficult to obtain on such matters as police abuse of authority, misuse of force, and corruption. There are, nonetheless, methods of obtaining informative estimates (see Geller, 1983; Barker and Carter, 1986; Sherman, 1974). Unfortunately, empirical evaluations of community policing programs have not taken a close look at how well the problems of control have been handled. Unexamined are the costs of greater rank and file autonomy and a more intrusive and proactive style of policing. Such an evaluation must go beyond resident and business surveys that assess the general population's perceptions and opinions. Needed is systematic in-person observation that describes precisely the nature of the treatment—who is getting stopped, rousted, arrested, and how these people are handled. Groups of at-risk citizens (e.g., street people and juveniles)—excluded or grossly underrepresented in door-to-door and telephone surveys—should be interviewed. How have their experiences with the police changed under the order maintenance regimen, and how, if at all, has it altered their behavior? Citizen complaints of police abuse and misconduct should be monitored. There is at least some indication that aggressive order maintenance programs generate community criticism about police fairness and civility, although whether it is justifiable remains an open question (Skolnick and Bayley, 1986:175).

THE PROBLEM OF LEGITIMACY

Justifying police and what they do has always been problematic in democracies, and this has been particularly true of the United States, where ambivalence about government authority is a persistent force. Under the law enforcement model, police derive their legitimacy in two ways, one process-oriented and the other outcome-oriented. The former attaches to democratic sentiments and the latter to professional ones of efficiency and effectiveness. The police authority to intervene in the affairs of private citizens and sometimes even coerce them is legitimated largely by the complex democratic processes that produce the laws that police enforce. The police act to implement the will of the governed, who—through a delicate balancing of majority rule and protection of constitutional rights—accord to the police those special powers required to enforce the law and take action where peaceful means have not or may not be effective to secure good order (Bittner, 1970). The second source of legitimacy derives from the sense of mission embraced by police. Manning's (1977) description of the adoption of the crime-fighting mandate by U.S. police is illustrative of many occupations that seek resources and status by claiming professional domain—responsibility and capacity for the production of certain outcomes, lower crime in this case.

Community policing also derives its legitimacy from both process- and outcome-oriented bases. To the extent that law is peripheral to order maintenance, the process source of community policing shifts to a form of direct democracy of the community will, the methods of which have been discussed in the section of this chapter on role definition. The second source—and the focus of discussion in this section—is the attachment of the police to producing or facilitating order. Klockars (1985:312) argues that the strength of the crime fighting mandate is so compelling that community policing advocates have been obliged to justify proposals at least partly in terms of their impact on crime. Advocates respond, however, that regardless of the crime control benefits of community policing, it is justifiable in its own right to the extent that it frees citizens from the fear of crime and sense of disorder that prevent them from enjoying their legitimate pursuits in public places (Sykes, 1986; Kelling, 1987a:93). It is this new subjective touchstone of police legitimacy that I wish to explore in the final section of this chapter.

In the last decade or so, fear of crime has assumed an increasingly important role as an index of police success. It has been institutionalized in annual U.S. Department of Justice surveys and is monitored by at least some policy makers and researchers. Perhaps the most obvious manifestation of its national priority is the funding of a large, expensive assessment of community policing projects in Houston and Newark—termed fear-reduction experiments.

What is interesting about the explosion of interest in fear of crime and the research industry that has accompanied it is that the concept is fuzzy, and much more is assumed than known about the merits of trying to reduce whatever its operational manifestations represent. It has been characterized as cognition, behavior, emotion, and attitude. It is perhaps most often measured as an attitude, where a distinction is made between personal worry and general concern about crime in areas such as one's neighborhood (Skogan, 1987:145). Operationally, fear is usually measured as a response to survey questions such as, "How safe would you feel outside alone in this area at night?"

The justification to use the reduction of fear is that it is "often far out of proportion to the objective risks of crime" (Williams and Pate, 1987:53; see also Brown and Wycoff, 1987:71). This so-called irrationality issue has been researched and debated for some time. Skogan (1987) recently reported results from a panel study that suggested that people's fear of crime may not be so irrational after all—that individuals' experiences with crime show a strong, consistent relationship with their attitudes and behaviors about it. Whether or not people are rational about crime in this sense is really irrelevant to the usefulness of fear of crime as an index of policy success or failure, however. Unless we are willing to assume that fear of crime is inherently and always undesirable, then we must ask ourselves—not whether people's anxieties about crime are accurate—but whether they mobilize people to take dysfunctional or functional courses of action regarding the quality of their lives. If fear is relevant to crime as an adoptive or mobilizing response, we must learn at what levels it produces a functional response and at what levels it proves dysfunctional. This is an enormously complex problem, for this surely varies a great deal among individuals and even with the same individuals in different circumstances. The problem is further complicated by the fact that avoiding criminal victimization is not an equally high priority for all people. It is only one among many simultaneously competing objectives people hold. Decisions such as where and how to live, work, recreate, and with whom to associate require a balancing of personal priorities and an assessment of the expected values of different alternatives.

Regrettably, we know very little about the functionality/dysfunctionality of the fear of crime (Garofalo, 1981). Until we do learn substantially more about it and can validate thresholds of dysfunctionality, we would seem best advised to avoid efforts to manipulate it. In this light, antifear programs appear to make as much sense as putting pain killers in the public drinking water to reduce headaches in the population at large. Indeed, reducing fear of crime on a mass basis may do as much or more harm as good, or it may be completely irrelevant to any objective indicator of life quality.

A response to this line of argument might be that regardless of our knowledge of fear's dysfunctionality for individuals, it is clear that civil society avoids public places out of fear of crime and disorder, which deteriorate the value of those spaces for vital economic, political, and cultural activities. Lessened fear among individuals will lead to the use of those spaces and thus, even if in some cases dysfunctional, it will contribute to the general public welfare. Whether or not the gathering of honorable citizens reduces crime and disorder—an unproven thesis—it remains a questionable business for the government to ask its citizens to make individual sacrifices regarding personal safety without advising them of the risks involved.

Other subjective measures have been widely used to assess community policing programs; they warrant careful scrutiny as well. Chief among these are perceptions of the extent of crime and disorder and evaluations of police service. When coupled with objective indicators of crime, disorder, and police practice, they provide a useful tool for learning how accurately changes in objectively measured levels of performance are perceived and weighted in citizens' evaluations. Substantial incongruities between objective and subjective measures deserve attention if for no other reason than police should be interested in why apparent program successes are not appreciated by the public and apparent failures are. What is bothersome about many of the recent assessments of community policing is their tendency to focus on subjective indicators and downplay or avoid altogether objective indicators of crime control, order maintenance, and police practice (see, for example, Pate et al., 1986). At best, this presents an incomplete and distorted picture—often of positive program effects—when the complete picture is far more equivocal. In general, the movement toward subjective indicators of police performance as a source of professional legitimacy seems a risky odyssey. A cynic might suggest that it merely exemplified an era of "feel-good" politics. But governments have always been in the business of shaping the perceptions, expectations, and feelings of the governed—for both good and ill. What is called for here is a balance that allows the public to distinguish a government's success in persuading people that their communities are safer from actually producing those conditions.

IMPLICATIONS: AN AGENDA FOR REFORMING THE REFORM

A Newtonian image of the brief history of U.S. police reform is that of a giant pendulum that describes its slowly changing arcs through symbols, myths, and metaphors, and other rhetorical edifices designed to house, structure, and facilitate real-world changes in what police do and accomplish. But as Manning and Klockars argue in Chapters 2 and 13, respectively, this volume, the relationship of rhetoric to reality either cannot be known or is at any given time known to be only partially true. Each time we learn our lessons from the failures of the pendulum's previous swing, we in fact seem to overlearn them and proceed anew to change the course of reform to pass through yet other rhetorical edifices of dubious or unknown relationship to reality. To draw upon a cliché, we seem forever in the process of throwing the baby out with the bath water when it come to learning from police history. Kelling and Moore (Chapter 1, this volume) offer a description of the process, suggesting that with community policing we have finally learned to limit reform excesses. I submit that despite laudable efforts to seek a balanced historical perspective for community policing, we are still faced with a reform that has been oversold. It may be that there is a certain inevitability to this process as Klockars (Chapter 13, this volume) suggests. Perhaps neither individuals nor societies can sustain a course of action without the sort of resolve that myths so powerfully reinforce. But as this reform is yet in its infancy, we might strive to make some midcourse corrections.

To begin, one must acknowledge the benefits as well as the limitations of community policing. First, it redresses the previous reform era's obsession with law enforcement as the core police role. It attempts to direct more administrative attention to the order maintenance activities comprising a major but latent part of the police work. Yet it fails to recognize that order is hard to define and manufacture, particularly when one hopes to produce it by means of systematically applied police aggression. It reaches for a sword when a scalpel will often do.

Second, community policing is valuable in its recognition that police purposes and practices must be formulated with an awareness of the expectations, perceptions, and values of the policed. It acknowledges that the capacity of police to reinforce order and enforce laws is severely limited without public support and participation. Yet it oversimplifies the difficulties of knowing and acting on a community will—especially in areas most afflicted by crime and disorder, and even in areas that appear to offer a coherent consensus on local problems. When communities are severely divided, simply harnessing the police to the will of one group on the basis of a community mandate risks exacerbating the situation in the long run.

Third, community policing recognizes that broad street-level discretion exists, especially in the handling of disorders. The many "Mickey Mouse" rules and regulations in police agencies do little to contribute to the most propitious street-level choices and are often counterproductive. Serious abuses are poorly controlled, and if so, often at the expense of proper police involvement when the situation warrants. Yet community policing has not developed means by which officers can be given sufficient autonomy to do good without also increasing the likelihood of doing ill.

Finally, community policing has encouraged the police to wrestle anew with the bases of professional legitimacy. Some, at least, have recognized the limitations of the crime control mission and sought other mandates. Unfortunately, the new alternatives, such as fear of crime, are just as grandiose, more nebulous, and less obviously as functional as the old measures of crime control.

What then is an agenda for reform? Some broad outlines are suggested here. First, we might restrain our appetite for lofty accomplishments and unburden the police of the glorious but futile missions of slaying crime, disorder, fear, or any other widespread social ills that plague our society. Were we to demonstrate conclusively tomorrow that what police do bears no relationship to those quality-of-life indicators, we would still find need of police. We are on strongest ground when we assess policing in the particular, micro-sense of their daily encounters with the public. That is not to say that police should never exercise initiative or try to address problems on a broader basis. Of course, criminologists should continue to gather data on crime, fear of crime, and so on to better understand any potential broader consequences of what police do. Yet what police officers themselves know about good policing has to do with how officers respond to the particular circumstances they are called to handle. This is the craft of policing, about which a great deal is known, yet uncodified (Bittner, 1983): making good arrests, deescalating crises, investigating crimes, using coercion and language effectively, abiding by the law and protecting individual rights, developing knowledge of the community, and imparting a sense of fairness by one's actions. These should be our first concerns when judging community policing or any other reform. As any piece of craftsmanship, the police officer's work can only be appreciated when examined at close range.

Second, we would do well to resign ourselves to the need for police to struggle continuously with the dilemmas of governing communities that are, in fact, complex, ambiguous, diverse, and highly stratified. As long as community-as-consensus is perceived as a prerequisite for governance, police will be burdened with the necessity of fabricating one where it does not exist. Any good police officer who has labored on the toughest beats knows that consent, not consensus, is his or her license to govern effectively. Consent is rendered when the *process* of government is known and accepted, even when there is discord over the substance of policy. In a practical sense, this calls for a high degree of openness by individual officers who must let citizens know what they are doing and why they are doing it. Muir (1977) offers a detailed description of how "professional" officers accomplish this on a daily basis in their personal dealings with the public. Another requisite of policing by consent is ensuring that citizens have the opportunity to voice their reactions to what they see and hear about their police. This is particularly important for those with grievances and whose poverty, powerlessness, and unpopularity make it particularly difficult to be heard. There are, of course, things that might be done by police themselves to ensure that these people are not ignored, but there are limits to any organization's capacity to receive and act on grievances against itself and requests that run counter to agency priorities. Police reformers could strengthen their cause if they attempted to improve the criminal courts to increase both the visibility of police practice and give voice to citizens with grievances. Lazy, incompetent, and corrupt officers of the court make no mean contribution to the cynicism of police and public. Community policing has attempted to strengthen some direct citizen-department linkages, but it has studiously avoided any attempt to revitalize traditional channels of political input, which, in fact, have formal responsibility for the police—local elected officials, such as mayors and legislators. Community policing reforms appear to thrust these officials even further to the periphery of meaningful policy making and operational oversight (see Bayley, Chapter 12, this volume). Alternatively, their role might be changed in ways that strengthen the consent process. Goldstein (1977: Ch. 6) suggests some ways in which this might be accomplished without opening the floodgates for corruption and incompetent administration. Some recent empirical evidence indicates that there is a capacity and willingness by elected officials in many communities to assume these duties in a responsible manner without making them mere cheerleaders of change (Mastrofski, forthcoming).

A third and final suggestion to reform community policing is to accept the paradoxical nature of the police role. We are in constant search of *the* police mission. In fact, as Bittner (1970) pointed out almost two decades ago, and many have reiterated in various ways since then, there is nothing that we wish our police to perform *too* well—be it control of crime, suppression or disorder, protection of individual rights, solving of social problems, or reinforcing "community." This does not mean that police should not endeavor to improve in these ways, but it does require that when a new reform rhetoric shifts our focus from one area to another, we take pains to note the consequences for those other objectives. Police agencies can play an important role in preserving this sense of balance and complexity, but it is also a responsibility to be taken seriously by those who do research on police and those who fund it.

The impact of community policing if widely implemented will not be known for a long time. Already the various proposals and pilot projects have stimulated more debate and innovation among police and researchers than the industry has seen since the days of August Vollmer. If the promise of community policing is great as Herman Goldstein (1987) suggests, so are the challenges and risks. Dealing with the problems raised here will go a long way toward making this reform more real and less rhetorical.

PART II

COMMUNITY POLICING PROGRAMS AND THEIR IMPACT

In a volume of this length, it would be impossible to present chapters representing all types of community policing programs, but this sampling offers an instructive variety. A chapter by Michael Farrell and one by David Weisburd and Jerome McElroy describe the Community Patrol Officer Program (CPOP) in New York City. Mary Ann Wycoff reviews the fear-reduction experiments in Newark and Houston. Timothy Oettmeier and Lee Brown focus on the Houston experience from the administrator's perspective. Gary Cordner assesses Baltimore County's experience with Community Oriented Police Enforcement (COPE). Finally, Part II is given an international flavor by contributions from Mollie Weatheritt summarizing the British experience and Chris Murphy reporting on Canada. Thus we have available reports on programs from old and densely populated central cities of the Northeast; a younger, sprawling urban center of the Southwest; a county in the Mid-Atlantic region with a mixed urban, suburban, and rural population; and programs in two nations sharing many cultural ties with the United States, but that also have major differences in their social makeup and the organization of their police.

Although they describe different programs in diverse environments, the chapters touch on several common themes: the impetus to develop community-oriented programs, the nature of program elements, the organizational scope of the programs, implementation problems, and assessments of what worked and what did not. These themes are briefly summarized below.

Nearly all the chapters report that the impetus for change emerged from perceptions of community dissatisfaction with police performance, but the particular elements on the agenda for change have been determined by police and police researchers. Several contributors report that a growing sense of danger, disorder, or rapid change stimulated departmental searches for alternatives to traditional approaches (Farrell, Oettmeier and Brown, Wycoff, and Cordner). In Britain, which had been experimenting with various aspects of community policing since the 1960s, the urban riots of 1981 intensified efforts to strengthen police-community linkages. Only in Canada did interest in community policing appear to develop without a perception of increased crime and disorder and eroding community support. None of the chapters report strong grass-roots pressure for a specific program of reform, but several do acknowledge the influence of police researchers, lessons learned from earlier program failures, and a few preliminary program experiments. Indeed, there appears to be a considerable cross-fertilization among departments, as program development characteristically included an intensive review of what other agencies were doing.

For many departments, the program elements were already operating in some form before community policing was used to describe them and an explicit philosophy was developed. Such strategies and tactics included foot patrol, proactive order maintenance, storefront operations, crime prevention, victim assistance, and community organizing. By the 1980s, however, these departments were looking for a comprehensive philosophy to undergrid, coordinate, and focus these strategies. In particular, most of these programs represent preliminary attempts to create an organizational environment that no longer makes these techniques tack-on frills but an integral part of mainstream police work (see Chapter 1 by Kelling and Moore). Wycoff describes how the idea of community policing was induced from several years' experiences with various program elements in Newark and Houston. Oettmeier and Brown note that the programs were already operational before a group of Houston police were convened to identify and define the conceptual umbrella, Neighborhood Oriented Policing. Cordner shows how Baltimore County shifted its orientation from a number of unfocused community-oriented strategies to a series of target-specific, problem-focused efforts. Murphy reports that the particular shape that community policing has taken in Canada has been little influenced by indigenous considerations, but mostly by continuing the tradition of importing reforms from the United States. The British experience reported by Weatheritt is significantly different than that reported in the other chapters. She suggests that in England and Wales there have been numerous ongoing efforts over the last two decades to promote a general community-oriented philosophy (unit beat policing, foot patrol, community constables, and community crime prevention), but that with few exceptions, these programs have suffered from a lack of tactical and strategic specificity. That is, program strategies are either not well defined or their linkage to program goals is poorly developed.

For the most part, community policing programs have been limited to narrowly defined experimental projects, making community policing officers—at least for the present—a special cadre. The Newark and Houston experiments targeted a few specific geographic areas and used small police task forces to implement program elements. New York City began with a pilot project of ten officers and a sergeant in one precinct, but quickly expanded it in less than three years to 85 percent of its precincts. Although the CPOP program accounts for a small proportion of patrol operations, it is now widely dispersed. Baltimore County began its COPE project with a jurisdiction-wide focus, but it evolved into a program requiring strategic target selection to maximize the impact of its 45 officers. Due in part to the greater influence of the central government, various aspects of community policing enjoy relatively widespread exposure in Britain: unit beat policing, foot patrols, community constables, crime prevention programs and planning, and community consultative committees. The centralized structure of rural law enforcement in Canada may give community policing reforms a boost there, while Canada's urban areas have already introduced many experimental features and begun to restructure some departments. Even in these departments, however, crime control and rapid mobile response still represent the core of the department's operations. Although community policing is still in the experimental stage in all of the departments discussed in these chapters, the contributors report growing interest among police administrators in expanding its scope in the future.

Several of the chapters deal with problems faced in implementing and operating community policing programs. Farrell discusses the New York agency's efforts required to overcome post-Knapp Commission rules to limit the risks of police misbehavior; he also describes how the department dealt with community pressure to expand the original pilot project. Weisburd and McElroy look at implementation problems in New York at the street level, finding that officers experience the greatest difficulty in organizing and coordinating citizen groups. Cordner reports that the COPE project's objectives lacked focus in its early stages, but the problem was overcome by employing a problem-oriented approach. Oettmeier and Brown identify the need to change the organizational culture to be consistent with community policing values. The idea is to infuse the entire organization with this perspective rather than merely to impose rules and programs from the top down. Weatheritt finds that despite a relatively lengthy history of experimentation with community policing tactics and substantial support from the Home Office, most community policing programs in Britain remain ill-defined on the operational level. For example, she finds that there is still considerable ambiguity about the role of the community constable and the purpose for making contact with the public. Similarly, Murphy argues that community policing programs in Canada face a variety of implementation hurdles because the theoretical and programmatic assumptions are not yet well articulated. Wycoff notes several severe consequences of failing to address these underlying problems, but she also suggests that the prospects for successful implementation are more positive than in the 1970s; police today are more educated and receptive to change, they can draw on the lessons of previous failures, and they have more evidence on which tactics work and which do not.

Finally, several of the chapters assess the impact of community policing programs. Farrell reports that community demand for and support of CPOP in New York City has been substantial. Weisburd and McElroy's fieldwork suggests that CPOP officers have used the program to increase the traditionally high-status activities of aggressive enforcement and arrest—a finding consistent with several evaluations of team policing in the 1970s (M. Brown, 1981:301). CPOs were able to use and coordinate existing organizations effectively but were not too successful in developing new groups. Cordner reports that the impact of COPE on officer attitudes toward the community improved significantly. Fear of crime showed modest decreases in targeted areas—the largest coming in the last stage when the problem-oriented approach has been implemented. Moderate reductions in reported crime were also reported in most targeted areas. Wycoff reviews the Houston and Newark fear-reduction program impacts. The experimental and quasiexperimental designs produced statistically significant effects for a variety of subjective measures of program effectiveness. The most successful strategies in Houston were the storefront station and the citizen contact patrol; in Newark (unlike New York's experience), greatest success was achieved with community coordinating and organizing.

Evidence is far less rigorous on the programs' impact on officers, but impressionistic evidence suggests that it was favorable, especially in replacing cynicism about the job and community with a positive outlook. Both Weatheritt and Murphy report a dearth of rigorously designed evaluations of community policing programs in Britain and Canada, respectively. They suggest a number of issues that future program evaluators need to address to give a more meaningful and comprehensive picture of program impact.

The reader will find some themes on which there is a fairly high degree of convergence among the contributors to Part II: the impetus for program development, program features, and the scope of organizational implementation. On the other hand, the chapters vary considerably in the methods of study and the conclusions drawn about program effects. All call for additional inquiry into community policing programs as departments continue to experiment and expand efforts in this direction.

4

THE DEVELOPMENT OF THE COMMUNITY PATROL OFFICER PROGRAM: COMMUNITY-ORIENTED POLICING IN THE NEW YORK CITY POLICE DEPARTMENT

MICHAEL J. FARRELL

The private homes and small apartment buildings on the 200 block of 45th Street in the Sunset Park section of Brooklyn look strangely out of place in what is primarily an industrial section of the city. Surrounded on three sides by warehouses and factories, and almost isolated from the rest of the community by the Gowanus Parkway, the residents of the block sometimes feel that they are living on an island, cut off from the safety of the mainland. The residents, mainly Hispanic blue-collar workers, struggled to maintain the residential character of their block against the onslaught of local drug addicts who congregated in a vacant lot on the corner, waiting to make their buys. Burglaries were too frequent an occurrence, and the people were afraid to let their children out of the house for fear that they would encounter drug addicts shooting-up in the hallways. The police from the local precinct did the best they could, chasing the addicts from the corner and making an occasional arrest. But the police couldn't be there all the time, and as soon as the radio car moved on, the addicts moved back. To some, it seemed that the only solution was to move.

In July 1984, Police Officer Robert Orazem was assigned to cover 45th Street, one of some 14 square blocks he would cover on foot in his new beat area. Orazem was a member of a new experiment in the New York City Police Department—the Community Patrol Officer Program. He was told to talk to the people on each block of his beat, find out what their problems were, and help them to solve them. It did not take him long to find out what the problems were on 45th Street, and he responded by spending a lot of his time on the block, keeping the corners clear and making arrests. But Orazem knew that he was having little impact on the problem. Every time he made an arrest he was off patrol for the rest of the tour, walking his prisoner through the maze of the criminal justice process. He soon realized that there just were not enough hours in the day to really clean things up, so he decided to take a different tack and try to do something about the focal point of the problem, the vacant lot.

Orazem tracked down the leadership of a then defunct Block Association and encouraged them to reorganize. He contacted the local Community Planning Board and discovered that the vacant lot belonged to the City of New York. Armed with that information, he began to contact other city agencies to find out what they could do to help eliminate the problem. Two weeks of making phone calls and talking to neighborhood residents culminated on a rainy Saturday morning when 50 block residents joined Orazem to clean out the tons of debris from the lot. The Department of Sanitation provided three teams to truck the garbage away. Other community groups enlisted by Orazem donated recreational equipment and the neighborhood eyesore was transformed into a community park for the smaller children. Orazem arranged to have the lot fenced by a City agency, and the keys were entrusted to the president of the Block Association.

The 200 block of 45th Street is still physically isolated from the main of Sunset Park, but the residents do not feel so cut off any more. The junkies are gone from the corner, burglaries have decreased, and both Orazem and the people who live on the block have begun to believe that there just might be hope.

THE COMMUNITY PATROL OFFICER PROGRAM

In July 1984 the New York City Police Department introduced a community-oriented patrol deployment strategy called the Community Patrol Officer Program. Almost from the very first day, the program received enthusiastic and vocal support from the residents of the community in which it was piloted. The program was also warmly received by the police officials in the area and, as a result, between January 1985 and December 1987, CPOP has been introduced into 64 of the city's 75 Patrol Precincts. It is the Police Department's intention to complete citywide coverage in the first half of 1988. This chapter reviews the origins and developments of the Community Patrol Officer Program in New York City and looks at the factors that have led to its wide acceptance by citizens and police officials alike.

Origins of the Program

In 1975 the residents of the City of New York were startled to learn that their city was teetering on the brink of fiscal disaster. Threatened with bankruptcy, the city's administration embarked on a fiscal recovery plan that in its initial phase required the city to curtail its services. For the first time since the Great Depression, municipal employees were laid off by the thousands. Some 3,000 police officers were furloughed, and a freeze was placed on new hirings. As a result of the layoffs and normal attrition, the once 32,000-member department was soon reduced by one-third. Responding to what was clearly a crisis in law enforcement, the department's administration eliminated several specialized units, cut back in others, hired civilian employees to replace sworn personnel in non-law-enforcement positions, and focused all of its resources in the Patrol Services Bureau in order to maintain a viable response to citizens' calls-for-service, which at that time amounted to over 6 million calls annually.

Despite the drastic reduction in manpower levels, the thinner blue line held, and the streets of New York were not plunged into chaos. Although the Police Department was able to maintain a viable response to citizens' calls-for-service and keep serious crime in check during the lean years of the fiscal crisis, it fared less well in dealing with the many order maintenance situations that arise on a daily basis in a city the size of New York. Focusing its limited resources on serious crime and service delivery, the department did not have the capacity to deal effectively with what became known as "quality of life" complaints. As a result, there was a discernible reduction in the peace and tranquility of the neighborhoods of New York City. Between 1975 and 1982, noncriminal infractions such as disorderly conduct and loitering increased by 181 percent. During the same period, arrests for these infractions dropped over 90 percent.

By 1982 the improved fiscal situation in the city allowed the department to begin rebuilding precinct resources. Additional personnel were assigned to each of the city's 73 precincts and more were promised in future budget allocations.[1] In anticipation of receiving new resources, the department began to search for ways of deploying them in a manner that would not only increase its ability to manage service demand, but would also directly influence quality-of-life issues. To assist in this effort, the department requested one of its consultants, the Vera Institute of Justice, to join with its Office of Management Analysis and Planning in reviewing current and prior deployment strategies and suggesting ways in which new personnel could be more effectively deployed.

Vera's staff approached the task from several directions. Senior staff members interviewed each of the department's seven patrol borough commanders, as well as a number of zone and precinct commanders to determine their view of current service needs and solicit recommendations for improving service delivery, particularly in the order maintenance area. In addition, a written questionnaire was drafted and administered to the commanders of each of the department's 73 patrol precincts to solicit information on current deployment practices. While these exercises produced a great deal of information, the most significant finding regarding service delivery in the order maintenance area dealt with the current use of personnel at the precinct level. In all of the precincts surveyed, the vast bulk of personnel were assigned to radio motor patrol, responding to citizens' calls-for-service at the direction of the central communications unit. A small number were assigned to plainclothes anticrime units, and a few officers in each precinct were assigned to traditional foot patrol posts at sensitive locations. In essence, almost all of a precinct's personnel were committed to basic law enforcement duties, and precinct commanders lacked any flexible resources they could deploy to deal with order maintenance conditions.

law + order

Vera staff also reviewed the major pieces of research on patrol conducted during the last 15 years or so. Three of these studies seemed particularly pertinent to the department's interests: the Newark Foot Patrol Experiment (Police Foundation, 1981), the Flint Michigan foot patrol study (Trojanowicz, 1983), and the Community Profile Experiment in San Diego (Boydstun and Sherry, 1975). In addition, essays by Wilson and Kelling (1982) and Goldstein (1979) provided provocative challenges to the way in which police agencies traditionally operated.

Vera's review of existing patrol operations and structures in the New York City Police Department, augmented by its review of recent experimentation in the field, led it to focus on creating a new role for individual patrol officers—the Community Patrol Officer, or CPO. That role was envisioned as improving police performance in several areas.

Increased Accountability

The then standard patrol practices, whether foot or motorized, did not foster beat accountability. The vast majority of the department's patrol resources were committed to responding to calls-for-service in radio motor patrol cars. During those times when officers were not on call, they were expected to patrol their sectors randomly and on occasion were given directed patrol assignments. Tour rotation on the department's duty chart did not permit assigning the same officers to the same beats or sectors on a daily basis, and in a given week, a motorized officer might be assigned to three or four different sectors. All of these factors mitigated against an officer either amassing a great deal of knowledge about conditions on a given beat, or being held accountable for correcting or at least properly handling conditions. Community Patrol Officers would be permanently assigned to beat areas, and would be responsible for both identifying and dealing with crime and order maintenance problems within their beats.

Identification with Community

Traditional deployment strategies do not provide much opportunity for officers to get to know community residents. Typically, officers and their partners drive from call to call attempting to address the immediate conditions presented. The officer's knowledge of beat conditions is limited to the identification of problem locations and problem people. He or she is neither required nor encouraged to form relationships with residents or the community and, in reality, the officer has little time to do so.

Community Patrol Officers would be required to get to know the residents and business people within their beat areas, and to attend community meetings. They would be required to determine the nature and extent of community problems by soliciting the input of the residents. In addition, they would attempt to work with community organizations in developing solutions to neighborhood problems, and where such organizations did not exist, to work with residents in forming them. To organize and facilitate this process, CPOs would develop and maintain Community Profile Records in which they would record information on conditions within their beat areas and the actions taken to deal with them. The Community Profile Records would also be used to record information on persons living and working within the beat area who might be encouraged to assist in improving conditions.

Developing a Proactive Approach to Order Maintenance

Traditional police patrol practices are essentially reactive. Officers respond to calls-for-service, deal with the condition presented, and move on to the next call. Tour and assignment rotation mitigate against individual officers adopting long-range strategies to deal with chronic conditions. In addition, while the department's allocation of personnel throughout the three-tour day is designed to vary the number of officers working on each tour in response to projected work load, the work load projections are based on citywide factors. In reality, temporal work load distribution may differ by precinct or by sector or beat area within a precinct.

Community patrol would be based on a proactive approach to dealing with order maintenance problems and neighborhood conditions. Officers assigned as CPOs would be required not only to identify crime and order maintenance problems within their beat areas, but also to devise strategies to deal with them. Each officer would negotiate a monthly work plan with his or her supervisor in which the officer would identify the principal crime and order maintenance problems in the beat area and establish objectives for the month. Officers assigned as CPOs would work flexible tours, adjusting their hours to meet changing conditions within their beats.

CONCEPTUAL DEVELOPMENT OF THE COMMUNITY PATROL OFFICER PROGRAM

In advancing a plan for the development of an experimental Community Patrol Officer Program the Vera Institute presented the Police

Department with an outline of how such a program would be structured and the duties to be performed by Community Patrol Officers. Conceptually, the CPO role was viewed as having four dimensions: planner, problem solver, community organizer, and information exchange link.

Planner

The first responsibility of the CPOs would be to identify the principal crime and order maintenance problems confronting the people within each beat area. Toward this end the CPOs would be expected to examine relevant statistical materials, record their own observations as they patrol their beats, and solicit and secure input from residents, merchants, and service delivery agents in the community. The problems identified would then be prioritized and analyzed and corrective strategies designed. These strategies would be reviewed with the Unit Supervisor and incorporated into the CPOs' Monthly Work Plan, which would form the focus of the officer's patrol for the coming month.

Problem Solver

CPOs would be encouraged to see themselves as problem solvers for the community. This begins with the planning dimension of the role described above, and proceeds to the implementation of the action strategies. In the implementation phase, the officer would be encouraged to mobilize and guide four types of resources against beat area problems: the CPO acting as a law enforcement officer; other police resources on the precinct and borough levels that can be brought to bear through the CPO sergeant and the precinct commander; other public and private service agencies operating, or available to operate, in the beat area; and individual citizens or organizations in that community. The strategies developed by the CPO could call for the application of any or all of these resources, and the CPO's success in resolving the problems identified would turn in large part on his or her success in marshalling them and in coordinating their application.

Community Organizer

Community resources cannot be brought to bear on crime and quality-of-life problems unless the community is willing to commit them for that purpose. Increasing the consciousness of the community about its problems, involving community people and organizations in developing strategies to address the problems, motivating the people to help in implementing the strategies, and coordinating their action so that they may contribute maximally to the solution are all aspects of the community organizing dimension of the CPO role. The CPOs would be required to identify potential resources and, where they are not adequate, to help in organizing and motivating the citizenry.

Information Exchange Link

Through his or her links to the community, the CPO would be in a position to provide the department with information about problem conditions and locations, active criminals, developing gangs, illicit networks for trafficking in drugs and stolen property, information about citizens' fears, and insights into their perceptions of police tactics. In turn, the CPO could provide citizens with information pertinent to their fears and problems, technical information and advice for preventing crimes and reducing the vulnerability of particular groups of citizens, information about the police view of conditions in the neighborhood and strategies for addressing them, and information about police operations in the community. This information exchange aspect of the CPO role was expected to result in arrests that might not occur otherwise, greater cooperation between the police and citizens in addressing crime and order maintenance problems, and a heightened sense in the citizenry that the police are a concerned and powerful resource for improving the quality of life in the community.

IMPLEMENTING THE PROGRAM

Vera's plan called for the implementation of a pilot project in one patrol precinct, and the assignment of one sergeant and ten police officers to man the pilot CPOP Unit. The operational specifications suggested are discussed briefly. The sergeant and the police officers selected for the pilot operation would be recruited on their agreement to work flexible hours in order to put the CPO in his or her beat area on the days and hours best suited to address beat conditions.

Under the supervision of the precinct commander, the sergeant would direct the program at the precinct, conduct daily roll calls for the patrol officers, supervise their activities within their beat areas, work with the officers on establishing patrol goals for each beat, and assist the officers in designing strategies to attain these goals.

One of the ten police officers would be assigned as program coordinator and would assist the sergeant in administering the program as well as acting as the sergeant's driver. The remaining nine officers would be assigned sizable beat areas of between 14 and 18 square blocks, depending upon population density, geographic and neighborhood boundaries, and the spatial distribution of crime and order maintenance conditions.

CPOs would be responsible for the identification of crime, order maintenance, and community problems within their beat area, and for devising strategies responsive to these problems. CPOs would be required to meet regularly with residents and business persons in their beat areas and to discuss community problems in an effort to determine the nature and extent of crime and order maintenance problems of concern to the community. The officers would also be responsible for attempting to involve the community in the solutions to those problems. Where citizen action groups currently exist, the officer would work with them on the design and implementation of neighborhood crime prevention programs. Where such organizations did not exist, the officer would assist community residents in organizing them.

CPOs would play an active role in crime prevention efforts in the community. They would attend neighborhood community meetings, conduct public education programs on crime prevention specifically geared to the various groups in the beat area, and conduct residential premises' security inspections, making recommendations to improve physical security.

CPOs would conduct foot patrol of some portion of their beats each day, covering the entire beat at least twice weekly. This would be a high-visibility patrol effort, planned and directed at focusing on community problems. Community patrol efforts would be based on each patrol officer's planning and organizing of his or her everyday activities with a view toward long-range peace-keeping and crime control objectives in the beat area. Random patrol activities would be replaced with more responsive and effective patrol strategies based on the CPOs' growing knowledge of the communities they serve.

CPOs would act as resource persons for community residents in other than criminal matters. They would be knowledgeable regarding both community and citywide resources for addressing community needs, and they would assist residents in contacting proper agencies or, in appropriate instances, initiate that contact on behalf of the community. The CPOP would function as an integral part of the precinct. Personnel assigned to the program would be assigned to the precinct and would work under the direct supervision of the precinct commander.

COMMUNITY PATROL OFFICER PROGRAM OPERATIONS

The Pilot Program

In July 1984 the New York City Police Department implemented a pilot Community Patrol Officer Program in Brooklyn's 72nd Precinct, covering the Sunset Park and Windsor Terrace sections of the borough. Following program design, one sergeant and ten police officers were recruited from among the members of the precinct's staff and were assigned to the new CPOP Unit. In addition, a police administrative aide was assigned to provide clerical support. Logistical support was provided in several ways. A CPOP office was set up in the precinct station house, and two dedicated telephone lines equipped with answering machines were installed. A marked 12-passenger van was assigned to the unit to serve both as the sergeant's supervisory vehicle and to support unit activities. Fliers announcing the introduction of the program and providing the unit telephone number were printed for distribution by the CPOs to merchants and residents within their beat areas. Finally, nine beat areas were designed, each covering between 14 and 18 square blocks, which covered approximately 70 percent of the precinct's total territory.

Field operations were preceded by a ten day training period, during which the new CPOs were oriented to their new roles as Community Police Officers and were provided with information on a number of public and private agencies they could use as resources in dealing with community problems. The training also included a number of meetings between the CPOs and representatives of community organizations located within the beat areas, during which specific community problems were discussed. On July 2, 1984, the new CPOs took their beats for the first time.

The pilot program was originally conceived as a one-year effort, during which program operations would be monitored both by the department and the Vera Institute. However, by October the pilot had produced such favorable response, both from the community and the department's command staff in Brooklyn, that a decision was made to begin replication of the pilot in early 1985.

The decision to expand CPOP operations to other precincts posed a new dilemma for the department's administration. New York City is made up of thousands of local neighborhoods, each of which is contained in several political subdivisions and represented by elected officials at the federal, state, and local levels—all of whom were requesting that CPOP be implemented in their areas. In 1985, immediate citywide expansion was neither possible nor desirable. While the city's fiscal recovery enabled the police department to begin rebuilding its forces and thus permit it to broaden CPOP coverage, this process would take several years to accomplish. More importantly, the department recognized that community patrol operations were still in a developmental stage and required careful nurturing if the program were to succeed over time.

To insure fairness in the process by which CPOP would be expanded to other precincts, the department adopted a three-part strategy. Initial expansion would involve replication of the pilot model—that is, the assignment of one sergeant, ten police officers, and one police administrative aide to CPOP operations in any given precinct.[2] While this insured fairness in the distribution of personnel, it also resulted in varying the degree to which CPOP coverage would be provided in the various precincts. In the geographically smaller precincts in Manhattan and Brooklyn North, nine CPO beat areas would encompass all of the territory within the precincts' boundaries, while in the larger precincts in the outer boroughs, nine beat areas would cover only a portion of the precincts' territory. Despite this, the pilot replication plan provided the fairest way in which the police department could address the political demands for program expansion and left the door open for the creation of additional beat areas in the larger precincts as additional personnel became available. The second feature of the expansion plan provided for an equitable distribution of the program between the several patrol boroughs.[3] Each planned expansion would be to six or seven precincts, one in each of the patrol boroughs.[4] Finally, the decision as to which precincts the program would be expanded in each of the patrol boroughs was delegated to the patrol borough commanders, who were directed to assess the need for the program within each precinct within their boroughs and establish a priority ranking of the precincts.

Program Expansion

In January 1985, CPOP was expanded to an additional seven patrol precincts. The process was repeated in March, June, and October, and by the end of the year, CPOP was operational in 31 precincts. The pace of expansion was slowed to a total of six new CPOP Units in 1986 because of a reduction in the number of new officers who would be hired by the department during that year. In 1987, 27 new units were added to the program, bringing the total in operation at the time of this writing to 64. The New York City Police Department has announced that it intends to complete citywide expansion of the program before the end of June 1988.

Although the rapid expansion of the Community Patrol Officer Program coincides with the restoration of strength levels in the New York City Police Department, there is evidence that the program would have been expanded even if new resources had not been available, although the pace of expansion would certainly have been slower. CPOP's acceptance and indeed popularity stems from a combination of factors. Community response to the program has been overwhelmingly positive. The police department has received thousands of letters from citizens throughout the city praising the efforts of the CPOs assigned to their precincts. Individual CPOs and CPOP Units have received a large number of citations from community organizations within their precincts. Community Planning Boards in those precincts in which the program has not yet been implemented continue to lobby actively for the program, and those Boards covering large precincts in which the original nine-beat model does not cover the whole precinct are asking when the remainder of the territory will be included.

These demonstrations of citizen support and satisfaction stem from the manner in which the CPOs have responded to the mandate to go on every block within their beat areas, ask the people who live and work there what their crime and order maintenance problems are, and do something about them. CPOP has given citizens more than just a specific police officer with whom to deal; it has given them a sense of some control over the quality of neighborhood life.

Police precinct commanders have also demonstrated overwhelming support for the program despite the fact that during the initial expansion stages many were required to remove personnel from other precinct assignments to staff the CPOP Unit. This support also stems from the manner in which the CPOs have adapted to the new duties and responsibilities assigned them. CPOP has filled a large void in police precinct operations in New York City. It has provided precinct commanders with the flexible resources necessary to deal with the myriad order maintenance problems existing in every neighborhood in the city—problems that are more oppressing than crime to the majority of citizens.

Day-to-Day Operations

To get some idea of what CPOs were doing to engender the support the program has received, the Vera Institute conducted a study of program operations in the first 21 precincts in which the program has been implemented. This study disclosed that CPOs perform a wide variety of tasks while on patrol. In addition to engaging in traditional law enforcement activities such as making arrests and issuing summonses, the CPOs do a number of things that traditional police officers do not ordinarily do. They attend community meetings and help to organize self-help groups such as block and tenant associations. They are also heavily involved in working with the youth and elderly in the neighborhoods, conducting safety programs and assisting in developing recreational activities. Most importantly, the study disclosed that the CPOs are taking their cues directly from the community, and are focusing their energies on those conditions and problems that the residents judged to be the most deleterious. In doing so, they are not only dealing effectively with a wide variety of crime and order maintenance conditions, but are also dealing with those conditions of greatest concern to the residents.

The above represents a composite picture of what CPOs do in the various precincts in which CPOP operates. Just as conditions vary between precincts, conditions vary between beat areas in the same precinct. As a result, beat priorities differ appreciably, and while one cop may focus almost all of his or her energies on dealing with crime and order maintenance problems, another will be able to devote more time to those activities designed to increase citizen participation in improving local conditions.

It is very difficult to measure the total impact of all of the activities of the CPOs in the various precincts. The substantial outpouring of citizen support for the program is certainly one measure, and the police command level support is another. Some CPOP activities are, however, quantifiable and review of these may present a clearer picture of what CPOP has done to gain the substantial support given it. During 1986 there were 327 CPO beat areas existing in 37 precincts, 273 in units that operated for the full 12 months of the year, and 54 in units that were added to the program in August. As a result, there were 3,546 man-months of CPO patrol during the year. During that time, the CPOs attended 4,419 community meetings, assisted in forming 113 new block and tenant associations, recruited 2,460 block watchers, conducted 680 residential security surveys, and arranged for the towing of over 7,300 abandoned vehicles. To support the law enforcement goals of the program, the CPOs issued over 83,000 summonses and made 6,465 arrests during the year, 968 of them for felonies. While these measures provide some insight into what CPOs are doing on their beat areas, they do not begin to explain what these activities mean to the residents of the various communities served by the program, nor can they begin to describe the impact that a skilled officer can have on every day life in a neighborhood.

Community Patrol Officer Cynthia Smith has worked a beat area in Brooklyn's 84th Precinct since October 1985. During her first few months in CPOP, she noted that there were few recreational opportunities available for the youth in the area and, as a result, the neighborhood kids hung out on corners, frequently getting into trouble. Cynthia reached out to other city agencies and began to locate programs that would serve the youth in her area. She also formed a girl's basketball league and got many of the neighborhood youngsters involved in it. While not all participate, there is hardly a youngster in the area who does not know Officer Smith and what she is trying to do for them.

Recently there were two burglaries in Cynthia's beat area, one in a community center and one in a day care center. Learning of them, Officer Smith began to ask the neighborhood kids if they knew what was going on. It didn't take long before she learned the identity of the burglar, a local youth. She then passed the word to tell him to come into the precinct and be arrested. The next day he surrendered to her.

THE PROGRAM'S EFFECT ON DEPARTMENT POLICY AND PROCEDURE

The proposal to implement an experimental community-oriented patrol program posed a number of policy dilemmas for the New York City Police Department. Some arose merely as a result of the differences between the proposed operating procedures and traditional department practices; others directly challenged long-standing policies.

As the purpose of traditional foot patrol is to provide a visible police presence as a crime deterrent, foot patrol posts in New York City have normally been designed as linear posts, five to six blocks in length. In addition to placing the officer in a position where he could observe his whole post from any location on it, the linear design also facilitated supervision. Patrol supervisors could merely drive the length of the beat to determine if the officer was indeed patrolling his post. The proposed CPO beat area configuration—square or rectangular areas of 14 to 18 blocks corresponding to community or neighborhood boundaries—raised a number of concerns with respect to the program: (1) the large beat areas would make supervision of the officers difficult, (2) the size of the beats and their configuration would provide the opportunity for officers to goof off rather than perform aggressive patrol; and (3) the size of the proposed beats raised questions as to just how effective an officer could be, given such a large area to patrol.[5]

Without experience as a guide, firm answers to these questions could not be given. However, it was suggested that design elements of the program directly addressed these issues. Community patrol did not rely on police visibility as the reason for its existence. Instead it focused on what the officer could do during his or her work hours to increase the crime resistance of a neighborhood during the times when he or she was not there. As a result, the configuration of the beat was less important than what the officer did on the beat. It was also suggested that the development of monthly work plans, frequent consultation between the CPO and his or her supervisor, and the daily update of portions of the Community Profile Record (in particular, the Beat Conditions Log and the Daily Activity Report) would facilitate supervision of the program and provide the unit supervisor with sufficient information to evaluate the performance of the individual officer.

Another issue of concern for the police department was the question of how community patrol officer performance could be evaluated. Officers assigned in traditional patrol modes are evaluated on a number of criteria, many of which are subject to statistical tabulation. Officers assigned to motorized units may be evaluated on factors such as response time, the manner in which specific calls are handled, quality of written reports, arrest and summons activity, and such. Clearly, many of the methods used to evaluate traditional patrol effectiveness would not apply to CPO performance, and new evaluation methods would have to be designed. More importantly, the department realized that one of its most difficult tasks would be to dissuade line commanders from using traditional measures to evaluate CPOP effectiveness.

Like many of the issues surrounding the introduction of CPOP, there was no easy answer to the evaluation question. The issue was temporarily solved by the police commissioner, who indicated that his evaluation of CPOP would not be based on productivity indexes such as arrests and summonses, but rather on the degree to which the CPOs were able to satisfy citizen concerns within their beat areas. To measure the level of citizen satisfaction, the department would require the Zone and Precinct commanders as well as the CPOP Unit supervisor to conduct regular interviews of merchants, residents, and civic leaders in the precinct, and solicit their views of the effectiveness of the new program.

The greatest concern for the department, however, stemmed not from these issues, but from the potential for misconduct made possible by the wide range of duties assigned to the CPOs. In the early 1970s, the New York City Police Department was the subject of an inquiry by a commission appointed by the mayor of the City of New York to investigate allegations of police corruption (the Knapp Commission). The Commission's investigation produced evidence of corruption, and in its report to the mayor, the Commission made a number of recommendations designed to prevent further abuses. Among these was the recommendation that "corrupt activity must be curtailed by eliminating as many situations as possible which expose policemen to corruption, and by controlling exposure where corruption hazards are unavoidable" (Commission to Investigate Allegations of Police Corruption and the City's Anti-Corruption Procedures, 1972:17). In the years that followed the Knapp Commission, the New York City Police Department promulgated a number of regulations designed to fulfill the Commission's recommendations. While these regulations succeeded in reducing the potential for corruption, some of them increased the separation between police officers and the communities they served. Many of these regulations, and indeed some that preceded the Knapp Commission Report, were specifically designed to reduce familiarity between police officers and community residents based on the belief that such closeness provided the opportunity for misconduct. Police officers were prohibited, for example, from entering business premises or private residences on other than police business, and from engaging in unnecessary conversation with citizens. The proposal to implement a pilot Community Patrol Officer Program seemed to many a regressive step that would bring patrol officers into greater contact with the community and increase the potential for abuse. In essence, the CPOP plan required the CPOs to do a number of things that police officers had theretofore been prohibited from doing: to enter all business premises on their beats on a regular basis, to go into private residences to conduct security surveys, to attend community meetings, to expend patrol time in trying to solve community problems, and so on. In short, they were to become deeply involved with the community and its residents in a manner, which if not carefully regulated, could plant the seeds of corruption.

Despite this concern, the Police Department decided to implement the pilot Community Patrol Officer Program. To address the potential for misconduct, the department adopted a number of preventive tactics, among which were: (1) careful screening and selection of personnel, (2) providing for functional supervision by all patrol supervisors in addition to the CPOP Unit sergeant, (3) providing staff monitoring of the program by an inspectional unit of the Chief of Patrol's Office, and (4) requiring the Unit supervisor, Precinct commander, and Zone commander to conduct weekly and monthly interviews of merchants and community residents within the CPO beat areas to determine the manner in which the CPOs were conducting themselves. While this final step imposed a burden on command and supervisory personnel, it was one they readily accepted. Precinct and Zone commanders in the New York City Police Department are held strictly accountable for the actions of the personnel assigned to their commands. The new CPOP requirements provided the commanders with an incentive and rationale for checking on the integrity of the officers assigned to the program, as well as a means of determining how the community responded to the program.

THE FUTURE OF COMMUNITY-ORIENTED POLICING IN NEW YORK CITY

The conceptual and operational development of the Community Patrol Officer Program has advanced considerably during the past three years. Given that this is the New York City Police Department's first large-scale involvement in community-oriented policing, more has been accomplished in this brief period than could reasonably be expected. Despite this, the police department recognizes that at this state of its development, CPOP is far from achieving its full potential. As a result, in the fall of 1987, New York City Police Commissioner Benjamin Ward implemented a series of steps designed to further the careful development of the program. In addition to establishing a CPOP orientation program as part of the department's Executive Development Program, the commissioner appointed an inspector as director of Special Programs, responsible for coordinating CPOP activities in all of the precincts throughout the city.

To further assist the department in its development efforts, the Vera Institute is conducting a large-scale evaluation of the expanded program, designed not only to determine what problem-solving techniques work in CPOP, but also to identify those aspects of the role that are most difficult for the officers and describe the kinds of assistance they should receive. Both Vera and the police department are also watching the community-oriented strategies being developed in other police agencies throughout the country and will undoubtedly benefit from what is learned in these jurisdictions.

NOTES

1. Between 1984 and 1986, two additional patrol precincts were opened, bringing the total to 75.

2. Although ten police officers are assigned as the initial complement of a CPOP Unit, twelve officers are given CPOP training, thereby providing the precinct with a pool of two trained members who may be used as replacement personnel.

3. The Patrol Services Bureau of the New York City Police Department is organized into several Patrol Borough Commands: Manhattan South, Manhattan North, Brooklyn South, Brooklyn North, the Bronx, Queens, and Staten Island.

4. As there are only three patrol precincts in Patrol Borough Staten Island, it would not be included in each planned expansion.

5. While the size of the CPO beat areas in the pilot precinct was limited to between 14 and 18 square blocks, the size of the beats in the expansion precincts varied in response to local conditions. In some of the more residential precincts outside of Manhattan, best areas of between 30 and 40 square blocks were found to be feasible, while in some of the more densely populated precincts in Manhattan, beat size was limited to between 12 and 14 square blocks.

5

ENACTING THE CPO ROLE: FINDINGS FROM THE NEW YORK CITY PILOT PROGRAM IN COMMUNITY POLICING

DAVID WEISBURD AND JEROME E. McELROY

The Community Patrol Officer Program was designed by the Vera Institute of Justice as a means by which the New York City Police Department (NYPD) could carry out community-oriented, problem-solving policing without a massive restructuring of the patrol force. Vera and the NYPD believed that these policing strategies would provide significant assistance to urban communities in controlling order maintenance problems and reducing the threat of crime. CPOP attempted to implement these strategies through the creation of a new and rather complex role for selected patrol officers who would be assigned to specific geographical areas ("beats") within a New York City police precinct.

As defined by Vera, the Community Patrol Officer role consisted of four principal dimensions (Farrell, Chapter 4, this volume).[1] Each CPO was expected to be a planner (identifying priority problems, analyzing them and developing strategies to correct them); a problem solver (managing the implementation of those strategies); a community organizer (working cooperatively with existing organizations on the neighborhood level and stimulating the establishment of such organizations where needed); and an information link (providing the police with information on and an understanding of community problems while informing citizens on how the NYPD can and cannot be of assistance to them).

CPOP was introduced as a pilot program, consisting of ten officers and

Research for this chapter was conducted at the Vera Institute of Justice. Points of view or opinions in this chapter are those of the authors and do not represent the official policies of the Institute.

a supervising sergeant, in one of the city's 75 precincts in July 1984. Vera research staff conducted an exploratory study of the pilot project during its first year of operation to see how the officers actually attempted to implement the new role and how the sergeant supervised their work.[2] Each of the CPOs and the sergeant were interviewed extensively using both structured and unstructured techniques. In addition, staff spent substantial periods of time accompanying officers on patrol, making notes about what they did and why they did it.

This chapter uses some of that data to describe how these community patrol officers carried out this new police role. While our observations are specific to the New York City pilot project, they have wider relevance to community policing in other settings, in that some configuration of these role dimensions is common to most other community policing programs. In concluding, we discuss the general implications of our findings for identifying those components of community policing strategies and operations that present the most (or least) difficulty to patrol officers.[3]

THE CPOP PILOT PROJECT

The pilot program included nine patrol beats, each consisting of 12 to 30 square blocks of residential and light commercial property. The nine CPOs that patrolled these areas were taken off the regular shift rational chart used by the NYPD and were encouraged to establish starting and finishing times for their tours that were appropriate given the needs and conditions of their beats. In addition, they were removed from a list of police units available for central dispatching in response to calls-for-service in order to provide them with time to carry out the CPO role.

Each officer was instructed to patrol the beat on foot, making a special effort to identify himself or herself to the residents and business people and to solicit their views regarding the major crime and order maintenance problems of the area. This information was to be entered in a Community Profile Record ("Beat Book") on a regular basis along with problem-solving strategies developed by the officer (in conjunction with representatives of the neighborhood) and approved by the supervising sergeant.

The officers were provided with 80 hours of initial training, which addressed a number of concerns: orientation to the rationale of the CPO program; a description of the tasks to be performed and consideration of procedures for performing them; discussion of the ethical concerns pertaining to the CPO role; an orientation to city service agencies and their representatives; and an orientation to community groups and organizations in the precinct.

ENACTING THE CPO ROLE

In the following sections we describe the efforts of the officers in the pilot program to carry out the CPO role and identify some of the obstacles they encountered in doing so. Our discussion is organized around the dimensions of the CPO role described above. However, the parallel is not exact. For Vera program personnel, "planning" included problem identification, problems analysis, and strategy development, while implementation of problem-solving strategies formed the principal tasks of "problem-solving." In practice, the officers treated problem identification as a distinct part of the CPO role, and they usually did not distinguish problem analysis and strategy planning from the actual problem-solving process. Our discussion below is consistent with how the officers themselves understood these role dimensions.

Planning: Problem Identification

The first task facing the CPOs after introducing themselves to the community was problem identification. As part of their role as planners, the officers were expected to identify the principal crime and quality-of-life problems confronting the people in their beats. Toward this end, the CPOs were encouraged to examine relevant statistical materials, record their own observations of beat conditions, and secure input from residents and business people in the community. The problems identified by officers were to be given a priority order and described at a level of detail appropriate for developing corrective strategies. We found in our evaluation of the pilot program that officers were indeed effective in rapidly identifying and prioritizing problems in their beats. However, they had much more difficulty with problem identification once obvious conditions were ameliorated and it was necessary to dig deeper into community problems.

In all of the beat areas the CPOs spent their first few months on patrol, identifying and addressing obvious problems and street conditions. All of the officers believed that the community should play a major role in this problem identification process, and indeed most of the problems CPOs encountered were identified by residents or business people. Of course, some of the conditions—for example, large-scale drug locations—while identified by residents, were known to officers before they entered the CPO program.

Most of the problems the CPOs focused upon were quality of life concerns that were seldom addressed by regular patrol officers. Some of these problems had not been responded to by the police because citizens failed to take the initiative in bringing these matters to their attention. For example, in one beat a CPO was told of a group of prostitutes that had been operating on a major thoroughfare for some time without police interference. This information had never been brought to the attention of precinct personnel. The CPO investigated and eventually arrested two women on disorderly conduct and drug possession charges. Other problems were not addressed by regular patrol personnel because they received a low priority as compared with other precinct conditions. In some areas this involved disorderly men on the street, or youths hanging out and playing loud radios in front of stores or residences. Importantly, residents often told CPOs that they were more disturbed by these problems than by some crimes, because the former represented constant annoyances.

A number of problems identified by CPOs would not be defined by all police administrators as police problems. For example, on more than one occasion, CPOs became involved in trying to clear up abandoned lots that had become serious health and safety hazards in the community. In three of the beats, such lots contained tons of refuse and were breeding grounds for rats and unsafe playgrounds for neighborhood children. In other beats, less serious problems—such as street hazards (e.g., large potholes), broken street lights, or areas overgrown with shrubs and weeds—were identified as priority problems by CPOs. Though not a priority for regular patrol officers, they were described by residents of the beat areas as affecting their safety and quality of life.

In a number of areas, officers were confronted with small-scale drug conditions, such as marijuana dealing in a local park. In other beats, the drug situation was much more serious, often including 24-hour traffic in narcotics. As a result, drug conditions were identified as a major priority problem by a number of the CPOs:

I had that one bad block and that's where most of my attention was. But that was everybody's problem, even the people who weren't living on the block. You know, the crime was just rippling from this block, so I figured if I could clean the block up a little bit. . . . So I spent most of my time on that block and the people who lived there were really thankful for what I was doing.

The process of problem identification became a much more difficult task after the obvious problems had been addressed and it was necessary to dig deeper into the needs of the community. This task was always difficult in quiet beats where there were few easily identifiable conditions even at the outset. In some beats, officers saw themselves being pushed to identifying less and less serious conditions as they ameliorated the more serious concerns of community residents. One officer expressed his resulting frustration in these words:

When you've solved a problem or addressed a problem and the community sees that it's addressed, they give you something else. I went from drug selling to beer drinking and loud radios down to the stupidest thing. Yesterday, a lady told me a Sanitation guy didn't pick up her trash can.

While the problem identification demands of the CPO role in some beats required more initiative on the part of the officers as the program progressed, CPOs were able to identify certain types of problems precisely because of their growing familiarity with the neighborhoods they patrolled. For example, officers were eventually able to identify outsiders in the neighborhood, or those who were seen as troublemakers.

I figure I was up there about six months. I knew everybody up there. I knew who was good and who didn't belong. As a matter of fact, that's how I made the burglary arrest I mentioned earlier. This guy just didn't belong on that block. I knew who lived in the house he was trying to get into. That's when I went in and challenged him. I asked him what his business was? So you get to know who's good and who's bad, who belongs and who doesn't.

A number of the officers developed new problem identification strategies once obvious conditions no longer occupied the major part of their time. To a certain extent, their concern with being pushed to deal with very minor problems led them to seek more serious issues to respond to. For some officers, this involved using crime statistics to examine such chronic conditions as car thefts and abandoned autos. For others, it meant seeking out special groups like senior citizens or teenagers in order to address their specific problems.

Problem-Solving: Planning Strategies and Carrying Out Actions

Once priority problems had been identified, the CPO was expected to develop and carry out strategies to address them. The officer was encouraged to see him- or herself as accessing and attempting to guide four types of resources that could be directed against problems: the CPO acting as a law enforcement officer, other police resources on the precinct and borough levels, other public and private service agencies in the community, and individual citizens and citizen organizations in the beat areas.

We found that CPOs were quick to develop problem-solving strategies, and that those strategies typically gave primacy to the officers' own law enforcement activities. Officers were also highly motivated and often successful in carrying out problem-solving strategies that relied primarily on CPO initiatives. They were less successful in motivating individual citizens to assist them in problem-solving. Traditional enforcement actions were initially presented to officers as only one of a number of potential CPO problem-solving tactics, and one that would play a less prominent role here than it does in regular patrol. In fact, CPOs were much more active in using enforcement actions, such as arrests, than were most motor patrol officers in the pilot precinct. In the view of the CPOs, these enforcement actions gained them respect and status from other patrol officers and precinct supervisors. As one of the officers noted:

I feel supervisors respect us more than they did prior to this. If you make collars, you're [seen as] involved and you're [looked at as] a good cop. That's the way most people think: guys who make collars, you know, they're good cops.

The largest part of CPO arrest activity arose in response to drug problems. A number of the officers were confronted with drug operations that had gone on relatively undisturbed for years. Generally, officers devoted significant portions of patrol time to individual locations, during which they would use a series of aggressive patrol tactics against those they believed were involved in the drug trade. The entrance onto the scene of uniformed police officers who were willing to confront small-time drug dealers was in itself something new in these areas. In New York City, patrol officers are discouraged from enforcing drug laws against street-level narcotics buyers and sellers.[4] Thus, when CPOs began to enforce such laws, it surprised many of these offenders. Indeed, a few arrests were made by CPOs precisely because dealers did not cease drug-related actions when they saw uniformed police officers.

While patrolling these drug locations, officers would generally stop and question anyone who looked suspicious. In making such identifications, officers were aided by their familiarity with the beat areas and citizens who lived there. Arrests were commonly made in the context of these sweeps:

I would tell them to get off the block and sometimes they wouldn't listen to me. They had drugs stashed somewhere and they'd say, "no, I'm waiting for somebody." I'd tell them again, "you don't live on this block, go wait for your friends on the corner." Again they would refuse and I'd take them in for disorderly conduct or loitering. I would never just grab someone and take him to the station. If they didn't give the right answer and they didn't move fast enough, then I would take them in. Most of the time they just left. . . .

When problems involved large numbers of perpetrators, the officers often attacked the problem as a team. This was particularly true with drug locations, though this strategy was also employed in response to disorderly groups. Generally, four or five officers would ride in a police van and address problems at a particular location. In some cases, they would leave the van and sweep a block, questioning everyone who was on the street. When the CPOs targeted a particular location, such as an apartment house entrance, the officers might surprise those involved by, for example, jumping out of the van after coming down a one-way street in the wrong direction. In one such raid observed by Vera researchers, five individuals were arrested, including one 20-year-old woman with a .22 caliber handgun.

In several instances the officers were quite successful in stopping drug activity, especially in locations that involved only a small number of dealers. Nevertheless, problems would often resurface either at the original location or another in the community. As a result, officers had to devote a great deal of time, on a continuing basis, if they wished to keep the drug problems in their beats under control. This point is well illustrated by one officer describing his feelings after coming back to the beat following a vacation:

I thought if I was going out there for a year, the drug problems were going to be gone, and they weren't. They might have been put back, they might have gone inside or whatever, but I was gone for a week and when I came back it was just as bad—well maybe not just as bad as a year ago. . . . It's the kind of thing that constantly needs enforcement. It constantly needs to be looked at.

Officers also employed enforcement actions to address a number of other problems they encountered on their beats. Intensive patrol on particular blocks was used to disband groups of drunk and disorderly men in front of stores or bars. CPOs found that bringing these individuals to the station house was an effective way of controlling this community condition because many of these men were embarrassed to be handcuffed and taken to the precinct house. The same strategy worked well in addressing the problems caused by loud radios and disorderly youths, though in these cases, arrests were seldom made. After being confronted daily by the CPO, these groups tended to move along or disband.

In several instances the CPOs' special knowledge of and contacts in the community produced arrests on conventional street crime complaints. In one beat, for example, the CPO's efforts led to the apprehension of a suspect who had shot a drug dealer. Police investigation immediately after the shooting failed to identify a suspect. The next day the CPO, who had been off duty when the shooting occurred, spoke to the victim and then patrolled the area directly adjacent to the incident. From conversations with people on the street who had revealed nothing to regular patrol officers and detectives (or were not interviewed by them), he identified the make of the car used in the shooting. Later he discovered the car a few blocks away and noticed some men hanging out nearby. The CPO had the victim brought to the area, the men were identified as the perpetrators, and the CPO arrested them for attempted murder.

Another enforcement action illustrates the importance of the ability of

CPOs to follow up situations that commonly fall through the net of traditional police activities:

There was one instance where two tenants had a fight. One tenant beat the other tenant up really bad. However, it worked out where it wasn't referred to the detectives. I picked up on it and I called the guy and spoke to him. It turned out there were two people who beat him up, so I went and arrested them. It was really a major thing. It ended up to be an assault and a burglary.

Officers used less-serious enforcement actions, such as summonses, to deal with a number of minor problems not often addressed on regular patrol, but which are annoying to community residents. This was particularly evident in the case of abandoned vehicles or cars that blocked driveways or obstructed street cleaning efforts. In one unusual case, summonses were used to disband an illegal video arcade that was operating on a quiet residential street.

CPOs elicited the help of other police officers in the precinct to deal with problems that occurred when they were off duty, or to follow up situations that could be better handled by specialized police units. Thus the CPOs would ask the youth car to pay special attention to a particular location, or contact the Narcotics Unit if they were confronted by problems they could not address.[5] Although officers generally believed that they were getting adequate help from other police personnel, the extent of that cooperation, at least on the precinct level, appeared to depend primarily on personal and professional contacts developed before the program began.

Other public and private agencies were used as well as CPOs in addressing quality-of-life problems ranging from potholes in the streets to broken street lamps, to abandoned lots that had become serious health hazards. The Community Board was the primary organization used by CPOs in addressing these problems, though they worked with a number of other private and public service agencies. At times it was not enough for the CPOs merely to contact these agencies. Often they had to do a significant amount of planning and persevere for some time to solicit a helpful response. For example, in one case where the CPO sought to clean out and secure an abandoned lot, he had to locate the owners of both the lot and the run down apartment building adjoining it. The owner of the lot had cleared out the debris once before and had a fence erected, but the fence was torn down by people who wanted to dump stripped cars in the lot. As the owner of the apartment house was eager to improve the security of the apartment building (in order to dissuade drug addicts from camping in the hallways), he gave the CPO authorization to enter the building and arrest trespassers. The officer urged the lot owner to clean the lot out again—or be subject to pay the city fee for clearing the lot. Eventually the lot was cleared out. In order to keep the area clear, the CPO also tried to close down some of the auto body shops in the area that were operating in violation of city ordinances.

In a number of cases, CPOs tried to enlist the help of citizens in their attempts to solve community problems, and at times they were successful. In the case of a deteriorating building, for example, a CPO helped to organize tenants who conducted a rent strike. This action eventually led to the building owner being taken to court by the tenants, and his being persuaded to put more money into the building itself.

In an unusual use of community controls, CPOs utilized beer drinkers in a local park to alleviate an on-going drug problem there. They told a group of young men that they could continue to drink beer in the park only if they were neat and threw away the bottles after they were done. The CPOs added another condition to their bargain: that the beer drinkers get rid of the drug sellers in the park. The latter group was, in fact, convinced by the former to cease sales in that public area.

While there were a number of instances where CPOs were able to mobilize citizens effectively to alleviate problems, officers were often disappointed in the community's follow-through in problem-solving. In at least two cases where lots had been cleared through the efforts of the CPOs, citizens failed to play the role expected of them in keeping the lots clean. One officer used the following story to illustrate the frustration CPOs sometimes experienced in attempting to use neighborhood residents and resources in problem-solving strategies. He had caught a teenage girl with a group of drug dealers. She had been carrying hypodermic needles for them. Rather than take her to the station house, the CPO decided to bring her home and talk to her parents. When he got there, he found that the only adult guidance in the home was an alcoholic older sister who was disturbed by the drug connection, but visibly drunk when the officer arrived. For this officer, this incident illustrated the fact that CPOs are many times confronted with people whose sadly disorganized personal lives prevent them from being able to assist officers in addressing community problems.

Community Organizing

The community-organizing dimension of the CPO role involved two primary features. In the first case, the CPO was encouraged to identify existing community resources and bring them to bear upon community problems. They were also expected to play a role in developing new organizations, such as block associations, that would eventually be a resource for officers in their efforts to carry out CPO responsibilities.

We found that CPOs were often effective in utilizing existing community resources, but had much more difficulty in establishing new community groups. CPOs were quick to identify community organizations within their beats and assess their strength and importance. In this regard, they worked with old-age homes, church groups, business organizations, drug rehabilitation centers, and the local Community Planning Board. CPOs used these groups to organize a number of community activities, including a major Halloween party that attracted thousands of youngsters in the precinct. They became involved with a number of organizations that had poor relations with local police officers prior to the start of the CPO program. For example, they began to refer teenagers in the community to a local pastor who ran a drug rehabilitation center. The pastor, who told us that he had not had cooperation in the precinct prior to the CPO program, eventually became an important resource for CPOs and a strong advocate for the program and its work with area youth.

CPOs had much more difficulty in getting citizens to organize and act where formal groups were not ongoing before they arrived on the scene.[6] Part of their difficulty in enacting this aspect of the CPO role may be attributed to the fact that this was a totally new police responsibility. Importantly though, officers were initially quite enthusiastic about this aspect of the program because they believed that the organizations they assisted and helped to develop would play a major role in assisting them in CPO work. One officer remarked at the outset of the program:

My major role will be as an organizer.... I'm out there to organize and get everybody to cooperate together. I see myself as an organizer, not as a police officer, although I will be enforcing the law. I feel once they see me on a regular basis, the laws themselves will be enforced by the people in the area. They won't tolerate things because there's a cop on the block and he's going to back them up and vice versa.

For a few of the CPOs, their lack of involvement in community organizing was the result of serious street conditions that demanded immediate attention and left them little time to invest in developing community groups. Yet in a number of cases where CPOs aggressively reached out to the community, they received little response. One officer, for example, distributed over 250 fliers proposing the establishment of block associations, but received just two inquiries from citizens. CPOs were particularly frustrated by this lack of response, because they originally had very high expectations for community involvement in CPO efforts.

I expected the community to be a lot more involved than they are. I figured, you know, in the beginning, everybody was very high on it. But as time went on, more and more people in the community were wrapped up in their own problems. I thought more people would want to get involved and have block association meetings. The energy just isn't there and there was nothing I could do to make them get involved.

Information Exchange

The CPO was expected to act as an information exchange between the police department and the community. This meant on the one hand that the CPO would provide the NYPD with information about crime and order maintenance problems in the community, as well as citizen attitudes toward police tactics and strategies. On the other hand, it meant that the CPO would provide citizens with information regarding police department activities and priorities. We found that the CPOs did collect information regarding the neighborhood, local crime patterns, and criminals operating in their beats that would not normally be received by other police department units. There was also evidence that these community patrol officers brought valuable information to citizens who would ordinarily not utilize police services.

Citizens developed greater trust in the CPOs as they saw them take action against community conditions. As a result, the CPOs gained access to information about criminal behavior in their beat areas that was unavailable to other patrol officers. As one CPO explained:

People get to know you. They get to trust you a little bit, and if something's going on, they figure, if they tell you, you'll act upon it—because you'll have to answer back to them in a couple of days....

Well basically, I have people calling me up ... and they say "Hey, this guy, he's dealing drugs right now in front of this address"—you would never get that on regular patrol.... They're also sending in anonymous letters, giving detailed descriptions of drug operations.

This information was passed on to other police officers and agencies and, as a result, the CPOs became a major information link between the public and the police department.[7]

While the bulk of crime-related information brought to the attention of CPOs in the pilot project involved drug offenses, useful information regarding other types of criminal activities was also received. Most of the CPOs, for example, worked with the precinct warrant officers and assisted them in locating offenders with outstanding warrants. Additionally, they were able to help other police units coordinate efforts in the precinct. One example of this came as a result of a tip given a CPO concerning an illegal license-purchasing operation. The CPO contacted officers from the Traffic Bureau and helped them coordinate operations designed to solve the problem.

The CPOs also provided information to the public. Some of the officers prepared crime prevention surveys for neighborhood residents, and all routinely advised citizens on crime prevention strategies. These activities were most often directed at helping senior citizens and children. In the case of children, they developed child safety and fingerprinting programs, which involved speaking at local schools, churches, and other community organizations about child safety and child abuse. In the case of senior citizens, officers developed an escort program and visited and spoke at senior citizen centers and homes.

CONCLUSIONS

Our research in New York City leads us to develop three general propositions concerning the work of community policing officers. First, when faced with choices of policing strategies and priorities, officers will choose those activities that have traditionally high status in policing. In the CPO program, officers became more involved in enforcement actions than was initially expected by program planners and even by the officers themselves. While this involvement was in the context of problem-solving efforts, officers were proud of their enforcement record, and they often defined problems that required aggressive enforcement strategies as more important and deserving of a higher priority.

Second, our research suggests that community police officers will perform most effectively those tasks over which they have most direct control. Initial problem identification, problem-solving tactics that relied on the CPO's enforcement of the law, or CPO utilization of other police or existing public resources, represented dimensions of the CPO role that were carried out most successfully in the program we examined. Information exchange between the police and the public, another aspect of the CPO role that officers carried out with relative ease, also relied primarily upon their own ability and enthusiasm in reaching out to the community.

Finally, we believe that community police officers will have the greatest difficulty in carrying out those functions that call for organizing citizen groups and coordinating citizen actions with those of the police. While CPOs were successful in utilizing existing organizations, they were generally unsuccessful in developing new community groups. Indeed, this was the case even where CPOs expended a great deal of time and effort on the community-organizing dimensions of the CPO role. In problem-solving efforts, CPOs felt as well that they were least successful in developing problem-solving actions that relied upon the assistance of individual community members, even in cases where this meant that community members needed merely to follow up on efforts initially carried through by the CPOs themselves.

We believe this latter finding is particularly important given the emphasis placed on community in community policing programs (Goldstein, 1987; Greene and Taylor, Chapter 11, this volume). Perhaps scholars have romanticized the concept of community in their effort to develop a more community-oriented policing strategy. The community is often identified as a resource waiting to be mobilized. Yet, as our findings suggest, community police officers are often confronted with settings of severe social disorganization. Such disorganization is not easily transformed into the kind of community organization envisioned by the community policing philosophy.

NOTES

1. These elements of the CPO role are described and examined later in this chapter.

2. For a discussion of supervision in the CPOP program, see Weisburd, McElroy, and Hardyman (n.d.).

3. Beginning in January 1985, the NYPD began to expand CPOP to other precincts. At the time this chapter was written, the program was operating in 44 precincts and the Vera Research Department was carrying out a more extensive study of its operations and effects.

4. This policy reflects the NYPD's concern with exposing large numbers of uniformed personnel to the corruption hazards involved in narcotics enforcement. Under the policy, such activities are the responsibility of a specialized and closely supervised Narcotics Unit deployed on the borough level.

5. For example, CPOs were not allowed to raid drug-dealing operations that occurred inside apartments in their beats.

6. This is not to say that all of the CPOs were unsuccessful in establishing community groups. One officer, in fact, managed over the year to organize five new block associations. Overall, though, CPOs themselves were frustrated with this component of the CPO role.

7. CPOs also acted as an information link for social service agencies. For example, a few CPOs played an important role in removing children from dangerous home environments by bringing information about child abuse to child welfare officers.

6

THE BENEFITS OF COMMUNITY POLICING: EVIDENCE AND CONJECTURE

MARY ANN WYCOFF

INTRODUCTION

The fear-reduction studies, funded by the National Institute of Justice, and conducted in Houston and Newark in 1983-84 by the Police Foundation, provide evidence of the efficacy of what the authors referred to as "community-oriented" policing strategies for reducing citizen fear, improving citizens' attitudes toward their neighborhoods and toward the police, and reducing crime (Pate et al., 1986). These community benefits may provide ample justification for a police organization to adopt such strategies; however, observations of these and other police-community interaction programs suggest they may constitute a "win-win" policing strategy, resulting also in benefits for the officers involved and, perhaps, for their departments. This chapter reviews evidence of benefits of community-oriented policing for the community and offers a rationale for testing the apparent benefits for police personnel.

COMMUNITY-ORIENTED POLICING: COMING TO TERMS WITH A TERM

"Community-oriented" is one of those terms that simultaneously suggests so much that is general and so little that is specific that it risks being a barrier rather than a bridge to discourse about developments in policing. Unfortunately, the barrier can assume the illusory shape of a bridge. Use of the same terminology may lead two people to believe they share a common interpretation of a subject. Should they be correct, the terminology is basis for an exchange of information. However, when people use terms with private, undisclosed meaning for each of them, they can converse at length before discovering they are talking about different entities bearing the same name.

This seems currently to be the risk in trying to discuss different experiences of what various observers may refer to as community-oriented policing. The term has rapidly and recently acquired vogue. In 1985 there were few references to it, at least in the empirical literature on policing; in 1987 entire conferences were devoted to it. In 1986 the authors of the fear-reduction studies (Pate et al., 1986) were looking for a label that might capture the more effective of several fear-reduction tactics tested in Houston, Texas, and Newark, New Jersey. They settled on "community-oriented," in part because the successful programs were similar to ones in Santa Ana and San Diego, California, and Baltimore County, Maryland, which were labeled "community-oriented" by the people who designed them and served as models for some of the fear-reduction strategies. All of these programs had in common positive, nonthreatening, two-way interaction between police and citizens. In each case officers were attempting to deliver services based on their understanding of what the residents in the program areas wanted done in their neighborhoods, and in each case officers were focusing their efforts on particular neighborhoods or communities.

In borrowing the term as a summary, we did not anticipate the variety of interpretations it might assume, nor did we expect that some readers would believe it to be synonymous with fear reduction. Both phenomena have occurred. In fact, since 1986 "community-oriented" has been both so broadly and so narrowly construed that it may now be a barrier to effective communication about police practices. One solution would be to discard the term and to search instead for others that more tightly specify the programs under consideration. Researchers may one day agree to do that, but for now it seems useful for expressing an emerging (or reemerging) attitude or orientation toward policing. If one thinks of community-oriented as characterizing an orientation rather than a specific tactic or specific set of outcomes, the term becomes a conceptual tactic or specific set of outcomes; it becomes a conceptual circus tent housing different and changing acts that can only be guessed at until one enters for a closer look.

In this respect, community-oriented is used in somewhat the way researchers a decade ago used—or should have used—the term "crime-fighting." Unfortunately, it took a long time to acknowledge that "crime-fighting" was a large conceptual tarp covering a broad range of programmatic approaches to crime prevention or reduction. We spun wheels trying to evaluate the "crime effectiveness" of police agencies without specifying the activities that were (or were not) conducted in efforts to cope with crime. In fact, it was impossible to evaluate the impact of the general concept because strategies—not general concepts—can be weighed and measured. If, in the early stages of interest in the community orientation, we view it as a philosophy to be operationalized and not itself an entity to be evaluated, the terminology may serve as a bridge rather than a barrier.

Discussing an orientation, however, does not eliminate the need to articulate the construct, at least to the point of determining that we are referring to a reasonably similar show or set of acts. My own sense of what we are talking about derives from exposure to several programs conducted by police organizations that have chosen to label their efforts as community- or neighborhood-oriented. Philosophically, the programs tend to have in common the belief that police and citizens should experience a larger number of nonthreatening, supportive interactions that should include efforts by police to

1. Listen to citizens, including those who are neither victims nor perpetrators of crimes;
2. Take seriously citizens' definitions of their problems, even when the problems they define might differ from ones the police would identify for them;
3. Solve the problems that have been identified.

Some programs go even further to incorporate the idea that

4. Police and citizens should work together to solve problems.

Judging from several current programs, listening to citizens and working with citizens tend to be done best within the context of communities or neighborhoods, thus requiring officers to concentrate their attentions on specific geographic areas. Eck and Spelman (1987b) point out that the problem orientation studied in Newport News can be used to focus on "communities of interest" (Newman, 1979) rather than on physically defined communities.

However community is defined, it is the commitment to *listening* to citizens (as opposed simply to talking to them) and to taking seriously citizens' definitions of their own problems that distinguish the better programs of today from "community-relations" programs of the 1960s and 1970s that too often lacked what Skolnick and Bayley (1986) refer to as "reciprocity" of exchange. This new commitment by police to listening may be based on a number of beliefs, among them that

1. Citizens may legitimately have ideas about what they want and need from the police that may be different from what police believe they need;
2. Citizens have the information about the problems and people in their areas that police need in order to operate effectively; and

3. Police and citizens each hold stereotypes about the other that, unless broken down by nonthreatening contacts, prevent either group from making effective use of the other.

Goals of the increased interaction between citizens and police may include:

1. A better attitude on the part of citizens toward the police;
2. A better attitude on the part of the police toward citizens;
3. More effective police service, with "service" and "effectiveness" being defined by the police; and
4. More effective police service, with citizens working together to define "service" and effectiveness." These definitions might include: (a) the provision of more or different types of service by police, (b) an increase in order, (c) a reduction of levels of fear among citizens, and (d) a reduction in crime.

It is especially the fourth goal, with its emphasis on the "collaborative process" (Murphy and Muir, 1985), that is the hallmark of the more compelling community-oriented efforts of the 1980s.

While the first and second goals focus on improving attitudes, both the third and fourth goals have as their primary objective the delivery of a tangible "good" to the community being served. Whether that good is the solution of a particular problem in the community, support for the development of social structure in the community, reduction of crime, or the reduction of fear among its residents, the police are attempting to *do something* for the community rather than simply seeking ways to improve their image among its citizens. In these programs, the efforts to listen and to improve attitudes are the means to better service. The successful programs in Houston and Newark were attempting to define and deliver goods as a result of listening to citizens, and it is programs that similarly combine listening with efforts to provide better service that this writer would define as community-oriented were the label hers to bestow. Just as there may be multiple notions of community and community good, there are a number of organizational arrangements, operational strategies, and activities used to accomplish the objectives of community-oriented policing, with the fear-reduction programs providing examples of only some of the options. Among organizational arrangements are the options of having special units conduct the program, of using designated patrol officers to operationalize the philosophy—as currently being attempted in Houston and Madison, Wisconsin—of training all officers to be community-oriented in the way they handle calls, identify community problems, and make use of uncommitted time. Under this department-wide approach, officers might work independently or as a part of an integrated team. In both Houston and Madison, physical decentralization as well as the decentralization of decision making are considered important organizational arrangements in support of the philosophy.

Operational strategies might include the use of storefronts, foot patrol, or combinations of foot and motor patrol. Among a variety of possible activities, officers might structure ways of meeting more business people and residents, publish newsletters, conduct community surveys, engage in community organization, attend community meetings, establish citizen advisory panels, work with Neighborhood Watch groups, participate in neighborhood social and athletic events, and work with other governmental or private agencies to enforce regulations and solve community problems.

All of the above has been said to underscore the point that the fear-reduction projects discussed below do not define or delimit community-oriented policing. Nor does fear reduction provide the only or even the central rationale for adopting a community orientation to policing. It happened that the successful programs could be described as community-oriented (as that concept has been outlined in previous pages) in that they promoted an increased number of nonthreatening contacts with citizens that: (1) involved listening to citizens, (2) took seriously citizens' definitions of problems, and (3) were intended to develop solutions, often in cooperation with citizens, to those problems.

BENEFITS TO THE COMMUNITY: THE FEAR-REDUCTION STRATEGIES

Seven strategies were tested in Houston and Newark. They are summarized briefly below.

Newsletters (Houston and Newark). These were tested with and without crime statistics. They were police-produced and provided residents of the test area with information about crime prevention steps they could take, the police department, and police programs in their area.

Victim Recontact (Houston). Patrol officers made telephone contact with victims to inform them of the status of their case, inquire whether they needed assistance, offer to send crime prevention information, and ask whether victims could provide additional information.

Police Community Station (Houston). A neighborhood storefront operation was conducted by patrol officers. The station provided a variety of services for the area.

Citizen Contact Patrol (Houston). Officers concentrated their patrol time within the target area where they made door-to-door contacts, introducing themselves to residents and business people, and asking whether there were any neighborhood problems citizens wished brought to the attention of the police.

Community Organizing (Houston). Officers from the Community Services Division worked to organize block meetings attended by area patrol officers. They organized a neighborhood committee that met monthly with the district captain and developed special projects ("safe" houses for children, identifying property, and a clean-up campaign) for the area.

Signs of Crime (Newark). This program focused on social disorder and physical deterioration. To address the first, a directed patrol task force conducted "random intensified enforcement and order maintenance operations" (e.g., foot patrol to enforce laws and maintain order on sidewalks and street corners; radar checks; bus checks to enforce ordinances and order; enforcement of disorderly conduct laws to move groups off the street corners; road checks for DWI [driving while intoxicated], improper licenses, stolen vehicles). Addressing physical deterioration involved an intensification of city services and the use of juvenile offenders to conduct clean-up work in the target area.

Coordinated Community Policing (Newark). This was the "kitchen sink" project that included a neighborhood community police center, a directed police-citizen contact program, a neighborhood police newsletter, intensified law enforcement and order maintenance, and a neighborhood clean-up.

The strategies the researchers considered community-oriented were the Police Community Station, Citizen Contact Patrol, Community Organizing, and Coordinated Community Policing.

With the exception of the newsletters, which were tested as true experiments, the strategies were tested as quasi experiments. They were implemented in target areas that were matched in each city with a program-free area that served as a comparison area for the target areas. Community surveys were conducted in each of the areas before and after program implementation. Surveys were conducted in person at randomly selected addresses with randomly selected respondents. Two types of samples resulted: two waves of a cross-sectional sample in each area, and two waves of panel respondents. Regression analysis of the cross-sectional data produced the area-level effects presented in Table 1. Regression analysis with controls for respondents' Wave 1 outcome scores produced the individual-level effects presented in Table 2.

At the area level, Houston's door-to-door contact strategy accomplished the largest number of primary goals. In terms of individual-level outcomes, Newark's Coordinated Community Policing program (the kitchen sink) was the most successful. Relative to the effort and resources required, most departments would consider the door-to-door contact strategy the big winner; it required no special facilities or training and a very small amount of patrol officer time (an average of three–ten minutes per

Table 1
Effects of Fear-Reduction Programs (cross-sectional results)

Programs	Reduce Perceived Area Physical Deterioration	Reduce Perceived Area Social Disorder	Reduce Fear of Personal Victimization	Reduce Worry About Property Crime	Reduce Perceived Area Personal Crime	Reduce Perceived Area Property Crime	Improve Evaluation Of Police	Increase Satisfaction With Area
Houston Newsletters With And Without Statistics	n.a.	n.a.						
Newark Newsletters With And Without Statistics	n.a.	n.a.						
Houston Victim Recontact Program	n.a.	n.a.						
Houston Police Community Station	n.a.	✓	✓		✓	✓		
Houston Citizen Contact Patrol	n.a.	✓	✓		✓	✓		✓
Houston Community Organizing Response Team	n.a.	✓					✓	
Newark "Signs of Crime" Program								
Newark Coordinated Community Policing		✓		✓		✓	✓	

✓ = Desired goal achieved; significant at .05 level
n.a. = Not applicable

Source: Pate et al. (1986), p. 27.

Table 2
Effects of Fear-Reduction Programs (panel results)

Programs	Reduce Perceived Area Physical Deterioration	Reduce Perceived Area Social Disorder	Reduce Fear of Personal Victimization	Reduce Worry About Property Crime	Reduce Perceived Area Personal Crime	Reduce Perceived Area Property Crime	Improve Evaluation Of Police	Increase Satisfaction With Area
Houston Newsletters With And Without Statistics	n.a.	n.a.						
Newark Newsletters With And Without Statistics	n.a.	n.a.						
Houston Victim Recontact Program	n.a.	n.a.						
Houston Police Community Station	n.a.		✓		✓			
Houston Citizen Contact Patrol	n.a.	✓					✓	✓
Houston Community Organizing Response Team	n.a.	✓			✓	✓	✓	
Newark "Signs of Crime" Program								
Newark Coordinated Community Policing		✓	✓	✓		✓	✓	✓

✓ = Desired goal achieved; significant at .05 level
n.a. = Not applicable

Source: Pate et al. (1986), p. 28.

munity-oriented policing, the desire to find ways of reducing citizen fear produced program elements that we would now identify as community-oriented. In Houston, the patrol officers who analyzed the fear problem and designed the strategies believed that an underlying cause of fear was lack of confidence in the police and the feeling on the part of citizens that police were remote from communities and uncaring about their problems. The intent behind every Houston strategy was to demonstrate the accessibility of the police and their concern for ordinary citizens. With this as the starting point, the officers sought to identify a number of different approaches that might accomplish these ends. The strategies that had measurable effects—all of which can be considered community-oriented—appeared to reduce citizen fear of crime, improve citizens' views of crime and disorder problems in their neighborhoods, and improve citizens' evaluations of the police.

BENEFITS FOR OFFICERS: CONJECTURE

The Police Foundation did not collect formal data on the effects of the fear-reduction strategies on the officers involved in them. Especially in Houston, the number of participating officers was too small to survey and the evaluation focus was on the effects for the community. However, working with the Houston patrol officers who designed and implemented the fear-reduction strategies allowed researchers to observe an evolutionary process among the officers that included the following features:

- Officer recognition (to their surprise) that most citizens welcome the opportunity to interact with police;
- A feeling that patrol work could be more interesting than they had realized;
- A sense of pride in their work;
- A growth in their sense of efficacy and personal competence (example of this being the officer who, over the course of the project, ceased referring to himself as a "plain ole, dumb ole cop" and began instead to think of himself as a leader in the neighborhood he served);
- A recognition that there are many ways to approach policing; and
- An identification with the profession of policing, which extended beyond the officers' own organization, as they became aware of officers in other departments attempting to conduct similar programs.

If Houston were the only source of data on officer effects, the generalizability of the observations would be questionable. Police Chief Brown had requested that the "brightest and best" patrol officers be assigned to the task force. The task force planning process that led the officers to research the relevant policing and fear literature exposed them to well-known people in the field. It gave them the opportunity to visit other departments and to plan and implement their own work. The special attention the task force officers received from Houston Police Department leaders, the Police Foundation, the National Institute of Justice, and media personnel could have been more than enough to create some of the changes.

However, I do not think that was all that happened to these officers. The attitude changes listed previously seemed to develop after the officers began implementing their strategies, and revealing statements on the part of the officers frequently made direct reference to their fieldwork. Robin Kirk, the Houston storefront officer, said: "It's given me the opportunity to do the best policing I've ever done." When he made that statement he was speaking to a group that probably wanted to hear just such a response. But three years later, when all the crowds have departed, you can ask him again about his work, and he will tell you that it just keeps getting better. That should be consolation for Officer Nilsson who works a problem-oriented foot beat in Evanston, Illinois, who says: "I often think I should retire now; it just doesn't get any better than this." Allow Kirk or Nilsson to elaborate on their feelings and they are much like Ron Cowart, a storefront officer in Dallas who said: "I used to think I was a mean and cynical cop; now I realize how effective I can be while still being a considerate human being." All three officers have substantial careers against which to measure their present experiences. All are veterans with 14 to 18 years in their departments, and all have been "tough" street cops with their share of the "good" assignments.

These three officers are not isolated cases. Listen to the officers speaking through the Mott (1987b) report. Talk with storefront officers in Detroit, COPE officers in Baltimore, Neighborhood Bureau officers in Madison, Senior Lead Officers in Los Angeles, officers involved in problem-solving policing in Newport News or St. Petersburg, and you will hear similar remarks. Are any of these officers "average?" In many cases they have been selected for the work they are now doing because somebody thought they would be good at it—and that seems appropriate. While the community orientation remains innovative and open to question, it should be implemented and marketed to other officers and agencies by those people who believe in it and are good at it. It is they who can develop the concept and provide the models on which selection and training of other officers will be based. Whether the practice of community-oriented policing will have the same effects on most officers as it appears to have had on some of the first who have implemented it remains an important empirical question.

In addition to the observations of individual community-based officers, there also are some survey data that reflect the impact of a community orientation on police personnel. In their evaluation of San Diego's community profiling project, Boydstun and Sherry (1975) surveyed officers in and out of the program and found that the participating officers were significantly more likely to report their work as "interesting" and significantly less likely to report it as "frustrating" than were nonparticipating patrol officers.

Schwartz and Clarren (1977:7) compared the attitudes of officers in and out of Cincinnati's team policing district and found that "positive changes were reported by officers in job breadth, independence, and influence over decisions, although most of the gain in job breadth reportedly was lost by 18 to 30 months. Some aspects of job satisfaction rose initially but all fell by 18 months." By the eighteenth month, the Cincinnati project had experienced managerial problems that adversely affected the program and officers' attitudes toward it. The departmental requirement that the program work within the framework of the management-by-objectives model, the refusal of the chief to modify decisions that affected project efforts, and the transfer of 40 percent of the sergeants out of the project area were all management decisions that caused the project officers to believe that top management had no real interest in the program—except as a way of obtaining Police Foundation funding. They understood that the problems that developed over the course of the project were not intrinsic to the program, and many of the officers reported at the end of the study that they wished they could work in a program like theirs had been "at the start."

In the study of Newark's foot patrol program, the Police Foundation (1981) found foot officers, as compared to motor officers, to be more satisfied with their work, to have a more benign view of citizens, and a more community-oriented view of the police function. Since officers were not assigned randomly to foot patrol and since the motor officers who participated in the survey were not selected randomly, these data can be viewed as only suggestive.

In their study of job satisfaction among Flint's foot patrol officers, Trojanowicz and Banas (1985:10) found that

to a statistically significant degree, foot officers, more than motor officers, felt they were (a) doing an important job in the Flint Police Department, (b) doing an important job in their patrol area, (c) keeping up with problems in their patrol area, (d) improving the police/community relations, (e) doing the job the police department sees as important, and (f) working as part of a police team.

Both foot and motor officers felt, to a significant degree, that . . . motor officers had more difficulty maintaining high morale and achieving job satisfactions.

As was true with the Newark officers, the Flint foot officers had, more often than motor officers, "chosen their own assignment as well as the area in which they worked." In Chapter 8 of this volume, Cordner reports effects of the Baltimore County COPE project on the officers involved in it that are consistent with the findings from Flint, Newark, and San Diego.

While observer impressions and the limited available data are illustrative of the advantages of the community orientation to officers who practice it, there has as yet been no test of the hypotheses that could be set forth. As the number of departments implementing community-oriented strategies and seeking evaluations of them increases, it will be possible to conduct such tests. In January 1988 the Police Foundation collected baseline data for assessing the effects of neighborhood-oriented policing on the approximately 40 Madison, Wisconsin, officers who began implementing it in February. In the Madison project, one-sixth of the department is working in what is being called the Experimental Police District (EPD), a geographical area constituting one-sixth of the city in which officers devise strategies for communicating with citizens, learning citizens' perceptions of problems, and working with citizens to solve problems. There is an emphasis in the EPD on participative management, with managers functioning as supporters of officers rather than as order-givers. Officers play a major role in determining the methods to be used in dealing with the community and its problems.

Based on the department's experience with a pilot project, members of the EPD Planning Team hypothesize that working in the EPD will cause officers to have greater:

- concern for citizens' problems
- concern for victims
- sense of independence
- self-esteem
- respect for their own skills
- sense of "ownership" of and responsibility for work
- organizational commitment
- a more positive view of citizens and of the way in which citizens view the police

The attitudes of the officers working in the EPD will be measured within a year of their assignment to the area. For comparative purposes, the attitudes of officers working in the rest of the department will be measured at the same times.

BENEFITS FOR THE POLICE ORGANIZATION: MORE CONJECTURE

If there are advantages for individual officers involved in community policing, these may result in benefits for the departments for which they work. Charlie Brown, the Kansas City officer who coauthored the report of the patrol experiment conducted there, used to join departmental colleagues in regaling researchers with tales of highly imaginative, non-productive activities in which patrol officers could engage. He would conclude, "If only you could harness that energy and intelligence for good police work. . . . " That harnessing appears to occur when officers are involved in policing neighborhoods they care about; energy goes into identifying and solving problems. Not only do officers have less time for pranks, but they would be less inclined to engage in them—at least in their own beat—where being seen by a citizen who knew them could be very embarrassing or worse. An officer who is known to the community is easier to report for either good or poor conduct than one who is not known. People engaged in community policing might have fewer incidents of damage to equipment and create fewer disciplinary problems. As officers identify more closely with their communities, become familiar with the residents and concerned about their welfare, they may be less likely to engage in the kinds of behaviors that can result in citizen complaints.

Additionally, the data for Newark foot patrol officers indicate that they have lower rates of absenteeism, an explicable finding if community-oriented policing increases job satisfaction as hypothesized. I will even be so flagrantly optimistic as to suggest that community policing holds the prospect of peer supervision among officers. To the extent that officers identify with the community, the we/they dichotomy many police use to characterize themselves and citizens is weakened. As the dichotomy is diluted, so *perhaps* is the power of the "blue code" to protect wrongdoing among officers. Observers have documented a case in which officers proud of their community program requested that a supervisor transfer an officer who was not performing to program standards. The rationale? "We've got a good thing going here; we don't want it messed up by some guy who isn't willing to work." A rare event? Probably, but researchers should remain alert to the possibility as they observe these types of programs. With this in mind, the Madison evaluation will monitor officer absenteeism, injuries, accidents, equipment damage, complaints, commendations, disciplinary actions, and attitudes toward controlling the behavior of peers.

Another possible organizational benefit is a workforce that becomes more interested in innovation and is more willing to consider flexible work arrangements. Officers who work community programs in which they are allowed to rearrange their hours to fit the needs of the job may be less inclined to support union demands for rigid schedules. As they see what their own "experiments" can accomplish in their beats, they may become more interested in organizational efforts to improve service delivery. Items in the Madison officer survey will assess receptivity to organizational change.

COMMUNITY POLICING: POSSIBLE DISADVANTAGES

To be taken seriously, any advocate of community-oriented policing must acknowledge potential problems with this approach. There is no point in extended discussion here of issues David Bayley covers so well in Chapter 13 of this book, but, briefly stated, a list of possible pitfalls includes:

1. *Illegal Policing.* This is possible in the event community-based officers become more responsive to local norms than to legal constraints (see McCoy, 1986).

2. *Inequitable Policing.* Many communities or neighborhoods are far from homogeneous, and it would be possible for some groups to benefit more than others from police service. We found this to be the case in Houston where blacks and renters were much less likely to be positively affected by the fear-reduction strategies than were whites and homeowners (Wycoff and Skogan, 1985a, b).

3. *Politicization of the Police.* Mayors and city managers have some reason to question the intent of community-oriented strategies. More than one politically ambitious chief has used the community link as a source of political clout—either in electoral or bureaucratic battles. Officers might find it tempting to use their community organizing skills and good relationships with the neighborhood to mount a campaign to accomplish political objectives whether it be a salary increase or the ouster of an unappreciated judge or chief.

4. *Corruption.* Close contact between police and business people or residents always makes an anticorruption manager alert to possibilities for unacceptable behavior, especially in communities in which the civic culture does not dissuade corrupt practices.

5. *Police Intrusion into Private Arenas.* Clearly, the better the police know us, the more they are able to know about us. In a democratic society, it is always appropriate to ask how effective we really want our police to be.

These are potentially grave problems and they are not hypothetical; most of them have existed and some still exist in the experiences of pre-reform cities. However, it is important to note that abuses and misuses of police power are not peculiar to the community orientation, nor are they inevitable. They are, however, the kinds of issues that could be used by its opponents to destroy a potentially valuable program. There are safeguards that can be employed against these problems, some of which are inherent in the community orientation itself. The strategies that may be most beneficial in avoiding the possible abuses of community policing may be the same ones necessary for success of the initial implementation of the program. Among these are: community/police coproduction of the program, appropriate management and supervision styles, and the development of appropriate performance measures.

When the public becomes closely involved with the police in dealing with community problems, the police will be known to the citizens and citizens will be able to take a more active role in holding police accountable for their behavior. Such accountability might be increased by regular reporting and discussion in city council meetings or council committee meetings of the kinds of problems police are dealing with in the community and how they are handling them. As occurred in the Community Organizing Response Team fear-reduction project in Houston, neighborhood representatives might meet periodically with the team of police officers that works their area or with the area commander. Or, as happens in Madison, citizens who receive police service might be mailed brief questionnaires about their opinions of the service they are given.

While greater police accountability to the citizenry will be beneficial in many communities, it will not serve to control corruption in those communities that tolerate such behavior. There are communities in which this continues to be enough of a problem to make community-oriented policing questionably suitable for these areas.

The only way to supervise and support a community-oriented officer is for the supervisor to be fully familiar with the problems the officer is handling and how she or he is handling them. This calls for a highly active and interactive style of supervision and management, one in which the supervisor spends considerable time conversing with the officer and with citizens in the officer's area. Effective management will not require that the supervisor or manager dictate what the officer should be doing or how the officer should do it. It will, however, require that the manager or supervisor be fully informed about what the officer is doing and capable of discussing with· the officer alternative means of responding to community needs. This greater familiarity with the officer's work and citizens' assessments of the work will place the manager in a better position to sense problems and to guide the officer in correcting them.

The same is true of the development of appropriate performance measures. If an officer is to be community-oriented, it seems logical that feedback from the community served should play an important role in the evaluation of that officer's performance. Gathering these data will be one of the ways in which supervisors will be more fully aware of officers' behavior than they now are in more traditional patrol systems. Performance evaluation should include assessments of the extent to which officers have been instrumental in dealing with neighborhood problems. The means for making these assessments—still to be developed in most places—will provide means for detecting problems that may be developing in the field.

THE PROSPECTS FOR
COMMUNITY-ORIENTED POLICING

The recent history of attempts to implement versions of community-oriented policing, most notably the stories of team policing efforts of the 1970s, breeds skepticism about prospects for success of the new programs of the 1980s. There are, however, reasons for optimism. Perhaps the greatest of these is the expanding capacity of the police profession to learn from its history. Police are an increasingly well-educated group, and with the growth of police education, there has developed in the last 20 years a literature that makes the lessons of the past accessible to a cohort of police interested in and capable of absorbing them. In a number of departments, managers now recognize that many of these earlier efforts failed because management systems and styles were not changed in support of what was to be a new work style. That departments interested in the community orientation are now consciously addressing this issue offers hope for successful implementation.

In addition to containing lessons about creating change, the literature now includes information about how to do a number of things more effectively in policing, whether handling spouse assaults, child sexual abuse, alcoholics, or the mentally ill; managing investigations; or responding to calls for service in a variety of ways other than sending officers to the scene. Goldstein's (1979) notation of problem-oriented police provides a critical conceptual umbrella over inquiries into handling more effectively the problems to which police are asked to respond. The problem orientation is a tool that helps police translate the philosophy of community orientation into service delivery that amounts to more than public relations.

Because of education, because of the literature, and because of almost 20 years of familiarity with ideas that were considered radical two decades ago, departments are now intellectually and psychologically prepared to test community-oriented policing in a way they were not in the 1970s.

Many of those earlier experiments were the result of the enthusiasm and commitment on the part of progressive police chiefs who believed or hoped they could develop the internal support for the new ideas. Most of them learned through painful experiences the enormity of the task of readying an organization for significant change. Some of them represented police departments that still faced the challenge of completing what Kelling and Moore (Chapter 1, this volume) have identified as the reform stage of police organizational development. There remained a lot of internal work to be done before the organization was ready to reshape its relationship to its external environment. Even in departments that were more organizationally advanced, the change-oriented chief was likely to have few on his staff who understood and shared his vision.

The environment for change has improved. There are more departments ready in 1988 than were ready in 1970 to move from the reform to the community stage of development (Kelling and Moore, Chapter 1, this volume). The chief does not stand alone in appreciation of alternative approaches to policing. The numbers of people at all levels of the organization who are willing to consider alternatives appear—at least in several departments with which we are familiar—to be much larger than they were even a decade ago. Innovators have internal resources that were not previously available to them.

The same factors that may make officers more receptive to new ideas also make them better prepared to carry them out. Educated officers should have more of the skills required for problem analysis and solution and for effective interaction with a diverse community than do uneducated officers. They are also the people who may be more likely to seek the challenge of a community orientation that gives them more responsibility for their work.

Innovators in the 1980s may also experience greater external support as well. Ironically, this comes in part as the result of shrinking financial resources. When departments were constantly able to expand their budgets, as many could in the 1970s, there was no need to struggle to find ways, as Stewart (in Spelman and Eck, 1987) put it, to "work smarter" and more efficiently. Today that need is more apparent to everyone, including officers, city officials, and citizens. This creates both more environmental pressure and support for innovation.

CONCLUSION

Chris Braiden (1987) has written that community policing is "nothing new under the sun" since the modern terminology only echoes Robert Peel's 1829 statement that the police are "only members of the public that are paid to give full-time attention to duties incumbent on every citizen in the interest of community welfare and existence." What *is* new—as exemplified by Braiden's own work and the Bramshill report on community-oriented policing (Jones et al., 1987)—is the understanding on the part of police professionals as to what is required to translate the philosophy into operations that work in the context of current social conditions and technology. Moreover, if we are correct in believing that context includes both greater police and public support for the philosophy and the practices of community-oriented policing, what we may be seeing is not a new concept under the sun but rather a new sunrise on a fine old concept.

ACKNOWLEDGMENT

Work on this chapter has been supported by a grant to the Police Foundation from the Charles Stewart Mott Foundation. Ideas expressed here represent cumulative conversations with colleagues (resulting in the intellectual symbiosis or theft) including: Keith Bergstrom, John Eck, Herman Goldstein, George Kelling, Tony Pate, Wes Skogan, Bill Spelman, Marilyn Steele, Mollie Weatheritt, and numerous police personnel interested in community-oriented policing. Thanks to Keith Bergstrom, Steven Mastrofski, and Bill Spelman for their comments on earlier drafts.

7

DEVELOPING A NEIGHBORHOOD-ORIENTED POLICING STYLE

TIMOTHY N. OETTMEIER AND LEE P. BROWN

OVERVIEW

Policing agencies, similar to other social institutions, are being forced to deliver their services in a rapid and ever-changing environment. Because of the complexities brought about by rapid social change, heretofore unknown pressures are placed on police agencies to meet the competing need to be flexible and, at the same time, maintain organizational consistency. Police agencies are better able to meet this challenge if they have a well-thought-out philosophy about policing that guides both the management efforts and the service delivery responses of the department.

Over the past few years, the Houston Police Department has addressed this need by developing as its overriding philosophy a commitment to manage its affairs and deliver its services in a manner that is responsive to neighborhood concerns. This commitment is clearly evident in the Houston Police Department's (1987) mission statement, which reads as follows:

The mission of the Houston Police Department is to enhance the quality of life in the City of Houston by working cooperatively with the public and within the framework of the United States Constitution to enforce the laws, preserve the peace, reduce fear, and provide for a safe environment.

The challenge to the management of the Houston Police Department is to ensure that all members accept their responsibility to conduct their business in a manner consistent with the department's mission. To assist in this effort, the department has promulgated a set of values. Collectively, these values represent a set of beliefs that govern the development of policies and procedures as well as affect the attitudes displayed by the members of the department. The values also incorporate a number of expectations held by the citizens of Houston. Foremost among these expectations is the desire and willingness to have the citizenry and members of the department work together to improve the quality of neighborhood life.

The commitment to developing and maintaining this relationship is quite evident in three of the ten department value statements:

- The Houston Police Department will involve the community in all policing activities which directly impact the quality of community life;
- The Houston Police Department believes that it must structure service delivery in a way that will reinforce the strengths of the city's neighborhoods; and
- The Houston Police Department believes that the public should have input into the development of policies which directly impact the quality of neighborhood life (L. P. Brown, 1983).

The department recognizes, however, that is is not sufficient just to articulate a philosophy; rather, the vision inherent in that philosophy must be reflected in the manner the department polices the city. For the Houston Police Department, the concept of neighborhood-oriented policing (NOP) became the philosophy from which a viable policing style was developed.

EXECUTIVE SESSIONS

As a concept, NOP evolved from within the department through the use of a technique known as an Executive Session. An Executive Session can best be described as a process designed to stimulate dialogue within the department. The dialogue provides answers to difficult questions that have a significant impact on the department and its operation. In the case of the Houston Police Department, the primary question centered on determining how a policing style could be designed that would incorporate active community participation in the identification and resolution of neighborhood problems requiring efficient service delivery methods.

Six Executive Sessions were conducted over a period of three months. A total of 28 sworn officers served as participants in the sessions. Each rank within the department was represented by two or more participants. Civilian personnel were also invited to attend the sessions. The following characterized the executive sessions:

1. The sessions were conducted off site (i.e., at an executive conference room within a hotel) to minimize interference from daily responsibilities.
2. The chief of police served as the chairman, emphasizing the importance of the commitment to the members.
3. An administrative coordinator was selected to oversee the administration and operation of the sessions.
4. Multiple representation from all ranks was required (however, each person left their rank outside the meeting room doors), participation was mandatory, no substitutions for excused absences were allowed.
5. Civilian resource personnel were present, lending their expertise to the subjects discussed.
6. Expert consultants were in attendance; they were requested to make formal presentations and respond to the questions regarding the topic in question.
7. Required reading assignments were made in order to expand the membership's understanding of particular topics scheduled for discussion.
8. Depending upon their experience and expertise, members were requested to make formal presentations before the group. Police officers consequently had an opportunity to convey directly to upper management their opinions on certain department issues.
9. Members were also required to respond periodically to key issues in writing and/or verbally during the course of the sessions. This promoted active participation by the membership and helped overcome rank consciousness.
10. Department personnel (regardless of rank) possessing unique experiences and/or qualifications relevant to the topic under discussion were requested to make formal presentations before the membership.
11. The sessions were recorded with transcripts returned to each member prior to the next meeting.
12. A final report was produced that represented the accomplishments of the sessions.

The Executive Sessions allowed participants the opportunity for an open discussion of ideas, facts, experiences, and values that would help shape the department's future style of policing. Consequently, the focal point of the Sessions rapidly centered upon an extensive review of four primary initiatives deployed within the department during the previous five years. Each of these initiatives sought to strengthen the relationship between the citizens and the police officers utilizing different types of operational strategies.

The first of the initiatives was known as the Positive Interaction Program (PIP). The primary goal of PIP was to develop a formal method of facilitating information exchange between beat officers and neighborhood residents. This was accomplished by arranging regular monthly meetings between police personnel and representatives of the neighborhood civic groups located within the officers' respective jurisdictions. Beat officers, their supervisors, shift lieutenants, and the division commander attended the meetings to discuss with the citizen representatives their needs and concerns. As a result of these meetings, civic groups became better organized to assist the police in improving the quality of life within their respective neighborhoods.

A second department initiative, entitled Project Oasis, represented a problem-solving process requiring involvement from a number of community organizations within the city in an effort to improve identified problems existing within low-income housing areas. As a problem-solving process, Project Oasis included the following steps: (1) an analysis of neighborhood problems, (2) developing an appropriate plan of action, (3) enlisting cooperation from other governmental agencies, and (4) assessing the results. Project Oasis required the officers to examine social, economic, and physical conditions affecting the quality of life in the target area. As officers began to understand the dynamic relationships between these conditions, neighborhood strengths and weaknesses were identified and responded to accordingly.

For example, officers discovered neighborhood weaknesses (e.g., crime, sewage, maintenance, utilities, etc.) requiring assistance from a number of different governmental agencies. Thus there was a greater advantage to working in cooperation with other agencies to resolve these concerns rather than having just one agency, such as the police, concentrate on their own agenda. Experience has also demonstrated that residents are much more effective at resolving problems if they have accepted responsibility for the long-term effect a given situation may have on the overall neighborhood. Furthermore, this type of concerted effort has a more permanent effect over the long term.

The third department initiative was known as the Directed Area Responsibility Team (DART) Program. As an experimental effort, the DART Program provided the department with a process of altering its service delivery methods in a manner consistent with flexible neighborhood needs. The service delivery methods were classified into five distinct categories: deployment, team interaction, job diversification, knowledge gaining/sharing, and community interaction. Interspersed throughout these categories were a total of 17 different strategies that provided the officers with the flexibility to cope with the demands of a changing environment in a growing city.

The DART Program introduced the line officers and supervisors to the importance of interacting with the public at the neighborhood level. This was accomplished by adding to the officers' regular responsibilities a number of new activities: establishing community contacts, attending neighborhood meetings, conducing security surveys, and sharing crime prevention information and techniques with neighborhood residents. The performance of these activities resulted in the officers and residents opening up multiple lines of communication. From this communication, officers developed greater empathy for residents and concern for their safety.

The final department initiative was known as the Fear-Reduction Program. Funded by the National Institute of Justice, the Fear-Reduction Program was designed to determine how police personnel could effectively address the problems of fear, disorder, quality of police service, neighborhood satisfaction, and, ultimately, crime itself in different neighborhoods. Community contacts, a community organizing response team, community storefronts, and newsletters were some of the strategies implemented throughout the City of Houston. Among the more successful strategies was the use of community storefronts. Because the storefronts were physically located within the "heart and soul" of the neighborhoods, beat officers had a golden opportunity to develop mutually rewarding and productive relationships with the residents.

In addition to these four initiatives, members of the Executive Session spent extensive time examining and discussing the ramifications of other community-oriented policing efforts being deployed by other police agencies throughout the United States. Presentations were also made regarding the relationship between the concepts of problem-oriented policing, managing patrol operations, and NOP.

As the members absorbed this information, they began to identify a number of common characteristics existing within each of the concepts, programs, and research findings presented to them. Discussions of these characteristics resulted in the formulation of emerging themes that emphasized the value of having the officers and the citizens work together to improve the quality of neighborhood life. It was from these beginnings that the members developed and refined the concept of neighborhood-oriented policing as it would pertain to the delivery of services within Houston.

DEFINING NOP

As characterized by the Executive Session Members, NOP represents a philosophy that guides and directs the delivery of police services throughout the City of Houston. As a philosophy, NOP seeks to incorporate the department's values into a responsive policing style that is dependent upon the quality of day-to-day interactions between the police and the public.

The key to defining NOP resides in the ability to recognize the need to establish rapport between the beat officers and the citizens who work and live within each of the officer's respective beats. It is the nature of this interaction between the officers and citizens that defines the quality of their relationship. It is through these relationships, either established in handling calls for service or in meeting with citizens when not on call, that officers can begin to identify and begin to think about the most salient service delivery needs in each of their respective beats.

From the collaboration among the Executive Session members, a definition of NOP was developed, which signified the importance of the relationship between the officers and the citizens:

Neighborhood oriented policing is an interactive process between police officers assigned to specific beats and the citizens that either work or reside in these beats to mutually develop ways to identify problems and concerns and then to assess viable solutions by providing available resources from both the police department and the community to address the problems and/or concerns (Oettmeier and Bieck, 1987).

The neighborhood residents' active participation is paramount to the successful implementation of the NOP philosophy for two reasons. First, community input is valuable to the department in that it offers a different perspective from that of police personnel as to what the local neighborhood concerns and problems are. It is naive to assume only the police are in a position to determine neighborhood needs. History has demonstrated repeatedly that police do not know everything transpiring within the neighborhoods, nor can they be everywhere at once.

Second, the police and the community work much better together when they know and understand each other. Effective communication encourages meaningful understanding. As so aptly noted by one of the Executive Session panel members, "The better we communicate, the more we communicate; the better we understand what problems are in the neighborhoods, the better we understand the community we are responsible to, and, the better the community understands us."[1] For too long, police officers have hidden behind a shroud of professionalism that is characterized by anonymity. This has served to inhibit their ability to interact and thereby develop a mutual understanding with the public. The philosophy of NOP addresses the traditional desire of the police to remain apart and aloof from the public. It recognizes the necessity of abandoning the noninvolvement syndrome that has become imbedded in the definition of professional policing.

Under NOP, the concept of professionalism is redefined in a manner designed to stimulate a commitment from both the officers and the neighborhood residents to communicate and interact. It envisions that the desire and willingness to work with the public will become an innate feeling within all officers. As a consequence of their mutual cooperation, the police and the neighborhood residents will learn and come to understand each other, and they will come to feel more comfortable with each other. This, in turn, should lead to the goal of creating a partnership of working together to improve the quality of life in the neighborhood.

In Houston, the concept of NOP is designed to serve as the foundation for the department's culture. The objective of the Houston Police Department is to have a culture that views all of its members and activities as a part of, and not a part from, the community. This is operationalized under the concept of NOP where each officer is expected to be an active partner in the neighborhoods he or she serves. The beat officer's attitude and behavior should demonstrate this expectation. This is best accomplished under a culture created by the NOP concept that calls for the residents to know the officers who provide services within their neighborhood.

The philosophy of NOP perpetuates this feeling of police-community teamwork by reinforcing in each officer that each and every contact is an opportunity to generate public support for cooperative police and citizen interaction. Whether the circumstances leading to the contact are positive or negative for the citizen, NOP recognizes that the behavior of the officer is what is often remembered. Thus officers must develop a full appreciation for the consequences of their behavior. The importance of establishing positive contacts with neighborhood residents was put into proper perspective by a member of the Executive Session when he stated from his experiences that

it is not how good you are, it's how good those people out there think you are that is important. Officers may think they are the best at what they do; however, if the people, the citizens, the community, and the civic groups do not think they are the best or do not think they are doing the job they should be doing, the officers have not accomplished anything positive.

As the officers and citizens begin to strengthen their lines of communication, the ability to identify neighborhood problems and concerns will improve. Responsibilities will also be more clearly defined for both parties. For example, acceptance of the NOP concept by the officers will be partially dependent upon their involvement in developing neighborhood plans, facilitating community participation, implementing new programs, and conducting evaluations.

Implicit within the NOP definition, consequently, are a number of prominent features:

1. To establish trust and harmony between the neighborhood residents and the beat officers;

2. To exchange information which will strengthen rapport and enhance neighborhood safety;

3. To address the problem of crime and reduce the level of fear associated with the criminal activity;

4. To help define service needs;

5. To help identify and resolve neighborhood problems; and

6. To clarify responsibilities on behalf of the citizens and the officers (Oettmeier and Bieck, 1987:10).

These features suggest that a number of traditional operational assumptions will be challenged. NOP implies a concern for reexamining how the traditional, total service delivery concept is defined. Furthermore, the focus of NOP suggests an altering of the orientation or perspective of the patrol officers. The new perception implies that officers must be encouraged to expand their responsibilities in concert with the needs of the neighborhood. Herein lie the seeds of rethinking how traditional roles would change for officers, supervisors, and managers alike.

ROLE EXPECTATIONS AND THE CONCEPT OF NOP

In analyzing the work of the Executive Session members, it became quite clear that NOP was not a new concept to the profession of policing. At least in theory, the idea of working with the public has been a long-standing goal of many police agencies throughout the country. In some instances, departments have developed and administered programs that emphasize the need to work closely with the public. Some of these programs were successful (e.g., Flint, Michigan's Foot Patrol Program, and New York Police Department's Community Police Officer Program) while others were not. Experience has demonstrated that, in part, success was based upon the ability of the department's officers to accept change, especially as it affected traditional role expectations.

Houston's experience in changing its policing style has clearly demonstrated that the process of change is both difficult and complex. It is complex because the alteration of a department's philosophy of policing will simultaneously affect numerous other variables. It is difficult because the manager of change must understand how the process of change will affect: (1) which strategies will be considered and actually implemented, (2) what skills will be used by the personnel to implement the strategies, (3) how the strategies and skills will define a management style for the department, and (4) how the shared values expressed by the officers will define the department's beliefs and desires to work with the community. Collectively, these variables have a direct effect on the accountability of the change process by department personnel.

Thus the department has recognized this type of change as requiring a gradual shift in emphasis from one operational role to another. The officers must believe the new role represents more effective and realistic means of achieving traditional objectives, as well as newly formed ones heretofore unknown to department personnel as being important in the eyes of the neighborhood residents.

In moving toward NOP as an operational philosophy, a shift in emphasis in the role of the Houston patrol officer will occur. This shift in emphasis will deemphasize the role of the officer as an "enforcer" and emphasize the image of the officer as one who provides help and assistance; someone who cares about people and shares their concern for safety; someone who expresses compassion through empathizing and sympathizing with victims of crime; someone who can organize, inspire, and motivate community groups; and someone who can facilitate and coordinate the collective efforts and endeavors of others.

The role of the beat officer, consequently, will be enhanced as a result of increased interaction with the citizens. Beat officers, for example, will be actively involved in the decision-making process involving the identification, prioritization, and selection of solutions for problems existing within the neighborhoods. Additionally, because of the officers' interaction with the citizens, they will be in an excellent position to determine what resources, if any, could be obtained from the citizens in combating neighborhood concerns. Since the beat officers are the most familiar with the citizens who work and reside within their beats, they are in an ideal position to develop programs and other initiatives to improve the quality of life within the neighborhoods. Success, however, is predicated upon an appropriate amount of direction and support from their respective supervisors and managers.

Bringing about a change in the role of patrol officers is not an insignificant undertaking. The goal is difficult because the evolution of bureaucratic and militaristic organizational structures in policing since the turn of the century has served to support and perpetuate traditional definitions of the police officer's role as being solely that of a "crime fighter." This notion, arising out of the 1930s, was instrumental in creating and reinforcing time-hardened assumptions regarding the effectiveness of random, preventive patrol in deterring crime and in the development of patrol management systems predicated on the basis of achieving rapid police response to all calls for service.

Traditional patrol work has accentuated random, preventive patrol and assumes that high mobile police visibility has a marked deterrent effect on the commission of crime. Officers are not expected to look beyond an incident in an attempt to define and resolve a particular type of problem. Once dispatched to handle calls, the patrol officers are encouraged to return to service as quickly as possible to resume random, preventive patrol.

Moreover, the organizational culture of municipal policing has continued to condition police officers to think of themselves primarily as crime fighters. Traditionally, police departments have attempted to identify and recruit individuals into policing who have displayed bravado. Organizational incentives have also been designed to favor self-conceptions of machismo; conceptions that are reinforced through pop art (e.g., detective novels, "police stories," and "Dirty Harry" movies). Many, if not most, of the approximately 500,000 law enforcement officers in the United States today have strong opinions about what constitutes "real police work." Because NOP is antithetical to traditional ways of thinking about police work, attempts to change these opinions may be met with resistance by some officers.

As the Houston Police Department begins to institutionalize NOP, we anticipate that resistance to change will take place throughout all levels of the organization, including management. Operationalizing the concept, NOP will challenge the traditional autocratic style of management perpetuated within most police agencies. NOP calls for a different, more responsive attitude and managerial style that will stimulate, accommodate, and perpetuate desired behavioral changes that will occur as a result of redefining the officers' role.

This new style of management must encourage a willingness within all managers to transform new concepts into attainable goals and objectives. Those goals and objectives must, in turn, be articulated within the organization *and* must be transformed into actions that are consistent with the service demands expressed by the citizenry.

To ensure that these actions are consistent with expressed service needs, NOP solicits organizational input from the "bottom up" as opposed to the traditional directions of "top down" so evidently displayed in most bureaucratic organizations. As noted among the department's values, "the Houston Police Department will seek the input of employees into matters which impact employee job satisfaction and effectiveness" (L. P. Brown, 1983). Effective management must include the active participation of the officers in policy development, procedure and strategy design, program formulation, and implementation. Since upper management personnel are removed from the officers' working environment, they cannot be expected to dictate service responses without first obtaining feedback from the officers as to what the neighborhood expectations and commitments are.

The Houston Police Department recognizes that there are no convenient solutions, no eloquent equations, and no magical formulas that upper management can employ to provide NOP services. The types of calls, types of citizens, and types of issues and problems that officers encounter will vary from one neighborhood to the next and, to a great extent, vary by time of day (e.g., across shifts). Consequently, this will require managerial resiliency and flexibility. By providing this flexibility, managers must also realize that a certain amount of risk taking will need to be allowed. We must remember that one can learn from failures as well as from success.

Upper management, on the one hand, has a very different role to play under the NOP concept. Managers must provide their subordinates with a process that encourages the officers to become involved in developing new and innovative ways to improve the quality of policing in the neighborhood beats. Top management can provide the patrol officers and their supervisors with an opportunity to design a custom patrol plan tailored to the needs of the neighborhood beats and sensitive to citizen concerns across all shifts.

First line supervisors and middle managers must realize their responsibility should be one of encouraging the officers to become involved in this process. A major portion of their role should be designed to support the officers' attempts to identify citizen concerns, assist in mobilizing appropriate resources (or removing the impediments) to address those concerns, and assess the effects of the assistance provided.

Upper management can also provide the right types of incentives to encourage officers to expand their roles and assume additional responsibilities. As these roles change, it will require a concomitant change in the officers' behavior. Research in the social science field has indicated that if behavior is to change, one's attitude must change first. Understandably, management cannot dictate attitudes; but management can provide the necessary support to facilitate the acceptance of an alternative style of policing such as NOP. The officers' acceptance of such a policing style will be primarily due to their belief that such an approach is an effective means of delivering services to the community.

Although NOP seeks to expand the role of the patrol officers to allow them more latitude in developing new ways to police their beats, it does not relax their compliance with the department's standards of professional conduct. While the image of the patrol officer as being dedicated full time to fighting crime and evil is expected to change, it does not mean the department will reduce its commitment in attempting to prevent crime and arrest criminal offenders. It is anticipated that by developing closer ties with the citizens in Houston, the department's ability to prevent crime as well as identify and arrest persons engaged in the commission of crime will be enhanced. NOP, in that context, is viewed as a better way of fighting crime.

CONCLUSION

Unlike a number of agencies across the country today, it is the position of the Houston Police Department that NOP should be treated as a process and not a program. Programs are too easily subjected to change and indirectly suggest a short term commitment. The life expectancy of any program is usually as stable as the administrator responsible for its outcomes. If you change the administrator, there is an increased likelihood the program will be discarded as there is no sense of continued ownership. If the new administrator is told to continue with the program despite personal preferences, marginal attention will be directed toward the effect, thereby suggesting to the participants that their commitment is not sincerely appreciated. This in turn eventually signifies the doom of the program as the participants lose interest and begin to move on to other endeavors that are more readily appreciated.

Another related concern is the fact that whenever programs are used within an agency, there is a tendency to split the patrol force. Officers assigned to the program are considered specialists, while those not assigned are left to perform the routine functions. This type of arrangement tends to place the patrol officers in camps of "us" and "them." Those officers not assigned to the program may become jealous and eventually seek to build a strong resistance to whatever the other officers in the program are doing. This occurs irrespective of how effectively the departmental program is being administered.

NOP, therefore, should transcend programmatical boundaries. As a philosophy, it must focus on the need to change attitudes before behavior. As a process it requires a commitment to identifying operational function before administrative accountability mechanisms. If agreement by all beat officers can be reached as to what NOP means in terms of job tasks and responsibilities, then a concerted effort can be made to design a management system that will not only structure those responsibilities, but will also provide an avenue of accountability for the actions taken. Herein lies another critical component of the NOP process.

If administrators wish to maintain a NOP style within their departments, they must be cognizant of the need to adjust their management system. NOP styles will not survive in a managerial atmosphere designed primarily to support a reactionary response mode to citizen concerns. Management that is characterized by a strict control orientation will not possess the flexibility needed to support the interactive concerns of the officers and the citizens. This will in turn break down linkages between the police and the community and thereby cause frustrations to exist due to unfulfilled expectations on behalf of the citizenry.

Houston's experience has clearly demonstrated that NOP represents a significant change from law enforcement's historical and traditional orientation in how and why police officers interact with the public. The implementation of such a change must by necessity be a gradual one. It involves not only a willingness on the part of the police to work with neighborhood residents, but it also requires the residents to be willing to make a similar commitment.

To achieve that end, the Houston Police Department's style of policing under the NOP concept addresses a number of objectives designed to facilitate and sustain the interactive relationship between neighborhood residents and beat officers:

1. Establish trust and harmony between and among neighborhood residents and the beat officer by establishing a positive, cooperative, and productive relationship between both parties;

2. Exchange information between neighborhood residents and beat officers which will strengthen rapport and enhance neighborhood safety;

3. Respond to the problem of crime and criminal activity by maximizing the efficient utilization of available department and community resources in enforcing the law;

4. Identify and resolve neighborhood problems which will reduce the fear of crime and enhance the quality of life within the neighborhoods;

5. Establish and improve communication linkages and working relationships between and among divisional and departmental personnel;

6. Establish an effective management structure which utilizes divisional and community input to define service needs, direct operational commitments, and clarify responsibilities on behalf of division personnel and the public in order to more efficiently respond to the concerns of neighborhood residents;

7. Facilitate the acquisition, analysis, and utilization of information in order to identify neighborhood crime and non-crime problems capable of being resolved through mutual participation on behalf of police personnel and community residents;

8. Develop and implement programs, strategies, and/or activities to efficiently use beat officers' uncommitted patrol time;

9. Provide safe and orderly traffic flow through the neighborhoods by enforcing violations and reducing the number of traffic accidents; and

10. Identify and utilize employee incentives conducive to improving employee morale (Snelson and Oettmeier, 1987:5-6).

NOP, as adopted by the Houston Police Department, represents a philosophy of policing designed to make the beat officer an integral part of the neighborhoods that exist in the city. The overall goal of NOP is to create a cooperative relationship between the police and the residents, to identify problems that impact the quality of life, to devise strategies to address those problems, and to work cooperatively to solve them.

In closing, NOP certainly poses more questions in need of attention than there are answers available. Among the more pressing issues are the following:

1. Do basic NOP principles exist that could assist administrators in the implementation process?
2. What will the new management system require in terms of responsibilities and accountability mechanisms? What ramifications must be addressed if the organization seeks to replace traditional service delivery methods with new methods?
3. How can the NOP style of service delivery be evaluated, what service delivery outcomes should be measured, how can the effectiveness of the management system be measured, and what criteria should be used to evaluate personal performances?
4. What are the training ramifications for new recruits, for Field Training and Evaluation Programs, and most importantly the veteran officers who have been subjected to traditional policing values for an entire career?

The Houston Police Department certainly does not possess the answers to these complex questions, but it is committed to addressing them. While it is too early to determine the ultimate success of their efforts, department personnel are committed to efficiently delivering services designed to improve the quality of life within all neighborhoods for all Houstonians.

NOTE

1. The panel member and others referred to within this Chapter were participants of the six Executive Session meetings chaired by Police Chief Lee P. Brown.

8

A PROBLEM-ORIENTED
APPROACH TO COMMUNITY-
ORIENTED POLICING

GARY W. CORDNER

This chapter presents an evaluation of the first three years of the Baltimore County, Maryland, Police Department's Citizen Oriented Police Enforcement (COPE) project. The COPE project began in 1982, is still under way in 1988, and is expected to continue indefinitely as a component of the police department's operational strategy. The COPE evaluation examined project effects on police officer attitudes, citizen fear of crime, crime, and neighborhood problems.[1] This chapter will present three effects following a discussion of the setting and development of the COPE strategy. One of the most interesting features of the COPE project is that what initially began as a community-oriented policing strategy evolved into a problem-oriented policing strategy. This aspect of the development of the COPE project will be an important focus of the chapter.

PROJECT SETTING

Baltimore County covers 600 square miles, has a population of 670,000, and includes urban, suburban, and rural areas. The county is a completely separate jurisdiction from Baltimore City and is governed by a County Executive and a County Council. The county government provides the complete range of public services, including police protection. There are no incorporated cities or towns within the county—the county government is the local government for all its residents.

Over the last few decades, Baltimore County has become increasingly suburban and, to some extent, urban. The county's population is densest near the Baltimore City line and generally decreases with distance from the city. Many of the county's residents commute to work in the city, although the county also has a substantial commercial and industrial base of its own. While the population of Baltimore City is about half black, county residents are overwhelmingly white. The Baltimore County Police Department has over 1,500 employees, including almost 1,400 sworn personnel. In 1984 the department responded to 296,908 calls for service that included 69,864 index crimes.

THE ORIGIN OF COPE

Following several sensational and highly publicized stranger-to-stranger murders (of whites by blacks) in Baltimore County in the early 1980s, a strong victim rights movement developed. Public meetings were held, considerable media attention was attracted, and demands for tougher laws and better protection were presented. Although most areas of the county did not have serious crime problems comparable to those in Baltimore City, and although the total number of murders in the county did not increase during this period, fear of crime seemed to have become a serious problem.

In late 1981 the county government authorized expanding the county police department by 45 personnel. Police Chief Neil Behan created a project team to develop alternative uses for these additional personnel, out of which came the COPE project. Three 15-member squads were created, one assigned to each patrol region (western, central, and eastern) in the county. To help distinguish the squads from regular patrol units, they were provided motorcycles and subcompact cars for transportation.

The veteran officers who volunteered for the COPE project were given some brief training in motorcycle operation, fear of crime, and problem solving, and were fully deployed in July 1982. Their primary mission was to reduce fear of crime; how they were to accomplish this mission was not rigidly prescribed, in part because proven methods were not available, and in part because the chief wanted those involved in COPE to participate in its development.

COPE EVALUATION

In its initial form, the COPE strategy differed little from the traditional police practice of saturation patrol. Part or all of a COPE squad would be assigned to a target area, and they would spend most of their time in that area performing mobile patrol. During this stage, target areas were typically selected on the basis of crime analysis information, strengthening the similarity of saturation patrolling.

The main vehicle for citizen-contact during the first stage of COPE's evolution was door-to-door surveying. This involved administering a short questionnaire to a portion of the households in target areas. The questionnaire dealt primarily with fear of crime and was needed to determine whether the COPE strategy affected citizen fears. This before and after surveying by COPE officers was not utilized in every target area, but rather was employed periodically for evaluation purposes.

The police department's own monitoring and oversight revealed the initial saturation patrol form that COPE had adopted. COPE's planners had intended that the strategy should emphasize citizen contact rather than mobile patrol. Consequently, the COPE units were directed to reduce their mobile patrol time and increase their citizen contacts. This was primarily accomplished through increased door-to-door surveying, some foot patrol, and a new emphasis on crime prevention activity. The latter included home and business security surveys, school programs, and public meetings on various crime prevention topics, including neighborhood watch development.

During this second stage of COPE evolution, the police department obtained the assistance of the Police Executive Research Forum (PERF) and Herman Goldstein for program development. A consensus was reached that COPE still had unrealized potential. Although in its second stage the COPE project had increased the level of citizen contact, it had really only replaced one traditional tactic (mobile patrol) with a more modern, but nevertheless commonplace, police tactic (crime prevention).

Goldstein argued that in both stages COPE was falling prey to the widespread fallacy of employing time-honored means without regard to the problems being confronted. He suggested that, instead, COPE units should first collect and analyze data about the specific problems in each target neighborhood, and only then choose tactics suited to these problems. In some target areas, saturation patrol or crime prevention might fit the problems uncovered, but in other areas completely different tactics might be necessary. Goldstein (1979) had previously described this approach as problem-oriented policing.

During its third stage, COPE did evolve toward this problem-oriented strategy. The COPE units began to collect more information, from more varied sources, before choosing their tactics. Door-to-door surveying and interviewing came to be seen less as onerous evaluation burdens and more as integral parts of the strategy. COPE also began to rely less on traditional tactics, and to enlist the aid of more public and private agencies in their problem-solving efforts.

COPE AS COMMUNITY POLICING

Before turning to the results of the COPE evaluation, it may be helpful to place the COPE strategy in the context of the general discussion and development of community policing. Those in the Baltimore County Police Department who helped originate the COPE concept were very cognizant of research challenging the effectiveness of traditional mobile patrol (Kelling et al., 1974) and supporting increased utilization of foot patrol (Police Foundation, 1981; Trojanowicz, 1983). COPE planners were also familiar with the "broken windows" thesis (Wilson and Kelling, 1982) that police attention to minor crimes and public order problems enhances neighborhood safety, forestalls decline, and indirectly reduces serious crime in the long run.

Research indicating that foot patrol is particularly successful at reducing citizen fear of crime was especially pertinent to COPE development, since fear of crime was the specific stimulus for the project. Not many areas in the county fit the stereotype of a densely populated urban neighborhood amenable to foot patrol, however. This accounts for the decision to utilize squads to saturate target areas and the choice of motorcycles and subcompact cars. COPE planners hoped that these types of vehicles would create less of a barrier between officers and citizens than traditional cruisers, and that officers would be more likely to exit these vehicles to "walk and talk" in target neighborhoods.

The focus of fear of crime makes the COPE project similar to recent projects in Houston and Newark (Wycoff et al., 1985). It also places COPE within the larger framework of police strategies oriented more toward order maintenance than toward crime control. In the 1960s and 1970s, police planning, resource allocation, and strategies were clearly concentrated on crime control (Kelling, 1978); more recently, arguments in favor of order maintenance policing (Kelling, 1985) and even "street justice" (Sykes, 1986) have gained increased favor.

COPE as a community-oriented police strategy falls in a long tradition beginning with the legendary beat cop and continuing through police-community relations programs to team policing and crime prevention programs. One view of modern community-oriented policing is that

it represents a substantial shift in the organizational model of policing, one where police strategy and tactics are adapted to fit the needs and requirements of the different communities the department serves, where there is a diversification of the kinds of programs and services on the basis of community needs and demands for police services, and where there is considerable involvement of the community with the police in reaching their objectives (Reiss, 1985b: 63).

This description of community-oriented policing contrasts with this century's dominant professional model that emphasizes crime control rather than service; police autonomy and authority rather than police-community power sharing (L. P. Brown, 1985); and a single legalistic standard for the entire community rather than neighborhood variation in enforcement practices and service provision.

One of the important features of problem-oriented policing, and of the COPE strategy, is its contrast with "single-complaint" policing (Sherman, 1986a). In typical police practice, patrol units are assigned to calls and they handle them as discrete units of work, often without realizing that over a period of days or weeks, numerous calls are generated by the same neighborhood condition or conflict. In problem-oriented policing, an attempt is made to identify the underlying patterns and causes of neighborhood complaints, and to go beyond superficial call-handling to more substantive solutions.

COPE as problem-oriented policing represents an important convergence of the community-oriented and problem-oriented themes in police strategy development. In their recent review of the COPE project and a similar problem-oriented police program in Newport News, Virginia, Eck and Spelman (1987b: 46) concluded that "problem-oriented policing is a state of mind, and not a program, technique, or procedure. The keys are clear-headed analysis of the problem and an uninhibited search for solutions." The inventor of problem-oriented policing, Herman Goldstein (1987: 8), recently observed of community-oriented programs that "the recurring themes in the newest projects (more involvement of the community, greater accountability to the community, and improved service to the community) are so synonymous with the values inherent in the policing of a free society, one could argue that the label itself (i.e., community policing) is redundant."

Thus, as problem-oriented and community-oriented policing the COPE strategy is simply rational police problem-solving consistent with democratic values. In many respects, COPE and similar strategies are attempts to capture the common sense of policing in bygone eras and small town settings and to institutionalize "the best potential inherent in good police practice, as seen from within the occupation" (Bittner, 1986). It is perhaps a telling commentary on the state of modern policing that such simplicity could be regarded as a major innovation.

COPE AND POLICE OFFICER ATTITUDES

As part of the COPE evaluation, a questionnaire was completed by COPE officers and by a control group of county police officers at four points in time during the first three years of the project. The questionnaire primarily investigated attitudes toward job satisfaction, the community, the police role, and the COPE strategy. COPE officer attitudes were examined over time, and constrasted at each point in time with those of control group officers. The findings are summarized below.

1. In general, COPE officers started out more satisfied with their jobs than were control group officers, and remained more satisfied.
2. At the start of the project, COPE and control group attitudes toward the

community were virtually identical, but as time went by, COPE attitudes toward the community became more and more positive, while control attitudes stayed the same or varied inconsistently.

3. COPE and control officers started out with somewhat different attitudes toward the police role, and over time their attitudes diverged even more. COPE officers became less likely to say that police should be aloof, less likely to characterize police work as law enforcement, and more likely to agree that police should get out of their cars and that police work is mainly a matter of providing services.

4. Multivariate analysis indicated that COPE and control officer demographics (age, experience, education) did not account for their different attitudes, reinforcing the explanation that the differences resulted from the COPE experience itself.

The effects of community policing on police officer attitudes are very consistent with those found in similar studies. Police officers in San Diego implementing a "community-profile" strategy developed more positive attitudes toward the community (Boydstun and Sherry, 1975), as have officers participating in recent foot patrol projects (Police Foundation, 1981; Trojanowicz, 1983). Foot patrol officers also commonly experience improved job satisfaction. Parallel findings for officers participating in a "community-oriented police education" program have been reported by Greene (1987), although he also points out the necessity of measuring the component dimensions of these attitudes, instead of relying on a few global measures. There seems little doubt, however, that police officers involved in community policing experience positive changes in their attitudes toward their work, their role, and the community.

COPE AND FEAR OF CRIME

The COPE evaluation employed before-and-after community surveys in target areas to measure changes in fear of crime, citizen perceptions of police presence, and citizen satisfaction with the police. Door-to-door canvassing was used to administer the surveys, which were conducted in 24 target neighborhoods. In 18 of these areas, all of the surveying was conducted by COPE personnel. In two of the areas, all of the surveying was done by evaluation staff, while in four neighborhoods, surveying duties were shared.

The reliability and validity of responses when COPE officers administered the community surveys is an issue. It can be noted that efforts were made to reduce unnecessary bias. Sampling procedures were outlined in advance, and officers were instructed not to mention COPE or fear of crime until after the survey was completed. Community surveying was presented as a routine aspect of COPE's tactics, downplaying the evaluative dimension. Most importantly, the pre- and postsurveys were used primarily to detect changes in fear and satisfaction, rather than to obtain a precise measure of these conditions in target neighborhoods. To the extent that respondents were affected by the COPE officers administering the surveys, they should have been affected equally in the pre- and postsurveys, thus still yielding an accurate measure of any changes in their attitudes.

For analysis purposes, each of the 24 COPE projects for which pre- and postsurveys were completed was classified according to the stage of COPE development it best exemplified. Seven of the projects best fit the saturation patrol mode, seven the crime prevention mode, and ten the problem-oriented mode. In the community survey analysis, changes in residents' attitudes from pre- to postsurvey were examined, and average changes during each stage of COPE development were compared. The findings were as follows:

1. During all three COPE stages, target neighborhood residents noticed increased police presence in their communities.
2. Residents of target neighborhoods started out very satisfied with the police department, and reported only slight improvements following COPE efforts. The greatest gains, however, were achieved during the problem-oriented stage.
3. Target neighborhoods experienced modest decreases on general measures of fear of crime during each stage of COPE. Each successive stage resulted in greater decreases in reported fear.
4. Following COPE's efforts, target neighborhood residents were somewhat less likely to report that they stayed at home due to fear of crime.
5. Following COPE's efforts, target neighborhood residents thought their chances of being victimized by personal or property crime were reduced. The largest reductions were achieved during the problem-oriented stage.
6. Measures of specific sources of fear all registered decreases following COPE's efforts. Once again, the greatest decreases were associated with the problem-oriented stage of COPE.

What is most telling in these findings is the very clear pattern of decreases in fear of crime associated with COPE's involvement in target neighborhoods. Further, decreases in fear were generally greatest during the problem-oriented stage of COPE development. Thus, what most reassured and satisfied residents was not simply visible police presence, or even personal contact with a police officer, but rather police efforts toward solving community problems. This interpretation should be tempered by the observation that the fear reductions achieved by COPE were not overly large. The actual reductions were in fractions of a point, and percentage reductions were mainly in the 5 to 15 percent range. Whether these fear reductions were substantial enough to be of practical significance is an important issue.

COPE AND CRIME

Because the COPE strategy was initially focused on fear of crime, and later evolved toward general problem solving, its effectiveness as a crime fighting strategy was not a central concern of the project evaluation. From the available data, however, COPE appears to have achieved moderate reductions in reported crimes in target areas. During the first two years of COPE, target crimes were monitored pre- and post-COPE for 37 projects. In 29 instances, target crimes decreased; in five projects, crime was unchanged; and in only three cases did reported crimes increase. This indicates almost ten projects with crime decreases for every one with an increase, a rather strong pattern.

A separate analysis of all crimes and calls for service was also done for 26 COPE projects conducted between October 1983 and April 1985. For each of these projects, data were collected for three time periods—the nearest complete month preceding the project, the complete month during the project in which COPE activity was greatest, and the nearest complete month following the end of the project. This analysis showed a 5 percent increase in reported crime (Part I and II) from pre-COPE to during-COPE, but a 12 percent decrease from pre-COPE to post-COPE. The increases during COPE are not surprising since Part II crimes were included in the analysis—COPE enforcement activity in some projects would lead officers themselves to "produce" these kinds of crimes in the form of arrests for disorderly conduct, drug violations, and similar offenses. Calls for service decreased 1 percent from pre-COPE to during-COPE, and decreased 11 percent from pre-COPE to post-COPE. These decreases in reported crime and calls for service in target areas stand in constrast with the countywide experience for 1984, which saw increases of 4 percent for Part I crimes and 6 percent for calls for service over 1983.

Because of the absence of control-group neighborhoods and the use of reported crime figures, these findings pertaining to COPE's effects on crime must be viewed cautiously.[2] The overwhelming pattern of crime decreases from pre-COPE to post-COPE, however, supports the view that the COPE strategy worked to displace or deter crimes from target neighborhoods.

COPE AND NEIGHBORHOOD PROBLEMS

As noted earlier, the COPE strategy evolved from saturation patrol to crime prevention to problem-oriented policing. During this evolution, the mission of the COPE units gradually changed from reducing fear of crime to solving neighborhood problems. COPE's tactics and operational habits also changed: projects became fewer in number and longer in duration; data collection and analysis became more extensive; and more attention was given to generating alternative solutions. COPE units increasingly went to other government and private agencies during the data-collection stage of problem-solving, and made more concerted efforts to find out what problems most concerned residents of target neighborhoods. The solutions implemented by COPE units also increasingly involved co-operative efforts with other government and private-sector agencies. Documentation of COPE's effects in neighborhood problem-solving must primarily rely on case studies. A few examples are recounted below to pro-vide some of the flavor of the problem-oriented version of COPE (see also Taft, 1986; and Eck and Spelman, 1987b).

Belmont

One early problem-oriented project involved juvenile conduct around a "tree house" along a stream in the neighborhood of Belmont. Older youths were openly consuming alcohol and drugs in and around the tree house (actually a shack), and brush fires and destruction of property had been observed. Neighborhood residents were afraid of the youths and also had restricted their younger children from playing in the area.

The COPE officers assigned to the project interviewed the com-plainants and wrote a "Public Nuisance" report. Except possibly for some enforcement activity, this would have been the end of the matter under traditional single-complaint policing. In fact, neighborhood residents had called the police numerous times before to complain about the situation, without any response approaching a lasting solution to the problem.

In this instance, however, the COPE officers next went to the county tax records office to determine who owned the property on which the tree house stood. When they contacted the owner, they learned that he was afraid of retaliation by the youths and thus was unwilling to remove the tree house himself. Next, the COPE officers contacted the county roads department, which agreed to assist COPE in removing the tree house. The COPE officers obtained written permission from the property owner to remove the tree house, assuring him that there would be no cost to him. Then the COPE officers and a county roads crew dismantled and removed the tree house.

While this process was under way, the COPE officer kept the community association and the complainants fully informed. They also arranged for extra patrols by regular precinct officers. They identified and monitored the youths who congregated at the tree house. Further, they learned that the property involved was located in a flood plain, and the county undertook negotiations to purchase the property, which will make it easier in the future to take prompt action. The youths probably still abuse alcohol and drugs, but they do so in private and no longer intimidate neighborhood residents and their young children.

Prior to COPE's involvement in this problem, the community association had contacted three other county government agencies besides the police department. Each had promised to take care of the problem, but none actually did. The COPE unit was able to remove the tree house and the problem in less than two weeks.

Garden Village

Another early example of COPE problem solving occurred in the community of Garden Village, a development of 342 federally subsidized town houses. The COPE unit initially knew that it was a high-crime area with apparent neighborhood tension. They learned that two families in the neighborhood were struggling for dominance, with other families fearful and forced to choose sides. They also learned of a recent shooting and a rape that had gone unreported to the police. Community residents complained of juvenile crime and disorderliness, narcotics activity, and lack of government services. COPE officers observed that streets, sidewalks, lighting, and other elements of the physical environment were in poor condition.

The COPE officers assigned to this project split into two teams—an intervention team to gather intelligence information on criminal activity, and an interaction team to develop communication channels with neighborhood residents. Together these teams were responsible for a number of actions and accomplishments:

- street lighting was repaired and improved by County Public Works and the local utility company;
- alleyways were repaired by County Roads;
- signs prohibiting ball playing in common areas were removed, giving children a place to play other than in the streets;
- town house management improved landscaping and trimmed trees and shrubs;
- a Garden Village Improvement Association was formed and legally chartered;

- four community meetings were held;
- 248 signatures were obtained on a petition to improve neighborhood parks and recreation;
- four burglary suspects were arrested based on information obtained from neighborhood residents;
- the subject involved in the unreported shooting was identified and arrested;
- a juvenile troublemaker had his probation violated and he was incarcerated; and
- COPE spearheaded the development and submission of a Block Grant proposal that resulted in the construction of a community park.

During this COPE project, the officers involved had some difficulties getting adequate cooperation from other county government agencies. As a result, the county administrator convened a meeting at which all department heads were instructed to cooperate fully with any COPE projects. In this and several other projects, COPE officers have adopted the roles of community advocates and ombudsmen.

Krone Drive

A project in the western part of the county centered on Krone Drive, a racially mixed neighborhood consisting of about 40 detached homes bordered by a high-density apartment complex. COPE became aware of community concern over lack of police protection and began to investigate. They learned that a crucial incident had been an assault and robbery of an elderly resident in her home. The victim believed that her assailant had been the same youth who had burglarized her home the previous year. He had received little punishment for the burglary, and police detectives did not seem to have pursued the investigation of the second case very energetically. The victim, seeing that the youth had retaliated after the first prosecution, was apparently unwilling to prosecute in the second case and moved 40 miles away to escape her predicament.

In this small neighborhood, many residents were aware of the situation in the case. In general, they regarded the apartment complex as the source of their problems. They had erected a fence to prevent apartment dwellers from taking a shortcut through Krone Drive to a nearby business area, but an opening had been made in the fence and "strangers" continued to pass through the neighborhood. COPE conducted a presurvey in the area and found unusually high levels of fear and low levels of satisfaction with the police.

COPE proceeded along several fronts to address the situation. First, they repeatedly visited the assault victim at her new residence, encouraging her to identify and prosecute her attacker. COPE obtained her commitment, arrested the offender, and provided the victim with protection and transportation to and from court. They also found 21 neighborhood residents who agreed to support the victim in court. The victim later moved back to Krone Drive, even though the prosecutor ultimately decided to drop charges because of doubts about the victim's identification of her assailant.

COPE officers also expended 172 hours on mobile and foot patrol in the community to reassure residents of police presence and concern. During the project period, only one crime was reported in the area, a sex offense involving fondling and indecent exposure. The young victim did not know the identity of her assailant. COPE officers took her with them on patrol several times and ultimately she did recognize the suspect. COPE officers arrested him and cleared the case.

COPE officers also engaged in crime prevention activities in the community. Residents had indicated on the presurvey that they thought their chances of being burglarized were high and that burglary was a major source of fear. COPE officers instructed residents in nearly every home on target-hardening techniques and followed up the home visits with a community meeting on crime prevention.

After consulting with neighborhood residents and the management of the apartment complex, COPE identified a number of environmental problems in the area, including poor lighting, missing street signs, and unsightly trash and underbrush. COPE enlisted the aid of the apartment management, county government agencies, and the utility company to correct these problems. COPE was also able to establish some communication between the Krone Drive community and the apartment complex management. As a result, both parties agreed to keep the fence through-way open, since closing it again would probably only heighten resentment among the apartment dwellers.

The postsurvey revealed substantial reductions in fear in the Krone Drive neighborhood and increases in satisfaction with the police. Direct measures of fear decreased 28 percent, perceived likelihood of crime victimization went down 35 percent, and sources of fear were reduced by 39 percent. Public awareness of police presence increased 161 percent, and citizen satisfaction with police service improved 50 percent.

Dundalk

Two interesting companion projects were carried out in the Dundalk community. One project focused on reported incidents of paint-sniffing in a wooded park near a senior citizen high-rise apartment building. A story had appeared in the *Baltimore Sun* newspaper entitled "Paint-Huffing High Blights Community." The story reported that both juveniles and young adults abused spray paint by inhaling its fumes in the park. Evidence of bizarre behavior and serious physical side effects was recounted.

When COPE officers began to look into this problem, they found that about 40 percent of neighborhood residents were at least concerned about the problem. COPE officers also observed that sections of the wooded park were littered with paint-soaked plastic baggies and emptied spray cans. Also noticed were old benches, chairs, and other amenities used by the paint-huffers.

Initial COPE efforts to deal with the problem included four-wheel drive and foot patrol in the park, which ordinarily got little police attention. Several arrests for paint-huffing were made almost immediately. The Department of Recreation and Parks was contacted and "No Trespassing After Dark" signs were erected. The COPE unit also contacted a summer Youth Jobs Program and got their assistance in cleaning up the park. On the first day of the cleanup, two tons of debris were removed.

COPE officers contacted the prosecutor's office and the district court to make sure that the paint-huffing cases did not get lost in the shuffle. At the same time, they enlisted the help of the county Drug Abuse Coordinator in establishing a prevention program in the community and in local schools. Because so little was known about this form of drug abuse, COPE officers also compiled case histories of paint abusers, including background legal information and interviews with the abusers themselves.

Perhaps most importantly, COPE officers acted to limit the supply of the preferred gold and silver spray paints. They learned that most of the abusers were local people without much mobility, and that they purchased their paint locally. One store in particular was convenient and popular with abusers. COPE officers talked to the store manager who agreed to remove gold and silver spray paint from the store's display shelves and to establish a policy of not selling these products to known abusers. He also agreed to monitor sales of other colors in case abusers made the switch. The COPE unit also contacted the Chamber of Commerce to make the situation known to the entire business community.

The COPE unit seemed to succeed in eliminating the paint-huffing problem in the park. Through COPE's efforts, the huffers who were arrested were placed in rehabilitation programs, and the unit's efforts got considerable media coverage. The media attention and community meetings sponsored by COPE brought the problem and its dangers to a higher level of awareness in the community.

An interesting sidelight to this project grew out of COPE interviews with neighborhood residents. While the paint-huffing problem concerned the people who lived on the streets around the park, residents of the senior citizen high-rise in the neighborhood were largely unaware of and unconcerned by the problem. Few of the senior citizens ventured into the park anyway, and none went at night. What did concern them, however, was the difficulty of crossing the main street between the high-rise and a nearby shopping area. Through COPE's efforts a crosswalk in the area was improved, and a massive enforcement effort was undertaken to get motorists to yield to pedestrians in the crosswalk. This COPE effort, together with political efforts by the senior citizens, attracted media attention and public support from a congressman, state senators and delegates, and a county councilman. Ultimately, a traffic signal was installed at the crosswalk to satisfy the senior citizens' concerns.

The second Dundalk project was brought to the attention of COPE by the local Chamber of Commerce. The complaint was that vagrants and alcoholics were panhandling and harassing shoppers, including the aforementioned senior citizens, in a business area. This shopping area was undergoing revitalization and trying to compete with more modern suburban shopping centers and malls. Merchants were very alarmed that shoppers would desert the area if the vagrants and panhandlers were not checked.

COPE officers learned that the problem was not a new one in the area, but that local people sensed it had recently gotten worse. COPE officers made covert observations in the area and concluded that about ten hard-core vagrants and alcoholics frequented the area, relying on panhandling to obtain money to purchase liquor. They found that these ten had from 6 to 113 prior arrests apiece. Obviously, regular patrol officers had been periodically arresting these vagrants without effect.

COPE officers also interviewed 200 shoppers, merchants, and residents. They found that 49 percent regarded the vagrants as a problem; 31 percent reported being concerned, worried, or fearful on account of the vagrants; and 53 percent had been solicited at least once by the panhandlers. They verified that the elderly were most fearful of the vagrants, some of whom panhandled rather aggressively. COPE took action on four fronts to deal with this problem. One approach was enforcement. COPE and precinct officers made arrests whenever possible and sought the cooperation of the prosecutor and the court in obtaining mandated alcohol treatment for those convicted.

COPE also organized a campaign to make panhandling less productive in the area. They produced and disseminated 15,000 "Stop Panhandling" posters (at Chamber of Commerce expense) and held several community meetings. They urged residents and shoppers not to give money in response to panhandling, if the practice really concerned them, in order to make it less lucrative. In addition, COPE officers contacted the Liquor Board, which in turn reminded establishments selling liquor that it was illegal to sell to already intoxicated persons. COPE officers also prepared legislation for consideration by the County Council making panhandling and especially aggressive-threatening panhandling misdemeanors. The legislation was carefully drawn so as not to infringe on legitimate exercise of freedom of speech.

Finally, the COPE officers working this Dundalk project realized that neither enforcement, new criminal legislation, nor the "Stop Panhandling" campaign were likely to result in permanent solution of the problem. The people creating the problem were hard-core alcoholics in need of serious treatment. Under Maryland law, they could be transported to a detoxification facility, except that no such facility existed in the county. Some local hospitals would accept emergency cases, but only for initial sobering-up. Further, the few long-term alcohol treatment programs available to the courts for committal of convicted persons were always full.

What COPE did was to develop proposals for a "street-level" detoxification center to which police could take skid-row drunks, and a court-committal program for both detoxification and rehabilitation. COPE obtained support for the proposals from various sources, including social service agencies and community groups. They also developed cost/benefit arguments in favor of their proposals and supporting information including an extensive review of existing facilities and programs. Their proposals were routed through the police department to the county administration, which created a high-level task force to study the situation. The COPE officers who developed the proposals were made members of the task force.

Whatever the final outcome of the task force, it is certainly noteworthy that the proposals for detoxification and rehabilitation programs came from police officers, and that they were presented before the difficult plight of the homeless became so widely recognized. The COPE officers in this Dundalk project started out with a problem and developed both short-term and long-term solutions. Some of the solutions used traditional police methods, while others did not. But most importantly, the solutions followed from analysis of the problem and employed a wide range of resources and talents beyond the boundaries of the police department itself. The incidence of panhandling and the presence of skid-row alcoholics decreased as a result of the project. A substantial cost savings was realized by the county ambulance service as a result of fewer calls for sick, injured, or unconscious intoxicated persons. Businessmen, residents, and shoppers reported less harassment.

Pre- and postsurveys were conducted in the senior citizen high-rise and in the residential area bordering the park discussed in conjunction with the paint-sniffing project. The two Dundalk projects were carried out during the same general time period so that the survey results may be as pertinent to one project as to the other. Direct measures of fear were reduced 5 percent, staying-in behavior went down 10 percent, sources of fear decreased 7 percent, but perceived likelihood of victimization went up 10 percent. Satisfaction with the police, which was quite high to start with, improved by 4 percent, while public awareness of police presence increased 9 percent. Perhaps the single most pertinent survey question for these projects was the one that stated: "What makes me afraid are groups of unruly kids and strangers who you see on the streets, sidewalks and parking lots." Responses to this question decreased 10 percent from pre-COPE to post-COPE.

OTHER PROJECTS

The projects described above dealt with unruly youths, neighborhood deterioration and tension, a specific criminal victimization, bizarre drug abuse, and aggressive panhandling. While these projects convey the range of problems addressed by COPE, a few more very brief examples may help round out the picture.

One COPE project focused on a particular youth who had intimidated an entire neighborhood. The youth was on probation for previous acts and was forbidden by the court from frequenting the neighborhood. Nevertheless, he routinely returned to the area and threatened residents. Regular patrol units had been unable to catch him in the area. COPE was able to invest enough time in the area to document his presence and get his probation revoked.

Some COPE projects involved very short stays in target areas. Once, for example, a murdered woman was found in a park, and residents of the surrounding neighborhood were greatly alarmed. When detectives quickly determined that the woman had been murdered elsewhere and simply "dumped" in the park, COPE officers went door-to-door to relay this information and reassure residents of their safety. Another project centered on fights between two groups of juveniles. COPE was able to eliminate this problem by getting a school bus stop moved so that the two groups were separated.

Several times COPE units were used in response to acts of racial or religious hatred. Following cases of cross burning or synagogue desecration, COPE units were deployed both to search for witnesses and to reassure the affected communities. These projects were meant as clear demonstrations of the police department's commitment to protecting all citizens and fully investigating all serious incidents.

Finally, immediately following the January 1987 AMTRAK train disaster northeast of Baltimore City, COPE units were used to help care for victims and the community. In particular, COPE officers canvassed the surrounding neighborhoods to check for additional victims, inform residents of the exact nature of the situation, and coordinate the community's care for the survivors. While other police and rescue units dealt with the situation at the site of the collision, the COPE units were able to help the community cope with the disaster.

CONCLUSION

The Baltimore County COPE strategy was initially aimed at the reduction of fear of crime, but this mission was later broadened to include all kinds of neighborhood problem solving. COPE's primary tactics evolved from saturation patrol to crime prevention to problem-oriented policing. The COPE evaluation demonstrated that the strategy became more successful as it evolved. In its problem-oriented form, COPE is at least moderately successful at reducing fear, satisfying citizens, and solving neighborhood problems, and may even succeed at displacing or deterring certain crimes.

As problem-oriented policing, COPE deals less superficially than traditional single-complaint policing with the kinds of problems that concern many neighborhoods. While the root causes of most neighborhood problems may be beyond the reach of COPE, the mid-range solutions typically implemented have far greater breadth and depth than those achieved by common police practice. COPE problem analyses and problem solutions depend in part for their success on the inclusion of information, resources, and efforts from other government and private agencies. COPE officers often act as advocates, ombudsmen, and brokers in order to obtain cooperation from other organizations. It should not be overlooked, however, that in response to some neighborhood problems, they also act as law enforcers and crime fighters. The key to the success of problem-oriented policing is matching solutions to problems.

The key to community-oriented policing is getting the community's views on problems and their solutions. The COPE strategy achieves this by surveying and interviewing community residents prior to defining problems and searching for solutions. Frequently, COPE units have found that what they thought was a fearful neighborhood was actually quite tranquil. On other occasions COPE officers have been startled to discover sources of fear quite different from those they had anticipated. The COPE experience has demonstrated the fallacy of assuming that a police department's sense of a community's problems matches community resident's actual concerns.

The COPE strategy should be understood as both community-oriented and problem-oriented. Based on the experience in Baltimore County, the strategy seems to have significant potential for delivering to communities the kinds of quality police services they need and want.

ACKNOWLEDGMENT

The author wishes to express deep appreciation to Chief Neil Behan and other members of the Baltimore County Police Department who initiated the COPE project and cooperated completely in its evaluation. The financial support of the Florence V. Burden Foundation was also greatly appreciated. The Foundation's director, David Nee, Charles Sorrentino of the U.S. Treasury Department, and the late Gary Hayes of the Police Executive Research Forum each provided valuable guidance to the project and its evaluation. The opinions and conclusions presented in this chapter are the author's and may not represent the views of the police department or the foundation.

NOTES

1. For a more complete description of the COPE evaluation, see Cordner (1985); the issue of the COPE and fear of crime is presented in Cordner (1986); the effects of COPE on police officer attitudes are discussed in Hayeslip and Cordner (1987); and a nice overview of the COPE project can be found in Taft (1986).

2. For further discussion of methodological issues in the COPE evaluation, see Cordner (1985).

9

COMMUNITY POLICING: RHETORIC OR REALITY?

MOLLIE WEATHERITT

This chapter sets out to describe and review what community policing is and how it has been implemented in the 43 police forces of England and Wales. I shall describe some of the pressures on forces to implement what amount to community policing programs and the political context in which they have done so. Community policing has its detractors but (for very good reasons) the stage of public debate has tended to be dominated by its enthusiasts. Community policing has reached the status of an orthodoxy in many English-speaking countries and as a result has tended to be seen as providing a coherent and self-evidently sensible and desirable set of answers to policing problems. I shall try to show that this is too simple a view both of the problems to which community policing is put forward as a response and of the policing solutions that it supposedly offers. Community policing ideas have been made an important contribution to debates about policing in Britain and have stimulated a considerable number of policing innovations, but community policing has ducked or fudged some fundamental questions about the police role and has failed to provide an adequate framework or set of concepts for considering those questions. Moreover, community policing ideas have sometimes been pursued and implemented with surprisingly little concern over how they might be given practical content.

Community policing is talked about at a number of levels and it is important to distinguish between them. At one level (on which I shall concentrate in this chapter) community policing is about developing a set of programs or activities for police: foot patrol, community-based crime prevention, ways of consulting communities about the kinds of problems they have and the kind of policing they want. The emphasis tends to be on the pragmatic and small-scale. Activities such as foot patrol or neighborhood watch are undertaken because they are expected to make the police more effective in preventing and detecting crime or in maintaining certain kinds of order. Such activities are also undertaken because they enable the police to present themselves in a way that will alter, for the better, public perceptions of them. On this second level, community policing is about promoting better police-public relations and a better police image. This promotional work is important not just because it is supposed to enhance police effectiveness. It is undertaken because community policing activities are seen as good in themselves in giving legitimacy to policing as an activity and to the police as an institution.

Community policing is also about changing the ethos of policing to emphasize notions of service, flexibility, consumer responsiveness, conciliation, consultation, and negotiation. It is contrasted with a policing rhetoric and style that are characterized as having lost touch with the public, as threatening of civil liberties, as invasive, oppressive, and alienating; or as slack, indifferent, and inefficient. Community policing is about encouraging the development of the preventive and nonconflictual aspects of policing and giving them more status, prominence, and importance within forces and more impact outside them. In contrast to the situation in the United States, aggressive or heavy-handed techniques of order maintenance have not so far been regarded as forming part of the community policing package in Britain. On the contrary, such techniques and the need to resort to them are regarded as the antithesis of what community policing is about. So strong is the identification of community policing with preventive, flexible, conciliatory, and consultative policing that its advocates sometimes seem to imply that if such an ethos is pursued and applied with enough seriousness and commitment, the conflictual and coercive aspects of policing will disappear.

Because many people are in favor of the kinds of policing values that community policing embodies and because they tend to feel uneasy about or are opposed to the kind of policing that is so often contrasted with it, community policing ideas have been influential in creating a publicly acceptable framework and language for talking about policing. More than this, community policing has come to be used as a consensual rallying cry with which to convey a sense of nostalgia and to create a climate of exhortation. The vision invoked is of a better yesterday that, at the same time, is contrasted with an unsatisfactory present and that provides the inspiration for a better future. The appeal is to a golden age in which communities were harmonious and cohesive and provided an unproblematic basis for policing by consent. The promise of community policing is that this ideal can be recreated in the future. This appeal tends to be the more seductive because it carries echoes of, or can readily be made to appear central to, a broader political vision in which the supposed ills of modern society can be cured only by a return to traditional standards of behavior and a renewed respect for traditional sources of authority. Community policing is essentially *celebratory,* both of the sources of authority that it invokes and, as I shall demonstrate, of the value and effectiveness of the kinds of activities and programs that are advocated under this banner.

Arguments in favor of community policing are conducted on the pragmatic level, on the level of community policing as an organizational style, and on idealistic and ideological levels. Advocates of community policing do not always distinguish between these levels. One of the consequences of this is that the question posed in the title to this chapter (community policing: rhetoric or reality?) cannot be answered. It cannot be answered because it is based on a distinction that cannot be made. The rhetoric of community policing—rarely, the persuasive devices deployed on its behalf—has come to be an important part of its reality: Its presentational aspects and its potency as a metaphor are as important (maybe more so) as its actual program. This does not mean that empirical examination of community policing programs is irrelevant. Indeed, one of the features of the current debate on community policing in Britain is the increasing attention that is being paid to what precisely community policing programs mean in practice and, more importantly, the implications of this evidence for the assumptions on which it is based. But it is clear that community policing is not just something that can be enumerated; it has to be elucidated too.

THE DEVELOPMENT OF COMMUNITY POLICING IN BRITAIN

The philosophy of community policing in Britain as well as important aspects of its practice (such as foot patrol) can be traced to the formation of a professional police in the nineteenth century and the ways in which the police mandate was established and legitimated. The process of legitimation that the early architects of British policing set in train has continued to draw on ideas that are commonly associated with community policing, most notably the idea that effective policing can only be done with the "consent" of the community. In this broad sense, community policing is neither particularly distinctive nor particularly new, although views of the means most appropriate to winning consent have clearly changed over time.

What *is* new is a language: the conscious linking of the term "community" to policing, to reproduce a phrase with a resonance and a presumed content that stands in contradistinction to other, less-desirable aspects of policing. In Britain, this seems to have happened in the mid 1970s. The term "community policing" is usually associated with the work and ideas of John Alderson, who, from 1973 to 1983, was chief constable of Devon and Cornwall Constabulary (a geographically large and mainly rural force of about 3,000 officers). In 1979 Alderson published *Policing Freedom,* which sets out a coherent philosophy and set of strategies for a community policing practice that he had begun to implement in his force in the mid 1970s. Alderson's subsequent speeches and writings have helped to popularize the term. Community policing (though often loosely used and in ways that mean different things to different people) is now part of the common coinage of public debate about policing.

Alderson's achievement was to articulate publicly a coherent philosophy and set of principles for policing. Although Alderson is widely regarded as the original architect of community policing in Britain, many of the activities that he argued for and supported were already well-established aspects of policing practice. Much of the rationale for these practices had begun to be made explicit in the 1960s. I shall therefore begin my history of community policing with this period, even though these practices had yet to achieve the status with which the term "community policing" has subsequently dignified them.

THE 1960s: REPORT OF A ROYAL COMMISSION

In 1960 a Royal Commission on the Police was appointed with terms of reference wide-ranging enough to enable it to look at the fundamental principles underpinning the police service. The commission was asked to review the constitutional position of the police and the arrangements for controlling and administering them. The years following the publication of the commissioner's report—and the subsequent enactment of its recommendations in the Police Act of 1964—were fertile ones for police innovation. Although the commission had little to say of direct relevance to the development of community policing, its recommendations have nonetheless had important indirect effects in helping to stimulate innovation in police forces and in lending cohesiveness and direction to British policing policy.

An important factor in the growth and spread of community policing ideas in Britain is the extent to which policing is subject to central influence and direction. The position contrasts markedly with that in the United States. Although British policing is essentially a local service, the financing of it is shared between local and central government with the latter contributing a little over half the costs in the form of direct grants. Thus central government has a direct interest in the nature and quality of local policing. Under the Police Act of 1964 (which sets out the respective duties of chief constables, local police authorities, and central government), the secretary of state (in practice the home secretary) is charged with a general duty to promote police efficiency.[1] The act provides him with a number of permissive and regulatory powers with which to do this. Although the act also gives chief constables an independent responsibility for the "direction and control" of their forces, a responsibility that is traditionally respected by the secretary of state, it is also the case that he is able to define police efficiency in such a way as to give him considerable scope for affecting police operational policies and deployment. The question is not whether the secretary of state has influence, but rather in what circumstances and in what ways he chooses to exercise that influence.

Central government influence may be exerted directly through sanction such as withdrawal of grant aid or a requirement that a chief constable resign in the interests of efficiency. Such sanctions are rarely contemplated and are even more rarely used. Instead central government influence is more likely to be exerted indirectly. The Home Secretary issues regular advice to police forces in the form of administrative circulars. He is statutorily permitted to provide certain common services such as training, and in fact does so.[2] He may also provide "research into matters affecting the efficiency of the police." I shall be concerned in the rest of this section to show how government-backed research and advisory circulars have been used to encourage the development of community policing practice and to foster common policies in forces.

A further influence on local policing is the work of Her Majesty's Inspectors of Constabulary (HMIs). Under the Police Act of 1964, HMIs have a statutory duty to inspect all police forces (excepting the Metropolitan Police), which they do annually, and to "carry out such other duties for the purpose of furthering police efficiency as the Secretary of State may from time to time direct." HMIs also have important advisory functions, what the 1962 Royal Commission described as "the encouragement of initiative forces and the sharing of new ideas or practices between one force and another [and] more particularly the responsibility for forward thinking about the demands of executive policing over wider areas than those of individual forces." HMIs are responsible for advising on arrangements for promoting collaboration between forces, for ensuring that the results of government research are made available to the police, and ensuring that new knowledge and up-to-date techniques are being applied. The intention is that by acting as purveyors of information to forces and identifying successful local initiatives and spreading the word about them, inspectors act as catalysts to innovation. HMIs are expected to be key figures in the business of identifying and disseminating good policing practice.

A final sense in which centralization has affected developments in policing derives from the relative cohesiveness of British policing. The relatively large size of police forces (the average provincial force has approximately 2,500 and the smallest force just under 1,000 officers) of itself lends an authority and importance to those in command. The chief officers' corporate body (the Association of Chief of Police Officers, ACPO) is relatively small, comprising the 44 chief constables of England and Wales and Northern Ireland, together with the rather larger number of deputy and assistant chief constables (total membership is 275). There is close liaison between ACPO and the Home Office and the association is regularly consulted, formally and informally, by government about matters affecting the police service. Government committees and working parties (even internal ones) will usually number representatives from ACPO among their membership. Government circulars on policing policy more often than not are agreed in advance with ACPO and serve to develop and articulate a policy consensus. A central conference of chief constables, chaired from the Home Office, meets regularly and provides an additional forum for discussing policy issues.

CENTRAL GOVERNMENT INFLUENCE AND THE DEVELOPMENT OF COMMUNITY POLICING

For all the reasons I have outlined above, a description of the development of community policing ideas and practice in Britain can hardly be attempted without reference to the role of central government in the process. In what follows, I shall try to assess government influence in respect of three main components of community policing: patrol, crime prevention, and (more briefly) structures of accountability.

Patrol

The 1982 Report of the Royal Commission on the Police recommended the setting up of a central government research unit to help plan police methods and study new techniques and to ensure that the results of its work were "speedily adopted throughout the country." By the mid 1960s, this unit (initially called the Police Research and Planning Branch) was involved in implementing, monitoring, or evaluating a number of experiments in different methods of patrol. One of these experiments involved controlled variations in the number of officers posted to foot beats in order to test the relationship between levels of foot patrol and crime (Bright, 1969). The study concluded that increasing the level of foot patrol did not reduce crime. Another experiment involved removing foot patrol cover and replacing it with 24-hour mobile patrol cover linked to a central point by radio. Here the results were presented as more promising: improved police morale, greater public confidence in the police, reduced crime and improved detection rates (unpublished research, reported in Weatheritt, 1986:89-90).

One of the reasons why the police were being encouraged to experiment with different methods of patrol was concern over shortages in police manpower. Police forces were under strength by about 15 percent. They had difficulty in recruiting suitable officers and many experienced officers were leaving prematurely. In 1966 a series of working parties was set up by the Home Office to look at ways of mitigating this situation by improving police officers' conditions of service and using existing manpower more efficiently. One of these working parties, on operational efficiency and management, was charged with looking at new systems of policing that had been or could be designed to increase the "productivity of every policeman to the maximum" (Home Office, 1967). At about the same time that the working parties were set up, the Home Office Police Research and Planning Branch began a second round of experiments in patrol, which built on what the branch had already learned about the relative effectiveness of different levels of foot patrol and from the car patrol experiment referred to above. The idea was to combine what was described as the best of two policing worlds: the increased mobility and communications provided by the cars and radios, and the traditional idea of the country police officer—to be imported into urban areas—who worked on foot and from a close knowledge of the area he patrolled. This scheme, known as unit beat policing, involved area beat officers, mobile patrol officers, and local detective officers working together as a team. Except in town centers that were difficult to patrol in any other way, general traditional foot patrol had no place in this new scheme of things. As earlier Police Research and Planning Branch experiments had shown, traditional foot patrol had failed to prove its deterrent worth.

The working party on operational efficiency had before it the results of a preliminary study on the effectiveness of unit beat policing that it claimed improved the ability of the police to prevent and detect crime. The working party recommended the virtual abandonment of traditional foot patrol, believing that it "embodies an idealization from the past that in the conditions of modern society . . . is no longer attainable." Patrolling on foot was, moreover, the working party said, boring and frustrating for officers required to perform it. The working party recommended a "radical departure" from the traditional form of beat patrolling on foot that would be more flexible and make greater use of technological aids, most notably the personal radio and the greater mobility provided by the motor car. The working party endorsed unit beat policing and recommended that chief constables consider adopting more flexible systems of beat patrol "as a matter of urgency."

Unit beat policing is referred to in at least two North American reviews (Wasson, 1977; Trojanowicz et al., 1986) as an example of community-based preventive policing, a somewhat ironic status in view of both its origins in a disillusionment with foot patrol and the criticisms that have subsequently been leveled at it (see below). Despite this, unit beat policing embodies several community policing ideas. Area beat officers are given overall responsibility for an area within which they are expected to live and whose people they are expected to get to know. They are supported by a system of mobile patrols with whom they are expected to work as a team. Detective officers are also integrated into this team. Communications between members of the team and between the team and headquarters are improved by issuing officers with personal radios and by setting up filing systems in which information they collect individually can be made available to all. The idea is that good police work is encouraged as a flow of information about the beat passes between members of the team. The work by the Police Research and Planning Branch suggested that this system was more than just an idea that sounded good on paper. The branch stated that the system also produced results: improved morale, better police-public relations, reduced crime, and improved detection (Home Office, 1967:117).

In 1967 the more flexible systems of policing of which unit beat policing was the most important example were, in effect, imposed throughout England and Wales by the Home Office. In an advisory circular, it exhorted chief constables to review their existing operational methods and the deployment of officers with a view to introducing new methods of policing based on the use of cars in conjunction with personal radios. The Home Office offered a financial carrot, in the shape of a central government loan, to offset the cost of buying this new equipment. In issuing the circular and making this offer, the Home Office was motivated by continuing concern over manpower shortages, the knowledge that impending public expenditure restrictions were likely to worsen rather than improve the manpower situation, and even a wish to create a market for the then ailing British car industry. The proposed changes were nonetheless sold to the police service and to the public using familiar community policing arguments that emphasized improved police effectiveness and better relationships with the public.

Within a very few years, however, the unit beat policing "solution" was beginning to look less promising. In 1971 the Home Office began a review of how areas in nine police forces were faring under the new system (Comrie and Kings, 1975). Although it had never been intended that the unit beat concept should be applied inflexibly, the researchers found that the model had been applied without regard to local circumstances. Haste and a tendency to regard unit beat policing as an operational blueprint had resulted in poor, patchy, and ineffective implementation.

The 1971 study pointed to the following advantages of unit beat policing. It had improved police efficiency and response times and had enabled the police to cope with an increased work load. But other distinctive features of unit beat policing—the role it assigned to beat constables and the idea of team working—had proved less easy to implement. In none of the study areas were detective officers and area constables integrated into the teams, and the latter, in particular, had become the "forgotten men" of the system. Perhaps most significantly, the Home Office researchers lamented the demise of general foot patrol and recommended that it be reintroduced on the grounds that it would make police officers more accessible to people and would be a more effective deterrent than mobile patrols.

From the 1970s onward, arguments in favor of a greater use of foot patrol have assumed an increasingly important place in public debate about policing in Britain. On the basis of survey evidence, "more foot patrol" is clearly what most people want (some of this research is summarized in Weatheritt, 1987). The idea of foot patrol and, in particular, patrolling by officers committed on a long-term basis to a small geographical area (community constables[3]) seems to be popular because of the friendly image it conjures up; and because it seems to provide a concrete and visible antidote to the negative consequences and pejorative associates of "reactive" or "fire-brigade" policing. (These presumed consequences are debated in almost identical terms in Britain as they are in the United States and are in essence to do with loss of police public contact.) But a greater emphasis on foot patrol has also become attractive for other economic reasons. The large increases in oil prices of the mid-1970s made mobile patrols more expensive and many chief constables began to see foot patrol as helping to solve some of their financial problems. As recession began to bite, local forces came under pressure to cut expenditures (as did other public services) and they began to introduce vehicle mileage restrictions and to cut vehicle fleets in order to save money.

One effect of these various factors is that a return to the bobby on the beat is a virtually unanimously accepted goal of public policy. Foot patrol is widely regarded as a key (and largely uncontroversial) feature of community policing. However, assertions about the importance and value of beat policing are relatively easy to make; giving a concrete and visible *content* to beat policing and demonstrating that its presumed benefits can actually be delivered have both proved to be more difficult. In Britain, community policing patrol initiatives (and especially the attempt to employ more community constables) have been pursued as though they raised few or no significant questions about how patrol can most effectively be done. We have been more concerned to pursue the question, How can we return more officers to foot patrol? than asking the more fundamental and difficult questions: How can patrol be made more effective? What should patrol officers do? and How do we know whether they are doing it well?

These issues can best be illustrated by considering the role and the work of community constables. The Home Office working party on operational efficiency and management referred to above defined a set of duties for such officers of which the most relevant are: to have overall responsibility for an area and to be familiar with everything on it; to see that this information is communicated to other officers; to maintain personal contact with members of the public so as to act as the "eyes and ears" of the police force to "show the flag" in areas where the public expects to see a police officer; and to report back to people who ask for help from the police what action is taken in response to their request. The officer's "primary role" is defined as being concerned with crime and criminals; and his effectiveness is to be judged by the amount of information he passes on to colleagues (Home Office, 1967:142). The emphasis is largely on crime and information gathering, and contact with the public is to be fostered mainly (though not entirely) in terms of its contribution toward meeting these ends.

The mandate is clear and it is largely a crime fighting or law enforcement one. Over the years, however, this emphasis has tended to become overshadowed and downplayed by the idea that making more contact with the community is to be pursued either as an end in itself or as a means to longer term (and often more contentious and ambiguous) goals such as citizen education. Thus, the role of community constables has expanded both to acknowledge and to develop the social service role of the police. In many forces, community constables are now expected to regard making contact with "the community" as *the* major justification for their existence. But one of the problems with this aspect of their role is that its purpose tends to be only vaguely or ambiguously defined and its content may hardly be defined at all, except at the most general level.

In 1981 the Home Office carried out a survey in five police forces of 300 community constables, which looked at how they spent their time and how they were supervised (Brown and Iles, 1985). Despite the greater importance that community policing ideas have assumed in public debate since the 1960s, the status of community officers as "forgotten men" seemed hardly to have improved. Community constables did not have much contact with their fellow officers. They believed that their career prospects were poor and they were not properly supervised. The research found community officers' role to be a surprisingly empty one. Officers spent half their time away from their beats, most often on entirely unrelated duties. Most of their remaining time was spent patrolling, but they made very few contacts with members of the public when doing this. Ten percent of their time was spent dealing with offenses and offenders. Although they spent a certain amount of time making informal contacts with members of the public (an average of three hours per officer per week), more formal involvement with community groups, schools, or statutory agencies was relatively uncommon: officers spent only two hours a week doing this.

The problems identified by this research are essentially to do with a lack of coherent, readily definable, and specific expectations of community policing constables. Instead, what is expected of them, although undoubtedly worthy and high-minded, remains in practical terms vague, ambiguous, or vacuous. It is therefore not surprising that community policing activities have proved difficult to supervise, remain unrewarded, and are regarded as marginal to "real" police work. Before community policing work can be properly integrated into mainstream policing, much more thought has to be given to endowing this work with more practical content and to tying that content to some clearer idea of what the police are for. Such a rethink will, I suspect, involve community constables in a return to the kinds of policing activities to which community policing is currently regarded as an antidote: in particular, reactive or response policing and criminal intelligence gathering.

Crime Prevention

While it is the primary duty of every British police officer to prevent crime, every force also has a specialist crime prevention department whose sole function is to devise and implement more focused preventive strategies. Crime prevention departments have their origins in a Home Office Committee, the Cornish Committee, set up in the early 1960s (Home Office, 1965). This recommended that every force appoint a small group of specialist officers to be responsible for crime prevention publicity and for keeping up to date with developments in crime prevention technology. Crime prevention was not to be a specialization pursued in isolation from other policing tasks. On the contrary, crime prevention officers were to be involved in training and one of their most important functions was to stimulate and maintain interest in crime prevention among their colleagues, particularly at the beat level.

The committee was very aware that crime prevention was not just the responsibility of the police service but ought to be taken seriously by everyone. It recommended that a central advisory body be set up (established in 1967 and now called the Home Office Standing Conference on Crime Prevention) that would stand as evidence that the central government took prevention seriously and that commercial and other interests needed to be involved in and coordinated with a national crime prevention effort if that effort were to be successful. The conference runs national and regional crime prevention publicity campaigns and, since 1985, a rolling program of working parties has reported annually to it on issues such as the prevention of burglary, car theft, shop theft, and child abuse.[4] In 1968, acting on one of the early recommendations of the Standing Committee (as it then was), the Home Office issued an advisory circular to all police forces, recommending that they set up crime prevention panels that would duplicate the Standing Committee's work by voluntarily involving members of local communities in the police effort to prevent crime. There are currently about 300 such panels throughout England and Wales. Crime prevention panels have become an increasingly important vehicle for broadcasting one of the central messages of community-based policing: The police must work with the community if crime prevention is to be successful.

The history of crime prevention within British policing can be interpreted as one of trying to give it status, importance, and impact that, nonetheless, seem to remain perpetually elusive. Partly because of the nature of the problem it sets out to tackle, crime prevention has always been longer on promise than on achievement. The size of crime prevention departments has been kept small (crime prevention officers from less than 0.5 percent of total force strength; compare this with detective strength at 12-15 percent) and the opportunities for promotion within crime prevention are extremely limited. This would matter less if crime prevention officers were seen primarily as a specialist resource to be used by generalized patrol officers who are themselves fully committed to trying to make a success of crime prevention. But there is little evidence of crime prevention officers being used in this way. Despite the hopes of the Cornish Committee, specialist crime prevention has been the Cinderella of the British police service, waiting in vain to be wooed by the prince of mainstream policing.

Specialist crime prevention has also come to be associated with an approach to prevention that is increasingly recognized as limited. The bread and butter of specialist crime prevention has been publicity campaigns aimed at making people more security conscious and giving people advice on target-hardening measures. A series of research projects carried out by the Home Office beginning in the mid 1970s showed that this approach had no or few effects on crime. (The most important of these research projects are reported in Clarke and Mayhew, 1980.) A number of criticisms were advanced against the traditional approach. First, it was too diffuse and insufficiently problem-oriented: Limited resources were spread too thinly and without regard for the precise problems that needed to be tackled. Second, physical measures needed to be considered within a wider framework that took account of people's motivation to use them. Third, traditional crime prevention was too reactive and individualistic. It needed to be planned in collaboration with other organizations and with regard to the availability of other, nonphysical measures. Similar criticisms were later made of the work of crime prevention panels (Home Office, 1986), which, until relatively recently, were dominated by the police who chaired and serviced them and whose work has tended to reflect the dominant concerns of police crime prevention departments.

Crime prevention planning in the police service has been much influenced by the central government party through its training school,[5] partly through the Home Office Standing Conference, partly through the influence of research, and partly by advisory circulars. Since 1967 the Home

Office has issued six such circulars specifically on crime prevention. (This number may seem small, but so far as I am aware it is larger than the number issued on any other policy issue—as opposed to administrative or legal issues—over the same period.) All reflect the department's interest in what might broadly be termed community policing issues. The idea that crime can be prevented only by police and community working together and the exhortation that the community must play its part in crime prevention has been reiterated in each circular. These ideas currently form the main plank of the government's crime prevention strategy (and that of the police). Although the ideas form less of a break with the past than many commentators on the British policing scene imply, it is nonetheless the case that the current government has committed more thought and more resources than any previous one into translating these ideas into reality.

Social Crime Prevention

Social crime prevention—the attempt to tackle not just symptoms but the "real" or "root" causes of crime, through hearts and minds campaigns or through changing social conditions—seems to have become an explicit organizational goal of police in the mid-1960s. Social crime prevention programs are mainly, though not exclusively, aimed at young people. School liaison programs that are aimed at instilling respect for law are run by all forces. Many forces provide leisure facilities and run activities for young people: sport clubs, youth clubs, discos, and the like. Many forces have become involved in trying to plan and implement programs that aim to reestablish social integration or improve the quality of community life. Neighborhood watch programs are perhaps the most widespread example of this but such broader social considerations have also been behind attempts to work with other agencies to prevent crime.

Social crime prevention programs are contentious in areas where the police are mistrusted and they have formed a focus for arguments about the proper nature and extent of the police role and police accountability in Britain. (In some areas of London, for example, it is the policy of the local branch of the National Union of Teachers not to allow police into schools.) The difficulty is that social prevention programs are often espoused by police on grounds that have to do with the promotion of wider social goals. The reasoning goes like this. The police have a mandate to control crime. Crime is a product of social processes. The police therefore have a duty to intervene in those processes. In the words of John Alderson, they must "penetrate the community in a multitude of ways in order to influence its behavior for illegality and toward legality" (Alderson, 1979:39).

I have quoted Alderson because he is the most notable exponent of this point of view and because his arguments that the police should intervene proactively are often thought to be an important part of the community policing package. In Alderson's model, the justification for this intervention is based on the idea of a "common good"—a common set of values to which all social policy should seek to give expression. The problem Alderson sees is that in relation to crime at least, social policy has failed. This leaves the field clear for the police with their special knowledge and their traditions of political neutrality to take the lead. Alderson envisages both a moral and a practical role for the police. As moral leaders, they should seek to give expression to the virtues of self-reliance, judgment, sensitivity, fairness, courage, and overall caring instinct (Alderson, 1979: Ch. 3). As practical leaders, their job is to mobilize community resources, bring people together to act in the name of the common good, and stimulate social discipline and trust in communities.

In 1976 when he was chief constable of Devon and Cornwall, Alderson created a small unit to put some of his ideas into practice. The unit's first task was a proselytizing one, aimed at convincing people that crime mattered and that they could and should do something about it. From this starting point, two strategies emerged. One involved the police working directly with local residents in various crime prevention and community involvement activities, including play and recreational schemes organized by the police for young people in school holidays, and the setting up of a community association on a local authority housing estate. The other main strategy was to create a forum for improving cooperation and coordination between the police and local authority agencies. This group created a joint agency training program and provided advice to the local authority on the policing and crime implications of proposed new building programs.

Alderson's ideas have been criticized on practical and on constitutional grounds. It is clear, however, that the Devon and Cornwall experiment was highly successful in giving expression to the policing ideals to which he was committed. Both the account given by the officer in charge of the experiment (Moore and Brown, 1981) and the high (though no means universal) esteem in which it is held attest to this (see, for example, Baldwin and Kinsey, 1982: Ch. 8).

On a practical level, however, there is no evidence that the Devon and Cornwall experiment reduced crime or, in particular, that the police were able through the activities they initiated to stimulate the ability of communities to regulate themselves and to improve informal social control. On constitutional grounds, Alderson has been criticized for wishing to elevate the police above the political fray and for investing them with a unique moral vision and duty that (implicitly) stand in constrast to the partial and often self-interested vision of other social agencies (see Baldwin and Kinsey, 1982; Bradley, Walker, and Wilkie, 1986:104 ff). An excellent dissection of the potential dangers in the police taking on what amounts to a political role in relation to community policing programs in the West Midlands police is given in Short (1983).

The idea that there is a consensual community waiting to be discovered and, moreover, that the police are best placed to discover it and to give practical expression to it is not only a recipe for failure, it is to misunderstand the nature of social process and the place of the police in the political order. Social harmony is not waiting to be discovered and it cannot be engineered by the police. Community policing provides no magic formula for escaping the inherent tension between freedom and security. To pretend that it does so is to abrogate responsibility for devising a constitutional framework in which the resolution of genuine and difficult tensions can be explored.

THE GROWTH OF CRIME PREVENTION PLANNING

The 1980s have seen a renaissance in crime prevention planning and activity. The old idea that preventing crime is a task for the whole community has once more been taken out of the policy cupboard and has been given some new institutional clothes. In 1984, five government departments issued a joint advisory circular that argues the need for a corporate and more adequately research-based approach to crime prevention. The circular says that crime prevention is more successful where police and local agencies work together in a coordinated way toward particular ends. It says that local government should ensure that those involved in planning and providing services should *always* take account of the scope for preventing crime, *even where the potential for this may not be immediately apparent.* To this end, information about patterns of crime and its correlates needs to be more readily made available or collated. Agencies are asked to exchange relevant information with the police, to discuss and plan policy options in collaboration with them and, perhaps, to provide coordinated crime plans for local areas.

A clear message of the circular is that crime prevention deserves more status not just in police forces but also elsewhere: A climate must be created "in which crime prevention is seen as an accepted goal of public policy." Improvements in the status of crime prevention have also been sought in other ways. Crime prevention officers' training has been reviewed, more money committed to it, and the balance of courses shifted in favor of community-based approaches and the importance of research. Thus, crime prevention officers are no longer expected to be just experts in physical security, their horizons are to be broadened to include mobilization of the community. Probationary constables are also to receive more crime prevention training. Crime prevention panels have been issued with new guidelines aimed at making their work more professional. They are expected to bring a more focused problem-oriented approach to their work and to evaluate the success of what they do (Home Office Standing Conference on Crime Prevention, 1985 and 1986). Contrast this situation with the 1970s when crime prevention panels were merely exhorted to "experiment with enthusiasm." The Home Office Standing Conference on Crime Prevention has been given a higher profile—it now holds a annual meeting in public and its chairmanship has been upgraded from official to ministerial level. More money (an additional £4 million) is being spent on officially funded crime prevention propaganda. The emphasis of Home Office funded research has changed, away from critical assessment of the assumptions on which traditional crime prevention is based, toward a search for best practice. (The two approaches are not, of course, mutually exclusive but the shift is discernible nonetheless.) Information about local crime prevention initiatives (particularly those involving cooperation between several agencies) is collated centrally by the Home Office (See Home Office Crime Prevention Unit, 1985). The Home Office has funded the post of coordinator for five local experimental multiagency crime prevention initiatives. There has been an explosive growth in neighborhood watch: the first scheme was set up in 1982; at the last count, there were 28,000 schemes throughout England and Wales. Finally, numerous ministerial speeches and pronouncements attest to the vigor (and of course success) of the government's initiatives. Crime prevention currently has a higher political profile than at any time in its history.

A number of themes can be discerned behind this renaissance. There is *localism* and *consumer responsiveness,* the ideas that problems have to be tackled at the level where they are most likely to be felt and that, as the circular puts it, "the public can only be expected to help . . . where initiatives against [crime] reflect their own perceptions and concerns, otherwise their involvement will be minimal." There is an emphasis on *voluntarism* and *self-help,* expressed through the development of neighborhood watch and crime prevention panels. There is the government's wish to see that the police together with other public services become more rigorously managed financially. "Value for money" is the watchword; greater efficiency and effectiveness its corollaries. The government believes that crime prevention is a cost-effective activity in terms of resources saved at other stages of the criminal justice process and that there are financial advantages to be gained by doing more of it. If the police can be encouraged to share some of the costs of preventing crime with other agencies and individuals, then so much the better. Finally, there is a recognition that crime prevention has an important *legitimating* function for police, partly because of the consumer consultative mechanisms it implies, partly because of the conflict-free and nonadversarial image of policing that it promotes.

The Effectiveness of Coordinated Crime Prevention

The rationale for putting more emphasis on crime prevention and for bringing a greater number of interests into the act appears to be a commonsense one. If crime prevention has failed because of a tendency to regard it as an isolated and discrete activity, then it makes sense to try to make it a more integrated and pervasive one. If crime prevention has failed because it has not made adequate appeal to what motivates people to act in particular ways, then it makes sense to devise ways of consulting them and of formulating policy in which their motivations and concerns can be made manifest. If crime prevention has failed because it has adopted too broad-brush an approach, then a more targeted approach to local problems is sensible. The appeal of coordinated or multiagency prevention lies in its recognition of the complexities of situations in which crimes occur and in its promise that they can be dealt with in a program of action where the partial knowledge of interested parties can be pooled and their fragmented responsibilities reconciled. This approach has come to epitomize par excellence the idea that policing problems can be solved if a consensus can be reached by appropriate parties about how to proceed.

The appropriateness and sensibleness of the above policy prescriptions and the political head of steam behind them provide few incentives for inquiring too deeply into the assumptions that they embody. Yet, like the community policing solution to patrol, broader crime prevention policies are something in the nature of a black box. At a general level, we have been willing to treat such policy prescriptions as nonproblematic. At a more detailed level, people have found it convenient not to inquire too closely into how apparent promise gets translated into specific action.

Skeptics are, of course, aware that things are less straightforward. Some of the problems they point to were illustrated by a project in 1978 set up and subsequently evaluated by the Home Office and aimed at improving cooperation on crime prevention between local authorities, the police, and other local agencies. The project set out to reduce the incidence of vandalism in 11 schools. The problem in each school was carefully researched and a set of measures tailored to it was devised. Several different local authority departments and representatives from each school were responsible for devising these measures, which included fitting damage resistant glazing, erecting high fencing, and redesigning the school grounds. The departments that had decided what action needed to be taken also had responsibility for implementing that action (Gladstone, 1980).

As an exercise in rational planning, this experimental project seemed to have everything going for it. Yet, after two years, only half of all the preventive recommendations had been implemented. The preventive measures were mostly not taken because those responsible for ensuring the work was done were already fully occupied, or had other more pressing interests or constituencies to satisfy, or were unwilling or unable to give priority to crime prevention (Hope and Murphy, 1983; reprinted in Hope, 1985). The multiagency approach was, in fact, a major reason for the project's failure.

There is no other published research on multiagency crime prevention in Britain that matches the thoroughness with which this demonstration project was evaluated. Echoes of the problems it ran into can be found in Moore and Brown's (1981) account of the Devon and Cornwall multiagency experiment in a parallel account of the same experiment by Blaber (1979) and in a critical account of Blagg and colleagues (forthcoming) of some interagency initiatives on three "problem" public housing estates. The main message of the Home Office project seems likely to have much wider application. This is that communities of interest are difficult to create and difficult to sustain. Coordinated crime prevention is not a panacea. Rather, it entails a highly problematic set of prescriptions whose outcomes are by no means predictable.

Crime Prevention and the Local Community

Crime prevention policy seeks to create and appeal to not only new communities of interest but also geographic communities, most notably neighborhoods. Neighborhood-based crime prevention seeks to work in two ways: by making people in neighborhoods more aware of what they can do for themselves and motivating them to do it; and thereby stimulating, creating, or recreating mechanisms of informal social control. Community policing casts the police as catalysts in the process. In Britain, neighborhood watch forms the most common and popular form of community-based crime prevention, at least so far as the police are concerned.

In Britain we have virtually no accounts of how police *do,* let alone *could* mesh with informal mechanisms of neighborhood control.[6] The importance of informal controls has tended to be referred to in a general way without regard to what actually happens in particular neighborhoods, or how such informal controls can be manipulated by public policy and, in particular, by the police. Studies of neighborhood watch have skated over these issues, concentrating instead on output measures (crime rates) rather than on the motivations and activities of participants. Advocates of community policing need to be much more explicit about the kinds of controls they are seeking to identify and manipulate, how this might be done, and whether and how the police should become involved in this process.

Scarman and After

The urban riots of 1981 and, in particular, the report by Lord Scarman on the riots in Brixton are widely considered to be a watershed in the development of policing in Britain. Scarman's identification of the precipitating causes of the riots as police behavior, and the supporting operational justifications that the police offered for that behavior, paved the way for a series of reforms aimed at making policing more responsive locally and in which preoccupation with enforcing the law is expected to take second place to securing public tranquility. The Scarman reforms are explicitly intended as an exercise in relegitimation. As such, they can be readily placed within the wider context of the other developments I have outlined so far.

Lord Scarman (1981: paras. 5.3 and 5.56) said that the police

are now professionals with a highly specialized set of skills and behavior codes of their own. They run the risk of becoming, by reason of their professionalism, a "corps d'elite" set apart from the rest of the community. . . . if a rift is not to develop between the police and the public . . . it is . . . essential that a means be devised of enabling the community to be heard not only in the development of policing policy but in the planning of many, though not all, operations against crime.

Legal requirement to consult was subsequently enacted as section 106 of the Police and Criminal Evidence Act of 1984 and a (nonstatutory) blueprint setting out appropriate forms and terms of consultation was laid out in two Home Office advisory circulars. As a result, all but one or two of the 43 police authorities in England and Wales have set up formal police community consultative committees, which include representatives of local councils, the main statutory services (education, housing, probation, etc), the churches, residents' and tenants' associations, and neighborhood action groups. The Home Office has advised on the kinds of issues that could usefully be the subject of local consultation. They include ways of maintaining a relationship of mutual trust between the police and the community; ways of maintaining community peacefulness and improving the quality of life; promoting greater public understanding of policing issues such as the causes of crime, police procedures, and law enforcement policies; considering the pattern of complaints against the police; fostering links with local beat officers; promoting joint crime prevention efforts through community action; developing victim support services; and so on. The rationale is that effective policing depends on people's cooperation and their having confidence in the police. To secure this, policing policy must be sensitive to people's needs.

Research on how consultative committees are working began in 1984 (Morgan and Maggs, 1984 and 1985). The research has yet to report on the kinds of activities in which consultative committees engage with police, or the full range of issues that they discuss. But in a highly critical review, Morgan (1987) reports on the professional and political competence with which the new committees discharge their functions. The picture he gives is not an encouraging one for the future of open and informed discussion of policing policy at a local level.

Morgan says police community consultative committees lack professional competence because they are ignorant. They are totally reliant on the police for information that is often unavailable or is not forthcoming or is aimed primarily at educating them into the police view of things. Their ignorance means that committee members are not competent to question and that consequently discussions do not happen or are vacuous. Committees' political competence is circumscribed by the fact that their members are those people who are already well-disposed toward the police. Groups who might be more critical or who are hostile (in other words, one party to the conflict that consultative committees are aimed at resolving) refuse to be involved. A result of these two factors is that consultative committees have in effect come to serve as little more than a forum for consensual impression management. Since community policing is about reinforcing the importance of the consensual aspects of policing, consultative committees are clearly effective in community policing terms. That they fail to provide an adequate forum for the resolution of conflict tells of a fundamental problem of community policing theory to which I return below.

CONCLUSION AND OVERVIEW

Throughout this chapter, I have been concerned to show how ideas that are associated with community policing have developed in Britain to produce a practice that emphasizes foot patrol and promotes crime prevention and better consultation. Because so many different rationales underpin these developments, the various elements that are said to compromise the community policing approach may be left vague or tenuous or may even be coincidental. On the other hand, community policing may be presented, as John Alderson had done, as a more or less coherent set of ideas, ideals, and practices that draw on a clear, if debatable, definition of community and a view of the right relationship of the police to that community.

Community policing is an elastic term that is often used to give a superficial coherence to a wide and disparate set of policing activities and various forms of police community dialogue. There are, however, some general themes that run through community policing literature in Britain and that inform—but also limit—the terms of public debate about it. The most important of these themes concerns the failure of community policing theory and practice to acknowledge that policing is about the regulation of conflict, if necessary by resort to force. This failure to engage with an important aspect of policing has implications for the debate at a number of levels.

At beat level—where there has also been a tendency to treat patrol activity as a given that does not need to be explicated—it has resulted in a failure to define a proper and therefore workable role for community beat officers, except at the most general and idealistic level. For many advocates of community policing, the combative and adversarial aspects of the police role have simply been wished away and have ceased to exist. Important law enforcement aspects of community constables' roles, particularly those deriving from their local knowledge or intelligence-gathering activities, have been ignored. In the fashionable rhetoric, such activities have become associated with "hard" policing to which community policing is counterposed as a softer and less-intrusive alternative. It is customary to characterize community policing as something different in both emphasis and essence from traditional policing. One effect has been to marginalize it. Restoring status to community beat work may mean accepting that it needs to become more, not less, like mainstream policing. At the very least, we need to define more coherent and detailed tasks for community constables that adequately reflect the law enforcement as well as the other aspects of their role. Certainly, if there is nothing but idealism to show for community policing, then it is destined to remain in the marginal position that its advocates currently lament.

At the level of police policy making, community policing has failed to deal adequately, if at all, with the fact that policing affects different publics in different ways and that law enforcement is bound to impinge on some groups more than others. There are different interests to be reconciled and the appeal to an ideal of a consensual community made by advocates of community policing does not provide a method or a means for doing this. Community policing is often seen as being most necessary in areas where sections of the community are hostile to the police or where informal social controls have broken down so that some sections of the community feel preyed upon or threatened by others. Yet the idea of community that is implicitly invoked by advocates of community policing is inadequate for dealing with these tensions. Of course, the police may deliberately act so as to try to impose one group's definition at the expense of others. But to call this "community policing" seems misplaced; it adds a harmonious-sounding gloss to an activity that is instead about the imposition of a nonconsensual definition of order by methods that in the end may only be successful because they are backed by the threat of resort to force.

Many individuals, groups, and agencies with whom the police seek to work in cooperative forums of various kinds are all too well aware that policing is about conflict regulation and that the police are given coercive powers to resolve those conflicts (at least in the short term). They know that it gives the police the upper hand in encounters and they feel that because the police are accustomed to taking charge where it matters, they will come to dominate in forums designed for dialogue and for planning joint action on a broader front. Accounts of multiagency initiatives show that this does indeed happen (Moore and Brown, 1985; Blagg et al., forthcoming). Agencies are often suspicious of working with the police and do not want to share information with them because they feel the police will use that information for purposes they do not approve of. They are concerned that the police view of problems will prevail. Theories of community policing typically emphasize the proactive role of the police but they do not have much to say about what the practical and constitutional limits to police action should be. The more thoroughgoing versions of community policing define the scope of that action as potentially limitless. On the whole, community policing fails to acknowledge or to deal with these problems or to provide a set of principles from which to address them.

Despite these difficulties—perhaps because of them—at the level of general policy declaration, community policing ideas are enormously seductive. They provide for the police a set of symbolically appropriate clothes that appeal across the political spectrum. In Britain there has been a tendency to avoid giving these ideas too much of a practical content or to think through their difficulties and their limitations. This process is now beginning (Willmott, 1987), but arguments about community policing will no doubt continue to seduce *because* they are vague. If more concrete progress is to be made, the mechanics of community policing need to be made visible and the principles they embody more openly and skeptically debated.

NOTES

1. The Police Act of 1964 sets out the arrangements for the 42 provincial police forces in England and Wales and the City of London force. It does not apply in the Metropolitan Police District (which covers all of Greater London except the City of London) where the Home secretary acts directly as police authority. His statutory relationship to that force is governed by the various Metropolitan Police Acts. The Metropolitan Police is the largest force in England and Wales, with a complement of 27,000 officers, a little over one-fifth of the total police establishment for those countries.

2. The Home Office provides basic training for probationary constables on a regional basis and supports a Police Staff College that trains senior officers from all forces for various levels of higher command.

3. "Community unstables" is used here as a generic term to describe what, in different police forces, are variously known area beat officers (compare unit beat

policing), resident beat officers, home beat officers, permanent beat officers, and neighborhood beat officers.

4. A diverse range of interests is represented on the Standing Conference. These include representatives from four government departments (education, environment, health and social security, and home affairs), local government, the Trades Union Congress, the Confederation of British Industry, the British Insurance Association, and the police. An equally diverse, though more specialized, range of interests is represented on the working parties. Their reports can be obtained from the Crime Prevention Unit, Home Office, Queen Anne's Gate, London SW1.

5. All newly appointed crime prevention officers are trained at the Home Office Crime Prevention Centre, which also runs courses for more senior officers, including some who are not crime prevention specialists.

6. A notable exception is some recent work of Shapland and Vagg (1987), which arrives at similar conclusions to those drawn by Kelling (1986b).

10

THE DEVELOPMENT, IMPACT, AND IMPLICATIONS OF COMMUNITY POLICING IN CANADA

CHRIS MURPHY

In a relatively short time, community policing has replaced professional crime control policing as the dominant ideology and organizational model of progressive policing in Canada. This chapter critically examines the development and impact of community policing on Canadian police ideology and practice, and identifies a number of conceptual and operational issues that will influence its future development.

The term "community policing" conveys a variety of metaphorical, ideological, programmatic, and pragmatic meanings (Manning, 1984). Based on a critique of crime control policing and modern bureaucratic police organization, community policing is a loosely related body of philosophical principles regarding the role, authority, and mandate of the public police, and the related set of internal organizational and operational reforms. Community policing advocates a broad, social role for police and enhanced community responsibility and participation in policing. It is argued that to meet the policing requirements of different citizens and neighborhoods effectively, public policing should become more visible, accessible, and responsive. This is accomplished by adopting various organizational strategies such as management decentralization, planned police response, mixed neighborhood patrol strategies, and mechanisms for community accountability and consultation. It is presumed that by increasing police-citizen involvement in neighborhood policing problems, public policing will more efficiently and effectively control crime, enhance public order, reduce crime fear, and increase neighborhood safety.

The recent emergence of community policing as the new police reform agenda of the 1980s has been associated with a number of distinct social, political, and economic factors. Expensive and expansive police services, declining neighborhood safety in core urban areas, class- or race-based social conflict, and a convincing academic critique of police efficiency and effectiveness have created public and political pressure for changes in conventional police ideology and practice, in both the United States and Great Britain (Manning, 1984; Weatheritt, 1986). Thus community policing can be seen alternatively as an ideological response to the ongoing search for community and order in modern urban society; a political promise of responsive and responsible police service; a programmatic set of internal, organizational, and managerial reforms; and pragmatic, operational strategies aimed at enhancing police effectiveness.

THE DEVELOPMENT OF COMMUNITY POLICING IN CANADA

In Canada, community policing has developed with relatively little external social or political pressure. For a variety of distinctive historical, political, and cultural reasons (Hagan and Leon, 1981; Lipset, 1986), Canadian police are publicly popular, well-financed, politically autonomous, organizationally stable, and ideologically powerful. Most urban core areas in Canadian cities, with few exceptions, are unarmed, orderly, and safe, and present police with relatively few serious policing problems. While Canadian crime rates and policing costs have increased, and some critical police research has been done (Shearing, 1981; Ericson, 1982; I. Taylor, 1983), policing in Canada has not yet become a serious political or public issue. It is necessary to examine some unique aspects of Canadian policing in order to understand why, despite the lack of external pressure for police reform, community policing has nevertheless been adopted and developed in Canada.

The United States has historically been a stimulus and source of innovation and criminal justice in Canada. With some exceptions, Canadian policing is typically a modified response to, or copy of, U.S. police ideology and practice. This perhaps unavoidable importation of police ideology, research, and technology, though sometimes modified and reformulated to meet Canadian conditions, explains the origin and pattern of much development and innovation in Canadian policing over the last ten years.

Canadian policing has benefited from this relationship by having the luxury of being able to pick and choose police innovations, technologies, and strategies after they have been field tested in the United States. U.S. police research agencies, such as the Police Executive Research Forum, the Police Foundation, and the National Institute of Justice, provide readily available sources of research, documentation, and information that are closely monitored and utilized by Canadian police, academics, and government officials.

There are, however, some distinct disadvantages to this one-sided relationship. Failure to develop in Canada, a vigorous and aggressive indigenous tradition in either applied police research or innovative police leadership, is in part explained by this easy reliance on U.S. based information and research. Innovation through imitation encourages the tendency to import wholesale policing philosophies, technologies, and strategies, which in some cases are inappropriate for the Canadian police environment. This has been particularly true of conventional crime control philosophies and strategies, born out of particular U.S. urban, social, and political conditions. Indeed it is arguable that Canadian police have adopted the U.S. crime control, bureaucratic reform model, without any real need for organizational reform, given the relative absence of violent crime, racial conflict, police corruption, or police/public alienation. The enthusiastic adoption of aggressive crime control strategies, such as SWAT teams, rapid response, and sophisticated police weaponry are an imitation of U.S. police strategies and not an indigenous response to Canadian policing problems. Community policing is also primarily U.S. police reform strategy but its emphasis on community-specific policing promises at least the possibility of a "made in Canada" policing style.

Explaining the source of innovation in Canadian policing does not adequately explain its development and apparent acceptance by both the Canadian public and police. The promotion of community policing as both an ideology of policing and a source of organizational and strategic innovation has actively been pursued by Canadian governments at both the federal and provincial levels. The Ministry of the Solicitor General, through its Research Division, and the Canadian Police College have been responsible for funding a variety of community-based policing projects, research studies (Murphy and Muir, 1984), and conferences (Murphy and Loree, 1987), and actively distribute information and materials on police innovation. Regarded as a potentially more effective approach to crime control, community policing is consistent with traditional government concerns regarding police efficiency and effectiveness. The possibility of shifting some policing responsibilities and costs back to the community, and reducing reliance on government-funded public policing, makes community policing a highly pragmatic as well as a politically appealing reform.

Despite its public popularity and government support, it is the police who ultimately choose to make community policing an operational reality. Community policing's status as the current definition of progressive policing provides an important new source of institutional legitimation. Chiefs of police who wish to be regarded as progressive, modern, and innovative must adopt the vocabulary of community policing or run the risk of being viewed as traditional or old-fashioned. While for some police chiefs community policing is mainly a rhetorical issue useful for negotiating new budgets and programs, for others it is a strategy for implementing organizational change and management innovation.

Community policing also provides a new source of management ideology and information, which legitimizes organizational change both within the department and outside in the political community. To rank-and-file police officers, community policing promises to provide a less-bureaucratic and -militaristic management style, enhanced occupational participation and control over their work, and greater job satisfaction. Community policing is, therefore, as much a force for organizational and management reform as it is an attempt to reform the police role in the community. The structural conditions that have inhibited indigenous police innovation in Canada may provide ideal conditions for its successful implementation and development. Institutional legitimacy, organizational stability, management tenure, public support, and an orderly urban environment may prove that while necessity may be the mother of invention, stability and legitimacy are the mother of implementation.

THE IMPLEMENTATION OF COMMUNITY POLICING IN CANADA

To describe the nature and scope of implementation of community policing in Canada, it is important to deal separately with urban and rural policing, given their distinctive task environments, organizational requirements, and policing traditions.[1]

Small Town and Rural Policing

Either assumed to be a scaled-down version of urban policing or a nostalgic remnant of traditional "village" policing, policing in rural areas and small towns remains ignored by most contemporary police literature and research. This is ironic, as much of what community policing is attempting to accomplish is what small town policing has been presumed to be about. Policing stable integrated communities, active police-citizen contacts, decentralized management, responsive police services, and community accountability would appear to make small town or rural policing an ideal model for community policing. However, this traditional stereotype of small town policing may be outdated and inaccurate.

Over the last ten years, policing in many small towns has become increasingly isomorphic with its urban counterpart. Efforts by provincial police commissions to upgrade and standardize small town police services have effectively promoted the dominant urban model of crime control and bureaucratic legalistic professionalism. In addition, policing in many small communities and rural areas in Canada is conducted by either centralized federal or provincial police organizations. The small towns or rural areas are policed in accordance with centralized management policies and standard operational procedures, which in many ways undermine traditional local policing practices and minimize local community influence.

As a result, small town policing in Canada is increasingly characterized by many of the organizational and operational practices of conventional urban crime control policing. This is evident in the growing dependence on computerization, the movement from foot patrol to rapid mobile response, increasing reliance on law enforcement rather than informal dispute settlement, the rapid adoption of professional management ideology, and increasing organizational bureaucratization (Murphy, 1985). While the degree to which this transformation from traditional village or small town policing to more modern standardized urban crime control policing undoubtedly varies across different communities, it would be safe to say that small town policing in Canada can no longer be assumed to represent the traditional ideal of community policing.

However, since the introduction of community policing as a competing ideology of urban policing, there has been a definite reappraisal of the virtues of traditional small town policing. Community policing offers an authoritative alternative to the urban professional policing model. Styles of policing that conform to the unique needs of particular communities that emphasize personal police contact, discretionary and informal order maintenance, and political accountability can now be recast as progressive and modern police practice.

As a result, larger centralized police organizations like the Royal Canadian Mounted Police (RCMP) and the Ontario Provincial Police (OPP) increasingly recognize the need to emphasize more flexible and community-specific policing policies and accommodate more local citizen input. A recent report on Native Policing in Canada has argued strongly for the adoption of community-based policing as an alternative to the prevailing standardized law enforcement model practiced in many rural Native communities (Depew, 1986).

While a number of questions remain concerning the compatibility of community policing principles with provincial or national policing standards, and the relevance of traditional police practice to changing rural environments, community policing appears to have at least diminished the dominance of urban policing as the only legitimate model for organizing and managing small town policing. It may be that small town policing is "so far behind urban policing, that it can now be seen as being ahead of its time" (Braiden, 1986).

Community Policing in Urban Police Departments

Developed to address the policing problems of diverse neighborhoods and the management of large centralized police departments, community policing has had its most visible impact on urban policing. Community policing has been formally adopted by a number of major urban police departments in Canada over the last five years. The following is a descriptive and selective overview of how some police departments have chosen to operationalize community-based policing principles and practices.

Since 1982, Canada's largest police force, the Metro Toronto Police Department, has formally been involved in implementing a number of significant organizational and operational changes associated with community policing. The management of police operations has been decentralized to zone or neighborhood districts, community planning officers have been created to generate community-based policing strategies, two experimental police storefront operations have been successfully implemented, foot patrols have been increased in specific neighborhoods, and community advisory committees have been established in some policing districts.

The Halifax Police Department in Nova Scotia is in the final stages of transforming its traditional organizational structure and operational philosophy to a community-based policing model. Changes include the adoption of zone-based team policing, generalist constables, decentralized criminal investigation, crime analysis and directed patrol at the neighborhood level, an expanded crime prevention function, and a reemphasis on foot patrol in the core urban area.

In Fredericton, New Brunswick, a small municipal police force has introduced a variety of innovative specialized police programs emphasizing community service and involvement. In addition to programs aimed at wife assault, sexual assault, and child abuse, Fredericton's Police Department has introduced an innovative storefront police operation in a low-income housing project that has had dramatic results.

The Halton Regional Police Force, an amalgamated police force in Southern Ontario, has introduced a number of community-based management and operational innovations. The Halton police chief has developed a unique participatory management process, extensive community-based crime prevention programs, split force patrol deployment, directed patrols, and recently a storefront operation in a high-rise apartment complex.

Other major Canadian police forces in Edmonton, Montreal, Winnipeg and Victoria are also in various stages of introducing community-based policing initiatives, focusing on core urban areas, specific community groups, and employing a variety of standard community policing strategies such as foot patrol, home visits, storefront operations, community councils, and directed patrol. In summary, community policing in a relatively short time has become a national focus for the development of progressive policing in Canada.

EVALUATING THE IMPACT OF COMMUNITY POLICING ON POLICE IDEOLOGY AND PRACTICE

As community policing is an attempt to reform both the philosophy and practice of contemporary policing, assessment of its impact must address changes in police philosophy and ideology and its impact on actual organizational or operational practice.

The adoption of community policing in Canada has had an identifiable impact on the rhetoric and ideology of public policing. The philosophical values of community involvement, responsive policing, public account-ability, and community-defined policing priorities have become an ac-cepted part of the political dialogue regarding public policing. Public statements by chiefs of police, police commissions, annual reports, and organizational mission statements indicate a definite rhetorical shift in the way policing is currently justified, legitimated, and promoted. While rhetoric is not necessarily an accurate indicator of operational reality, it typically precedes and justifies related organizational and operational changes. Though experience suggests that community policing principles have been conservatively translated into modest changes in police prac-tice, their articulation and promotion at the rhetorical level have made it possible for both police and communities to engage in a modest reform process that would not have been possible using the conventional crime control ideology.

If community policing is an attempt to change the role and relationship of the police and the public, it also implies a reform of traditional police management and organization. Community policing has introduced a variety of modern management principles such as decentralized author-ity, management planning, participatory management, flexible organiza-tional structure, and a more open organizational environment. However, evaluations of community policing programs in Canada suggest that im-plementing and managing fundamental change within a police depart-ment require a level of management skill and sophistication that is beyond the capacity of some police departments. This explains a tendency to adopt community policing strategies and incorporate them within traditional management philosophies and organizational structures. Thus, despite rhetorical change in management philosophy, community policing can have limited impact on traditional management practice.

Community policing has, in some cases, resulted in a shift in the way police departments structure and manage their operational activities. The growing acceptance of neighborhoods as the basis of operational planning and resource deployment in police departments such as Halifax and Toronto has led to the decentralization of management and operations to the district or neighborhood level. The redistribution of both administrative and managerial functions to district or zone teams is considered an essential element of a community-based police organization. Whether these organizational changes will eliminate the centralized bureaucratic model remains to be seen; however, the concepts of organizational decentralization, participatory management, limited functional specialization, and neighborhood-based police operations are now no longer required as radical or particularly threatening organizational concepts.

What the police actually do rather than what is said or how the department is managed or organized is of course the most critical dimension in evaluating community policing's actual impact. Community policing emphasis on more visible, accessible, and responsive police service has been operationally translated to mean increased foot patrol, police storefront operations, and an expansion of various crime prevention programs. While these efforts have been well-received by the public, they remain in most cases isolated police strategies, unrelated to the general philosophy or operational practices of the department as a whole. As a result, most police departments remain committed to crime control and mobile rapid response to calls for service as their basic operational philosophy, while community policing strategies remain a specialized adjunct unrelated to the core crime control model.

Community policing's endorsement of broad community involvement, accountability, and participation in police policy has to date been conservatively interpreted by Canadian police. While there has been aggressive promotion of neighborhood involvement in Block Watch programs and other crime prevention programs, these remain typically police-managed community programs that seldom translate into broader public involvement in policy and accountability issues. Community involvement is a modified version of the traditional police-community relationship in which the community is viewed as a resource, a support group, and an information source rather than as an authoritative body. For example, there is nothing in Canada comparable to England's citizen police councils (PACE), nor has there been the kind of active public involvement in police programs exemplified in some U.S. cities such as Flint (Michigan) or Detroit. However, given the traditional political and pragmatic problems associated with operationalizing community political involvement, and a comparative lack of public demand for this kind of involvement, it is not surprising that Canadian police have chosen to interpret this element of community policing reform cautiously and conservatively.

Finally, a word on empirical evaluations of community policing. To date, there exists in Canada no evaluation of the impact of community policing that would meet classical evaluation standards (Weatheritt, 1986; Sherman, 1986b; Rosenbaum, 1987). While the Ministry of the Solicitor General is currently attempting to document and evaluate a number of community policing projects, these undoubtedly will also fail to meet the scientific canons of classical evaluation methodology. Community policing is difficult to evaluate empirically as it remains a broad ideological phenomenon with a loosely linked set of objectives and varied programmatic strategies. As most community policing programs are in the early stages of development and implementation, the focus of research to date has been on documenting the implementation process rather than the impact or possible organizational change. Community policing programs or projects are typically a well publicized product of community or institutional politics in which various parties have a vested interest in the success of the program. Impact evaluations using survey data alone often fail to provide information or analysis that would allow the police or communities to assess either the actual impact of the program or the reasons for its relative success or failure. If community policing is to progress, both police and funding agencies will have to pursue more critical but methodologically sophisticated evaluation studies.

UNRESOLVED ISSUES AND PROBLEMS

Community policing, despite its limited development and implementation, remains an elusive yet potentially powerful source of police reform. The ambiguous rhetoric and vague theorizing that dominate much of the academic and programmatic literature too often obscure considerable confusion and conflict about the basic assumptions and implicit values inherent in community policing. That so many different political and institutional interests can agree about community policing suggests that they could very well be agreeing about different things. Community policing's emphasis on community consensus, citizen involvement, police accountability, and discretionary policing amplifies rather than resolves traditionally problematic issues. Any shift in the nature of police role in modern society that is as dramatic as community policing advocates and critics imply, and as diverse as operational experience indicates, deserves more discussion, debate, and clarification. There is evidence, however, that these issues are now becoming the subject of a growing body of more critical and sophisticated literature (Cohen, 1985; Goldstein, 1987; Kinsey, Lea, and Young, 1986; Klockars, 1986; Manning, 1984; Mastrofski, 1984). Without ongoing attempts to articulate and debate these issues, the police alone will be forced to develop their own operational interpretations.

The following are some of the problematic issues that have in various ways been raised by recent Canadian efforts to implement community policing:

What is a Community? The wholesale endorsement of community as both the means and the end of community policing projects and programs presupposes some agreement about the conceptual and empirical validity of community as an identifiable and viable concept. While ideologically appealing, the image of community used in much of the literature is often nostalgic, consensual, geographically limited, and value-laden. Police experience to date suggests a more realistic and perhaps useful conception of community as that of a community of interests, united on a temporal basis, in relation to specific interests, requiring some degree of mutual collaboration and agreement. This more limited, yet more empirically precise, conception of community, while less ideologically appealing, may more accurately reflect the reality of the urban policing environment and encourage community policing programs to espouse more modest and achievable objectives.

Who Represents the Community? Community policing endorses the legitimacy of collective community representation and consultation regarding police services and policing problems. Communities are to be consulted, surveyed, organized, and negotiated with, in order that their interests, needs, and concerns are incorporated into neighborhood police priorities and strategies. This vision of a more active, democratic, and politicized community, however, begs the question of who legitimately represents that community. Traditionally in Canada, citizens' input into policing issues are formally represented to police by government, police commissions, and committees. However, research (Stenning, 1981) suggests that government-sponsored police committees are a limited and sometimes ineffective means of community representation, and that other forms of direct citizen involvement may be more effective. This issue is particularly problematic in low-income communities that are often poorly organized and politically unrepresented. Democratic community representation raises a number of important and pragmatic questions. Should the police where necessary organize communities to represent their own interests? How should police assess public opinion? How do police balance their formal commitments to local governments and neighborhood politicians, versus informal representatives of the community? How do police reconcile representative but competing public interests in the community? Alternative strategies to deal with these issues need to be forthcoming, as we encourage police to venture into the difficult world of community politics.

Community Standards Versus Individual Rights. Community policing ideology endorses the collective rights or norms of the community as an authoritative basis for police response. This has been translated operationally by police to mean an emphasis on public order maintenance and/ or selective enforcement of some community standards on some citizens (juveniles, prostitutes, drug users, and drunks). This political or ideologi-

cal commitment to collective or neighborhood rights and norms sometimes conflicts with the official and legal mandates of governments and
the police to protect the rights of individuals and minorities from the ar-
bitrary power and standards of the majority. In Canada, this movement
toward individual versus collective rights has been encouraged by the recent introduction of the Canadian Charter of Rights. Thus when the
Toronto Police aggressively enforce community norms against young
black juveniles, they are accused of racism and abusing individual liberties. While the issue is receiving some critical attention (Sykes, 1986; Klockars, 1986), it remains both philosophically and operationally problematic to police who are expected to enforce these sometimes conflicting philosophical and political principles.

The Community Role in Policing. Community policing suggests a shift in
the authoritative power of the community to control or influence policing
by emphasizing that policing is both more effective and legitimate when it
responds to community-defined issues and that police should be seen as
essentially an agency of municipal and local government (Goldstein,
1987). Community policing suggests a number of possible readings on the
relationship between police and the community with substantially different implications. Is community policing meant to empower the police,
the community, or both? The following possible formulations of this
relationship illustrate the range of interpretation that can be abstracted
from community policing literature:

1. Community as an extension of police surveillance and response
   capabilities (Neighborhood Watch, Operation Identification).
2. Community as consumer and/or client of police services (Goldstein,
   1979, 1987).
3. Community as partner, coproducer of neighborhood order and safety
   (Murphy and Muir, 1984; Wilson and Kelling, 1982).
4. Community as a source of authority, influence and control over
   neighborhood police policy (Kinsey, Lea, and Young, 1986).
5. Community as an alternative source of order, policing, and law enforcement (I. Taylor, 1983).

Unless the relationships implied in community literature or programs
are made explicit and the mechanisms for establishing these relationships
are developed, the vague rhetoric concerning this complex relationship
will remain a source of considerable confusion and conflict.

The Expanded Role of the Police. Community policing advocates and
legitimates a broader social and political role for police than the legally
constrained crime control model of conventional policing. The broad
organizational mandate of maintaining order, peace, and security extends

the police role into proactive preventative problem solving and the general dynamics of community organization and politics. The police officer as community organizer, problem solver, social service provider, and local politician inevitably enhances police power and influence within and over the community. This is typically justified as a more effective way of reducing crime and stabilizing community order as a protective government service, particularly in low-income communities. Depending on one's political view of the role and responsibilities of police and government versus that of community and citizens, this enhancement of police power and influence is either intrusive and dangerous or protective and responsible. Therefore, an expanded police role does raise a number of important philosophical and pragmatic policy and operational questions.

Should police provide social services that other agencies or government institutions have a responsibility to provide? Does the expansion of police social service inevitably reduce government expenditure on other social services? Does expanding the role of police in community issues and problems politicize policing and give the police too much influence over neighborhood politics? If community policing expands police power and influence over the community, are there adequate safeguards or means of making the police accountable for this power? Does limiting police involvement in community problems mean an abdication of government and police responsibility to provide all communities with a certain basic level of service, order, and safety? In Canada to date, there has been little public, political, or academic debate on these issues.

CONCLUSION

The recent development of community policing in Canada marks a significant shift in contemporary police rhetoric and practice. Supplanting crime control policing as the new definition of progressive policing, community policing has been enthusiastically adopted by police, governments, and citizen groups as a means of reforming public policing to meet varied public and institutional interests. Whether community policing can possibly satisfy these diverse expectations remains to be seen. To date, Canadian police have conservatively and cautiously translated community policing as a mandate for modest organizational reform and limited community involvement. The future of community policing in Canada, as a more radical reform of police theory and practice, will ultimately depend on citizens' demands for such change and a more satisfactory articulation and resolution of the problematic, ideological and operational issues that continue to limit its potential development.

NOTE

1. There are 53,464 police officers in Canada and 591 police departments or detachments. The Royal Canadian Mounted Police (RCMP), Canada's largest police force, employs 18,497 people in various federal, provincial, and municipal police functions. The provinces of Quebec and Ontario have their own provincial police forces with rural and limited municipal policing responsibilities. The five largest urban police departments in Canada are in Toronto (6,935), Montreal (5,005), Calgary (1,469), Edmonton (1,333), and Vancouver (1,237). Some 72 percent or 410 of all police forces have fewer than 19 employees and police approximately 25 percent of the Canadian population. The RCMP are responsible for policing rural areas outside of municpalities, in all provinces except Ontario and Quebec, and also police on a contract basis in 195 primarily small municipalities in these same provinces (Statistics Canada, 1986).

PART III
THE PROSPECTS OF COMMUNITY POLICING

Chapters in Part III take stock of community policing and look for implications for the future. As the number of studies evaluating community policing programs grows, it is difficult to get a feel for what they mean and how to make sense of their diverse findings. Further, much in program evaluation tends to assess only bottom-line outcomes without examining the validity of the theory that underlies the program model.

The chapter by Jack Greene and Ralph Taylor is a corrective to this state of affairs. The authors carefully reconstruct the "broken windows" theoretical model underlying many community policing proposals and then critique the empirical research that might shed light on the model's validity. Greene and Taylor find little or no evidence in extant research to support the processes hypothesized by the broken windows model. The linkage between incivility and weakened informal social control has not been empirically established; the linkage between incivility and fear of crime appears to be limited to those neighborhoods that are neither poor nor well-off; and the linkage between incivility and crime cannot be separated from the effects of the neighborhood's socioeconomic profile. In reviewing eight empirical studies of the impact of community policing programs, the authors find little consistency in findings across studies. They note a number of methodological deficiencies plaguing this research and offer several recommendations for theory development and testing. They conclude that until the issues they raise are addressed, there can be little advance in knowledge about what works and what does not.

In his chapter, David Bayley—who with Jerome Skolnick recently rendered a generally positive and hopeful prognosis for community policing

(1986)—takes the devil's advocate position, suggesting a dozen ways in which the reform could go wrong. Acknowledging that community policing may more often than not be a catchy phrase to generate enthusiasm for the same old techniques, he does suggest that several profound changes have occurred in some innovative departments throughout the world (community crime prevention, proactive policing, public participation in policy development and oversight, and decentralization of command). These changes constitute the core of the real reform with great potential to have a significant impact on what police do and accomplish. Yet Bayley cautions that these changes may also have no impact on crime, reduce the police capacity to deal effectively with disorders, provide a continuing rationale for inefficient public resource allocation, enable police to mobilize interest group support for self-serving causes, promote vigilantism, and produce a number of other equally unpalatable changes. Noting that these problems are not yet documented, Bayley suggests several precautions to avert them.

In the final chapter, Carl Klockars offers Part III's most pessimistic appraisal of community policing. Drawing on Egon Bittner's seminal analysis of the modern police function, Klockars understands community policing as first and foremost a rhetorical device that mystifies and conceals fundamental contradictions between society's aspirations and reality. In a society aspiring to achieve peace by peaceful means where that is not always possible, the police have been given the responsibility to use force and violence. Faced with a society that has never been able to resolve its ambivalence about the police role, police have always been vulnerable and have historically felt the need to justify themselves by employing circumlocutory devices that hide the true nature of their role. Community policing, for Klockars, follows in the footsteps of previous circumlocutions: legalization, militarization, and professionalization. He argues that legal considerations have little bearing on most of what police do, that the police have no demonstrable capacity to succeed in the war declared on crime or in the rhetoric of militarization, and that the professionalism that derives its support from the trappings of science, education, and training nonetheless demands but never really gets obedient bureaucrats. Turning to the rhetoric of community policing, he critiques several appealing but deceptive features: police-community reciprocity, decentralization of command, reorientation of patrol toward foot patrol and away from rapid response to calls for service, and civilianization. Acknowledging the appeal and goodness of community policing's aspirations, he condemns as excessive and unrealistic any claims that it can accomplish them.

The three contributions in Part III vary somewhat in perspective and tone, but all are critical in one way or another about community policing's accomplishments, past and future. Readers deeply involved in contemporary efforts to improve police through this reform may find this troubl-ing and wish that this section and the volume, in general, had more that emphasized the positive. However, our purpose in putting together this book was neither to sell nor sink the reform, but to submit it to careful scrutiny, broaden perspectives, provoke debate, and ultimately stimulate theory, research, and administration. If skepticism emerges in the early stages of a reform movement—as it has here—it strikes us as a healthy sign that processes are at work that may help avoid the errors and excesses of earlier eras of reform. The chapters in Part III—and the entire volume for that matter—do not offer the final word on community policing, but they do offer an agenda for debate and inquiry that may in the long run contribute to improvements in policing that are real as well as rhetorical.

11

COMMUNITY-BASED POLICING AND FOOT PATROL: ISSUES OF THEORY AND EVALUATION

JACK R. GREENE AND RALPH B. TAYLOR

INTRODUCTION

Recent developments in urban police strategies emphasizing community-based and foot patrol approaches have rekindled a debate over the role of the police in contributing to neighborhood social control. In this chapter we consider the current movement toward community policing and foot patrol programs, and touch on some of the general questions that have been raised about this new police intervention. We also consider the theoretical underpinnings of community policing, delineating the anticipated police processes and community impacts, and examining several evaluations of community policing with specific concern for methodology, analysis, and findings. In the closing section we identify several necessary theoretical and empirical improvements in community policing and in the evaluation of this important police response.

Origins of a New Policing "Philosophy"

The seeds of a new policing philosophy are visible in past attempts to decentralize and democratize police agencies through team policing (Angell, 1971; Sherman, Milton, and Kelly, 1973; Schwartz and Clarren, 1977). These programs sought to improve police and community communication, thereby making police agencies more responsive to the community and to rank-and-file police officers. More recently, an historical and often nostalgic view of greater police and community harmony has provided normative support for foot patrol programs (Moore and Kelling, 1983; Walker, 1984). Putting the police "back on the beat" has great public appeal, often stressing the imagery of the historical neighborhood cop.

Current attempts to make the police more problem-focused (Goldstein, 1979; Eck and Spelman, 1987a) have also contributed to the interest in community policing. These programs aim to reduce neighborhood-level problems that may eventually lead to community disorder and crime. The "new" community policing philosophy also suggests that traditional bureaucratic, crime-attack policing has failed. The police have lost their community context and this loss inhibits the police in their order maintenance and crime control functions (Wilson and Kelling, 1982).

Bureaucratic policing has been criticized on several dimensions, the most salient of which are police detachment from the community, the exclusion of police constituent groups from policy making, an emphasis on the means of controlling police behavior to the exclusion of the ends of policing, providing public safety, and a feel of security. Police patrol strategies that emphasize motor patrol, minimal police and citizen interaction, and a strict interpretation of law enforcement as the central role of policing are illustrative of this bureaucratic approach.

To the extent that distinct eras of police reform are identifiable (Fogelson, 1977), the last 10-15 years might be labeled the antibureaucracy era. Evaluation studies of police crime control activities have agreed that police strategies, whether they be preventive patrol (Kelling et al., 1974), rapid response (Pate, Bowers, and Parks, 1976), or follow-up investigations (Greenwood, Chaiken, and Petersilia, 1977) have not produced their desired results. These studies suggest that the deterrent capacity of the police has been largely overestimated and the traditional police response exaggerated. Collectively, these findings call into question the effectiveness of traditional policing in dealing with crime, disorder, or citizen fear of victimization.

A second complaint about bureaucratic policing accuses the police of mystifying their role and manipulating public expectations (Manning, 1977; Kelling, 1978), failing to consider the police role in light of other equally important social service and control functions (Goldstein, 1977), and drifting from the ends of policing, by placing too much emphasis on the means (Goldstein, 1979; Greene, 1981). Here, too, bureaucratic policing is challenged for maintaining an image of policing that does not reflect social and political reality. Bureaucratic policing, with its reliance on organizational control of the police response, the leveling of citizen demand, and a predominantly reactive response to community disturbance has indeed fallen on hard times.

Community-based and foot patrol programs of most recent vintage may be viewed as a continuation of the organizational reform of the police, based on the presumption of bureaucratic failure. Several of these programs reject traditional bureaucratic policing assumptions, and anticipate, among other things, an improvement in police officer job satisfaction and attitudes toward the community, and eventually an improvement in the crime effectiveness of the police. Although foot patrol and community policing are not synonymous (Goldstein, 1987), many of the efforts falling within the community policing umbrella have been foot patrol programs.

The new community policing approach also proposes that communities desire to be more responsible for social control. Through police actions that mobilize the forces of the community, it is presumed, the police can increase the community's capacity for exercising informal social control. Lacking a strict legal basis for these police order maintenance interventions, the police can draw from the community normative and moral support to legitimize their activities (Kelling, 1987a). Finally, this line of argument suggests that reducing community fear of crime will have a long-term stabilizing effect on the locale, eventually reducing objective criminality.

Questions about the Approach

This emerging community approach has several implicit assumptions and program requirements that have received scant attention. Those questioning the efficacy of community policing have begun to consider these assumptions and requirements. Manning (1984) has raised concerns with the presumptions that citizens desire close contact with the police and responsibility for social control; Walker (1984) questioned the historical accuracy of nostalgic interpretations of police and community relations, and their use of support of this new policing philosophy; and Klockars (1985) has called attention to the political consequences of order maintenance policing. Most recently, Goldstein (1987) examined community policing with concern for specifying the outer limits of the police function, the tension between police independence and accountability, the breadth of decision latitude accorded the police, and the role of the community in a community policing framework.

Although the debate over the direction and scope of community policing has attracted attention (see Sykes, 1986; Klockars, 1986; Skolnick and Bayley, 1986; and Kelling, 1987a), widespread support continues for this police innovation among researchers, police policy makers, and the citizenry. Perhaps less clear is the validity of the theory undergirding this approach and the empirical support for such programs.

ISSUES OF THEORY

Arguments in favor of community policing build on a new theoretical rationale. Although this new rationale is primarily oriented toward foot patrol, because of its emphasis on police-community contacts, it is also relevant to the changes sought in bureaucratic policing and to the wider issue of community-based policing strategies. This theoretical rationale, referred to variously as the "broken windows" or "incivilities" thesis, has been articulated most clearly by Wilson and Kelling (1982). The thesis is notable not only for what it proposes about how police should go about their business, but also because it gives some attention to the relations between police and actors in the community—merchants and residents.

In their 1982 *Atlantic Monthly* article, Wilson and Kelling proposed that police need to protect communities as well as individuals. They do this by assisting in the order maintenance function: "though citizens can do a great deal, the police are plainly the key to order-maintenance" (p. 36). Order maintenance involves taking care of disorderly behaviors—panhandling, soliciting, loitering, and public intoxication—and disorderly people—vagrants, drunks, and vandals. It is important to take care of disorders because they are presumed to play a key role in making communities ripe for criminal invasion.

The Sequential Model

The Wilson and Kelling model suggests a parallel between untended property and untended behavior. The former refers to physical incivilities—signs of disorder in the community such as abandoned houses, broken windows, graffiti, and playgrounds strewn with broken bottles. The latter refers to social incivilities—people hanging out, public drug use or drunkenness, or "hey honey" hassles (Hunter, 1978). Social and physical incivilities are similar, suggesting that area residents have little respect for the maintenance of public order, and that the larger municipal authorities are powerless to improve the situation (Hunter, 1978). Wilson and Kelling's untended property and untended behaviors are similarly defined: "Vandalism can occur anywhere once communal barriers—the sense of mutual regard and obligations to civility—are lowered by actions that seem to signal 'no one cares.' We suggest that untended behavior also leads to the breakdown of community controls" (p. 31).

Untended behaviors erode community control through a complex set of interactions and consequences. As social incivilities become more widespread and/or intense, residents make fewer efforts to exert informal social control over one another. For example, "adults stop scolding rowdy children" (p. 32). This lessening of regulatory efforts results in further expansion of incivilities; "the children, emboldened, become more rowdy," (p. 32). Faced with the spread of incivilities residents use the streets less, resulting in less eyes on the street (Jacobs, 1961). "Atomization" of community (Conklin, 1975) and the alienation of residents from coresidents will also ensue. The fabric of community is progressively abraded.

At this point in the process of community decay, Wilson and Kelling hypothesize that criminals may move into an area. "Though it is not inevitable, it is more likely that here . . . prostitutes will solicit . . . drunks will be robbed . . . muggings will occur" (p. 32). These developments further intensify residents' fears. "In response to fear, people avoid one another, [further] weakening controls" (p. 33). Given such possible scenarios, "a stable neighborhood . . . can change, in a few years or even a few months, to an inhospitable jungle" (pp. 31-32). More recently Skogan (1986) has made similar arguments about this cycle of neighborhood degeneration. Figure 1 graphically depicts the proposed sequence of neighborhood decay hypothesized by Wilson and Kelling.

In the Wilson and Kelling causal sequence, fear of crime plays a pivotal role for a number of reasons. First, fear of crime is crucial because it amplifies the impacts of incivilities. Were it not for fear, the consequences of incivilities would be much less dire for the community; the negative spiral would not be as ironclad, nor would it move as swiftly. It helps explain, in part, "how disorder and crime are usually inextricably linked" (p. 31). Fear is driven in large part by these incivilities. The incivilities are fear-inspiring because "serious street crime flourishes in areas in which disorderly behavior goes unchecked" (p. 34). Second, although not explicitly mentioned, fear of crime is an important concept because it is a construct that can (purportedly) be influenced by amount and type of police patrolling. The central status of fear in the proposed community disorganization sequence and its potential responsiveness to changes in police practices raises it to the conceptual status of crime, when considered as an output variable.

The implication in the Wilson and Kelling model is that in order to pro-

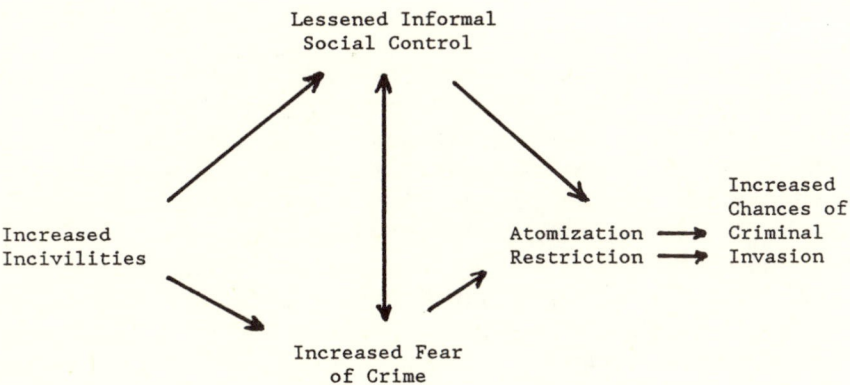

Figure 1
Wilson/Kelling Proposed Sequence of Community Decay

tect communities police officers need to be concerned about combatting fear of crime. The best way to do that is to work on reducing social and physical incivilities. It is suggested that police, if on foot patrol or through some other community attachment, can protect communities by reducing these social and physical incivilities. These community-based police tactics may deny opportunities for creating physical incivilities, while assuring the community that social incivilities will not be tolerated. Drawing from the moral order of the community, the police can restore the citizens' sense of public propriety and maintain respect for the police and the law (Kelling, 1987a).

The Roles of Patrol Officers

Wilson and Kelling argue that policing from the earliest days involved the maintenance of order, but that attention to this role waned subsequent to World War II. They argue that patrol officers should reassume this role. By doing so, they can help break the vicious downward spiral of community decay depicted above. How is this to be done?

"The essence of the police role in maintaining order is to reinforce the informal control mechanisms of the community itself" (p. 34). This is done by enforcing informal local norms of acceptable public behavior. Such assistance can take many forms (asking vagrants to move on, asking persons drinking in public to drink elsewhere, or kicking undesirables out of the community), but basically the officer is working with the regulars on the street to define and enforce rules. In walking with one foot patrol officer involved in the first Newark experiment, Wilson and Kelling note: "Persons who broke the informal rules . . . were arrested for vagrancy" (p. 30). Wilson and Kelling conclude that it was this elevation of public order by officers on foot patrol that caused the lower fear levels in the treatment neighborhood. Residents liked having the foot patrol officers around and appreciated their assistance.

Motorized patrol officers, it is further argued, cannot carry out the order maintenance function as effectively as officers who have greater community attachments, either through foot patrol or other community contacts. These community-based officers are said to be more familiar with local rules and community regulars, have a better idea of what response may be desired because they have spent more time in the community contact, and are better able to distinguish between regulars and strangers. This enhanced community sensitivity makes a successful resolution of incidents more likely. Community-based policing also lowers fear because there is more community exposure to police officers; they are a more salient presence in the community. On a daily or weekly basis, this police presence is more noticeable, making people feel safer.

Considering the Argument

The Wilson and Kelling model is the clearest statement of what community policing and foot patrol should be able to accomplish and why. Closer involvement with the community is expected to bolster community confidence and maintain social control while at the same time reducing the "signs of crime." Consequently, it is appropriate to consider carefully whether or to what degree the rationale they propose has empirical validity.

The Proposed Sequence of Decay

Two preliminary points need mention before considering the available support for the Wilson and Kelling community policing model. First, the sequence of events they depict occurs in neighborhoods or communities. Therefore, we should look to neighborhood or community-level analyses, or analyses of comparably sized areal units for evidence in support of the proposed sequence. There are three extant neighborhood-level studies that include more than just a handful of neighborhoods. The Northwestern Reactions to Crime (RTC) Project (Skogan and Maxfield, 1981), conducted between 1975 and 1980, included 12 neighborhoods from Philadelphia, Chicago, and San Francisco. A Baltimore, Maryland, study conducted from 1981 to 1984 included 66 neighborhoods (Taylor, Schumaker, and Gottfredson, 1985; Taylor, Gottfredson, and Schumaker, 1984a, b). More recently, Skogan (1987) has analyzed data from the 12 RTC neighborhoods merged with over two dozen other neighborhoods from different cities.

A second consideration is that although the Wilson and Kelling model is explicitly longitudinal, should longitudinal evidence be lacking it would be appropriate to consider evidence from cross-sectional studies. Such a move would be warranted if we were to include a large enough number of neighborhoods from a variegated urban area, such that the various neighborhoods were at different points in the downward spiral toward decay. It is hard to know exactly how many neighborhoods would be needed to ensure an adequate range on the spiral; nonetheless, if the sample of neighborhoods included both low- and high-crime neighborhoods, that at least would provide some assurance that neighborhoods at varying stages of dissolution were included. These two considerations help us better define the scope of evidence relevant to the proposed sequence.

The Wilson and Kelling model suggests that *as physical and social incivilities increase, informal social control weakens*. What evidence exists indicating such a linkage? In the RTC project, physical and social incivilities were measured via perceptions. No analyses reported on neighborhood-level links between perceived incivilities and informal social control. In the Baltimore study on-site, ratings of the objective physical environment, including social and physical incivilities, were made. Analyses of the ratings indicated a clear-cut incivilities factor and a separate land-use factor. Informal social control was one of the outcomes assessed in neighborhood-level analyses. Although there was a significant zero-order correlation between the objective incivilities measure and informal social control, the first-order partial correlation, controlling for length of tenure mix in the neighborhood, was essentially zero. This suggests that sociodemographic composition of a neighborhood as reflected in a high proportion of renters accounted for both weak, informal social control and a high incidence of incivilities, and that there was no independent link between incivilities and informal social control. In short, these studies provide no evidence supportive of the proposed link between incivilities and a weakening of informal social control.

The model further suggests that as *physical and social incivilities increase, fear also increases*. Skogan and Maxfield (1981) report for the 12 neighborhoods in the RTC project a sizable neighborhood-level correlation between perceived incivilities and fear. They neglect to report, however, the first-order partial, controlling for sociodemographic composition of neighborhood, between incivilities and fear. Fear was also an outcome examined in the Baltimore study. The zero-order correlation between incivilities and fear was quite sizable, as was the case in the RTC project; but, after entering a sociodemographic composite variable including tenure mix, racial composition, and income, the partial correlation was nonsignificant. In another analysis (Taylor et al., 1985) focusing on a subset of 45 of the 66 neighborhoods and excluding very poor and very well-off neighborhoods, incivilities and fear remained correlated after controlling for sociodemographic composition. This latter analysis confirms an independent linkage between incivilities and fear, but suggests that the linkage is conditional, obtaining only for particular types of neighborhoods. In short, the fear-incivilities linkage is context-sensitive and not unilateral as Wilson and Kelling have proposed.

The Wilson and Kelling model also suggests that *incivilities are linked with crime*. There is no evidence of such a linkage in the RTC analyses. In the Baltimore study, a strong zero-order link between crime and incivilities was observed; but, after controlling for social class, the partial correlation was nonsignificant. Incivilities were more prevalent in neighborhoods where income was lower, educational levels were lower, and the population was more black (Taylor et al., 1985). These three variables "explained" 63 percent of the variation in incivilities. The linkage between incivilities and crime appears to be largely driven by the linkage of both concepts with social class and does not exist independently.

Other linkages in the Wilson and Kelling model could be considered (e.g., between fear and behavioral restriction), but the above discussion covers the most central linkages in the model—those spanning fear, informal social control, incivilities, and crime. This research indicates no unique links between incivilities and informal social control, or crime, and a conditional linkage between incivilities and fear. The latter suggests the that fear-incivilities connection is context-sensitive, a possibility not addressed by the model.

Empirical evidence currently available suggests that social class factors are pivotal in determining fear, incivilities, and crime (Taylor and Hale, 1986). Therefore, Wilson and Kelling's focus on fear and incivilities is, at worst, misplaced, and at best, likely to yield less insight and guidance for effective policy than they anticipate.

Considering the proposed model as a whole, one aspect of it deserves further consideration: The model is naive with respect to the dynamics of neighborhood change. Much urban sociology has focused on how and why neighborhoods change the way they do; what factors lead to decline or revitalization or segregation, for example. Such research suggests two points, neither of which are taken into account by the proposed longitudinal model.

First, neighborhood change is, over a long time frame, largely predictable from the ecological (noncrime) characteristics of the neighborhood and its surroundings (Hunter, 1974). The Wilson and Kelling model suggests that the processes of neighborhood change are more volatile and undetermined than they actually are.

Second, impacts of incivilities and crime on neighborhood change are highly idiosyncratic, depending largely upon how these conditions *as part of a constellation of larger events* are interpreted by local residents (Taub, Taylor, and Dunham, 1981, 1984). The proposed model assumes a more simplified type of impact than has been suggested by research.

The Proposed Solution

The Wilson and Kelling model suggests closer contact between patrolling officers and community personnel as a way to avoid community decline. Such collaboration will, they suggest, enhance informal social control, thereby lessening fear and incivilities. But they ignore several problematic features of police-community relations.

First, there are fundamental conflicts between the police role and the community's reaction thereto (Menke, White, and Corey, 1982). Policing has been viewed by the public as a "tainted occupation" (Bittner, 1970). Although citizens may want the police close at hand during an emergency, there is little evidence to suggest that police/citizen interaction in nonemergency or need situations is desired. Citizens may want the police, but not too close. As Manning (1984) has suggested, there may exist some tipping point where citizen fear and concern with crime may actually rise with the additional presence of the police. Clearly, citizens have a difficult time determining whether police presence suggests increased safety or danger.

Related to the above, Wilson and Kelling assume that people *want* higher levels of policing or closer levels of contact with officers. This may not be so. In fact, among minorities, those who are afraid of the police are sometimes the same individuals who are afraid of crime (Block, 1971). Fear of or dissatisfaction with the police may be strongest in exactly those neighborhoods for which Wilson and Kelling propose their intervention. It seems overly sanguine to expect that a change in the method of patrol (e.g., foot patrol) without a major revision in the police role and citizen expectations of that role, will alter these attitudes.

Second, the police themselves have learned to be distrustful and wary of the general public. The social isolation of the police from the public is predicated in part on police officer perceptions of dangerousness, challenges to police authority, and a concern with maintaining the appearance of efficiency (Skolnick, 1966). In these situations, the police may actually seek to minimize their contact with the public because the more contact they have, the greater the likelihood of a complaint (see Muir's [1977] avoider police type).

Third, the proposed buttressing of informal social control by the patrolling officer is problematic. Informal social control as a system of norm enforcement operates independently of and perhaps as a result of a lack of formal agents of authority (Greenberg and Rohe, 1986). Given the independent or at best complementary nature of these two systems of social control, it is difficult to envision how the police as formal agents of social control can become effective agents of informal control. It seems more sensible to assume that community policing enhances the formal control system and the prestige of the agents of formal control, rather than the informal social control system.

However, suppose we assume for the sake of argument that police officers could become effective agents of informal social control. What steps would be necessary prerequisites to such a development? Two seem most pertinent. First, officers must learn what the "norms" are that bona fide residents or regulars wish to have enforced. Second, officers must learn to whom such norms should be applied. They must develop the ability to discriminate between insiders, those who belong and have legitimate roles on the street, and outsiders. The learning of both these matters—norms and insider/outsider distinctions—takes considerable time.[1]

In making decisions about insiders and outsiders, the officer is involving him- or herself in a high-context culture (Hall, 1966). This represents a considerable time investment. Exactly how much time is required before the officer can be an effective enforcer of local norms? Were we to admit that the patrolling officer could become integrated into the local system of informal social control, the time involvement needed to ensure effective functioning in this system is considerable, unspecified, and perhaps unrealistic.[2]

Some More Pervasive Problems in the Model

The preceding discussion has focused on particular problems of the proposed model. Also deserving attention are some more pervasive, yet perhaps less obvious, features of the model. The importance of these characteristics of the overall model may be more significant than the points raised above.

The treatment of the construction of community and/or neighborhood as ecological units and as social processes is inadequate. In the language of Cook and Campbell (1979:64-65), there is an inadequate preoperational explication of the construct of community. There is extensive sociological and community psychological literature on neighborhoods and communities: what they are (Hillery, 1955; Heller et al., 1984:131-140; R. R. Taylor, 1982; Suttles, 1972) and how they can be delimited. There are alternative ways of focusing on communities: for example, institutions versus composition of population versus land use characteristics, and so on. Further, there are nested levels of community ranging from the street block to major portions of a city.

The proponents of community policing and foot patrol make no cross-reference to this extensive literature. They make little attempt to specify the level of community at which it would be most beneficial to intervene, nor do they indicate the quality or dimension of community (social ties? commitment to locale? vitality of local institutions?) that these programs will buttress or enhance. Empirically, this means there is no guidance as to how the units of analysis should be defined, nor which qualities of community can be measurably enhanced by the proposed intervention. Yet the theoretical rationale is explicitly a community-level one.

Also receiving undifferentiated treatment is the concept of fear of crime. Along with enhanced informal social control, reduced fear of crime and a concomitant decrease in crime and restored neighborhood vitality are purportedly the main benefits of community policing interventions. But fear, like community, is a complex construct. DuBow, McCabe and Kaplan (1979), for example, distinguish between perceptions of crime (e.g., has crime increased or decreased in your neighborhood in the last two years?), affective reactions centering around perceived vulnerability (e.g., how safe do you feel or would you feel walking alone in your neighborhood at night?), and estimates of risk (e.g., what are the chances that you will be victim of a street crime or a mugging in the next two years?). Many studies of community policing measure fear of crime differently (e.g, perceptions, affective reaction, or risk assessment), and there is no theoretical discussion in any of these studies concerning why community policing should affect one particular fear dimension rather than another.

More troubling than the undifferentiated discussion of fear is the chance of a focus on fear diverting us from crime issues. The proponents of community policing and foot patrolling maintain that communities have a right to experience lower fear levels. Communities also have a right to lower crime levels. Implicitly, a focus on fear reduction siphons police energy away from concern about local crime rates. The focus on fear suggests that low fear is a construct more central to community health than low crime. On what basis can we argue this is so? Since fear and crime rates are only loosely coupled, reductions in a community's fear do not translate readily, if at all, into lower crimes rates. Therefore, the focus on fear is problematic because it potentially diverts conceptual and patrolling efforts away from crime prevention.

The Wilson and Kelling causal model provides the central rationale for community policing. The model is a neighborhood-level one, yet community theory and empirical studies of neighborhood-level processes provide either no or conditional support for the proposed linkages in the model. The model mistakenly assumes that citizens desire closer interpersonal contact with the police and that such contact will reduce fear of crime. It may also be erroneous to assume that police officers can function as agents of informal social control, and even if that were possible, the amount of training required to assure effective community responsiveness has not been demonstrated in most of these efforts. Finally, on a more general urban ecological note, the Wilson and Kelling model does not delineate how community is to be defined, nor does it specify which aspects of community structure are to be enhanced; its assumptions about the neighborhood-level change processes appear to be incorrect.

THE EMPIRICAL STUDIES ON COMMUNITY POLICING

We now turn our attention to the empirical studies that have examined the impacts of community policing. Eight studies bearing on this topic have been carried out in several cities across the country: Flint (Michigan), Newark (New Jersey—two separate programs), Oakland, San Diego, Houston, Boston, and Baltimore. In some cases, the only intervention implemented was foot patrol; in others, foot patrol was implemented along with other community policing strategies. The studies reviewed have a similar orientation: They were police-initiated programs aimed at realizing one or more of the community policing goals previously discussed.

We first provide a thumbnail sketch of each study, considering the type of community policing represented, the impacts associated with these programs, and the design of the research used to assess program effects. After this brief review, we come to some conclusions about the cumulative effects of these efforts. Table 3 provides a list of essential features of each of the community studies examined.[3]

A Thumbnail Sketch of the Studies

Flint, Michigan

The Flint Foot Patrol project (Trojanowicz, n.d., 1983, 1986) introduced 22 police officers and 3 supervisors into 14 experimental neighborhoods. Neighborhood land area varied widely as did the social and demographic characteristics of residents; some areas were ethnically homogeneous, while others were quite divergent in the mix of residents, types of residents, and mix of business and residental clients. The experimental areas did not conform to census tracts or other ecologically relevant neighborhoods, and the project had no control areas against which the effects of foot patrol might be tested.

Flint foot patrol officers were given wide latitude in defining and implementing foot patrol; therefore, it is difficult to assess the specific patrol tactics used by these officers. In addition to law enforcement responsibilities, foot patrol officers in Flint were charged with being "catalytic agents who encouraged citizens to band together in the effort to combat crime" (n.d., p. 75). Such activities reflect the expanded police role envisioned by Wilson and Kelling.

A panel of local community residents—6 from each of the 14 patrol areas—reported on citizen perceptions of crime and public safety. By the third year of the evaluation, the total number of panel residents had declined to 44. Such a high level of respondent mortality makes inferences about the program effects tenuous. A cross-sectional citizen survey was also undertaken in the second and third year of the project (Trojanowicz, 1986).

The area-level analysis suggested that, although reported crime for the City of Flint increased during the project, reported crime in the foot patrol areas declined by 9 percent. No tests of statistical significance or displacement effects were reported. Wide variations in reported crime across program areas were evident; in certain foot patrol areas, crime declined by as much as 66 percent, while in others, crime increased by as much as 52 percent. Crimes such as vandalism and assault decreased when examined across foot patrol areas, while robbery increased. This pattern suggests that crime rate changes in program areas were not influenced by the foot patrol program, but rather were driven by local dynamics in each area.

Foot patrol area residents perceived a decline in the seriousness of neighborhood crime between the project's first and second years. These

Table 3
Critical Features of Community Policing Studies

STUDY	UNIT OF ANALYSIS	NUMBER OF EXPERIMENTAL UNITS	ELEMENTS IN PROPOSED PROGRAM	RESEARCH DESIGN	OUTCOMES
Flint	Foot Patrol Areas of Varied Size and Composition	14	Foot Patrol Unspecified Treatment	Case Study	Crime Rate Fear Satisfaction with Police
Newark 1	Police Beats Matched by Residential/ Nonresidential	12	Foot Patrol Unspecified Treatment	Non-Equivelant Comparison Pre-Post	Fear Crime Rate Perception of Safety
Newark 2	Treatment "Neighborhoods" Matched on Unspecified Criteria	3	Foot Patrol Radar Checks Bus Checks Enforcement of Disorderly Conduct Laws Road (Driver) Checks	Non-Equivelant Comparison Pre-Post	Perceptions of Disorder, Crime, and Victimization Satisfaction with Area, and Police
Oakland	Portion of CBD (6-7 City Blocks)	1	Foot Patrol RID Program Other Patrols	One-Group Pre-Post	Crime Rate

San Diego	Northern Police District	22	Community Profile	Untreated Control Pre-Post	Police Values and Behavior, Organizational Change
Houston	Program and Control Areas	4	Newsletter Victim Recontact Station Contact Patrol Community Organizing	Non-Equivelant Comparison Pre-Post	Perceptions of Disorder Crime, and Victimization
Boston	Police Beats and Reporting Areas	105/ 296	More or Less Foot Patrol	Non-Equivelant Comparison Pre-Post	% Share of Calls for Service, Crime, Maintenance
Baltimore	Targetted "Neighborhoods"	24	Problem-Oriented Policing	One-Group Pre-Post	Fear Awareness of Police Satisfaction with Police Reported Crime

same respondents perceived neighborhood crime to increase above the first year levels during the third year's evaluation. Panel respondents reported low fear of crime across all three years of the evaluation, as well as a general awareness of the foot patrol program. The survey of citizens produced similar results: general satisfaction with the foot patrol program, a decline in fear of crime, and a positive evaluation of foot patrol officers. No tests for statistical significance in any of the observed changes were reported.

In sum, in the Flint evaluation, the *high* level of respondent dropout from the citizen panels, lack of statistical tests, and wide variations in crime rates across program areas preclude any confidence with respect to the effect of foot patrol in this city.

Newark 1

The first Newark Foot Patrol Experiment was conducted between 1978 and 1979 (Police Foundation, 1981). The project introduced foot patrol officers into Newark for the purpose of "upgrading and stabilizing neighborhoods" (p. 3). The Newark program addressed the two issues identified by Wilson and Kelling: untended property and untended behavior.

Eight patrol beats where foot patrol was in effect were matched into four sets of two beats each. Matching occurred according to the "number of residential and nonresidential units found on each beat" (p. 16). One beat from each of the four sets was then assigned to drop foot patrol while it was continued in the remaining four. Four additional beats, presumably selected on the same criteria, saw the addition of foot patrol officers—56 patrol officers and 3 commanders provided an unspecified foot patrol treatment.

The Newark evaluation used a quasi-experimental nonequivalent comparison group design and separate pretest/posttest samples. Individual level analysis was conducted for a residential and a commercial sample; area level analysis was conducted for beats. The relevance of beats to ecological neighborhoods was not demonstrated. Residents were found to recognize the manipulation of foot patrol in their neighborhoods. Residents in beats where foot patrol was added noticed a decline in street activity, a decrease in the severity of crime, and more positively evaluated police performance. These same residents reported less use of protective measures and crime avoidance efforts. Business persons, by contrast, were less likely to see street level activity change, saw street disorder and publicly visible crime increase, and "believed their neighborhoods had become worse" (p. 88). Reported crime and victimization were unaffected by the level of foot patrol in the resident and commercial samples. Area-level analysis produced few significant results.[4]

Newark 2

In 1983 and 1984 a second foot patrol study was carried out in Newark. This study was different from the first in that participating officers were instructed to give increased attention to social and physical incivilities (Pate et al., 1985:3; Williams and Pate, 1987). Three neighborhoods were selected and matched on several unspecified sociodemographic and crimes indexes.[5] A single control (nontreatment) area was also selected.[6] The rationale for selection of program areas was not fully explained, and it is not clear if they were ecologically valid neighborhoods. A group of 24 patrol officers received three days' training to prepare for their order maintenance role. The patrolling effort (coordinated community policing) was complemented by a cleanup effort involving city and community personnel and the distribution of a community newsletter. The coordinated community patrolling included several interventions: foot patrol, radar patrol, bus checks, road checks, and enforcement of disorderly conduct statutes.

Two evaluation designs were reported for study: an experimental design for assessing the newsletter program, and a quasi-experimental design for the patrolling and clean-up programs.[7] In the area-level analysis, pre- and postprogram responses were compared on eight outcome measures[8] across the three treatments (e.g., newsletter, patrol, cleanup). Statistically, significant changes were reported for four[9] of these outcome measures.[10] Correlations among the dependent measures were not reported. None of the outcome measures were affected by the cleanup or newsletter programs. The coordinated patrol program was said to have reduced perceptions of social disorder, worry about property crime, perceptions of area property crime, and improved assessments of the police.[11] In the "individual level" analyses reported in Williams and Pate (1987), no program effects were found for either the newsletter or cleanup programs. The coordinated community policing program was said to have magnified slightly the findings in the cross-sectional analysis reported above.[12]

Oakland

In 1983 a diversified patrol strategy intervention was implemented in a portion of Oakland's Central Business District (CBD). The implementation strategy included, in addition to foot patrol, mounted patrol, small vehicle patrols, and a RID (Report Incidents Directly) program. Twenty-eight officers were assigned to foot patrol. By means of these foot patrol officers, local business persons could report directly things that were bothering them, and about which they wanted the police to do something. The focus of the program was on "soft-crime" (Reiss, 1985a:6-8) and the social and physical incivilities referred to by Hunter (1978) and Wilson and

Kelling.[13] The target on "soft-crime" was justified on the grounds that it was particularly fear-inspiring, representing a major reason why people were reluctant to work or shop in the CBD. It was felt that foot patrolling would be particularly effective in dealing with soft-crime (Reiss, 1985a:10).

As a measure of implementation, arrest reports per officer were examined. Felony and misdemeanor arrest records were "surprisingly high" (Reiss, 1985a:39). Felony arrests averaged one and a half per officer in a three-week period, and misdemeanor arrests amounted to roughly two per officer during a three-week period. The outcome assessed was crime rate (Reiss, 1985a:39-41). "Overall, there have been substantial drops in the rate of crime against persons and their property in the central area comprised of Beats 1, 3, and 4 [the program area]" (p. 39). The drops in crime in the treatment area from the preprogram to program time frame were more substantial than the declines noted citywide. No statistical tests were reported.

San Diego

The San Diego Community Profile project was conducted between 1973 and 1974 (Boydstun and Sherry, 1975). Community profiling was designed to improve the interactions between the police and community by making police officers responsible for knowing the community and its problems. Twenty-four patrol officers and three sergeants were randomly selected for participation in the program and provided with 60 hours of "community-oriented" training.

This program had three objectives: (1) change police officer attitudes toward and interactions with community residents, (2) change the role of the police department itself from law enforcement to community service, and (3) change the climate of the police agency by improving job attitudes among the police (p. 1). Understanding of and accountability to the community were the community policing objectives of this program.

Two groups of patrol officers, one employing the community profiling orientation and the other traditional police patrol, were compared in the evaluation. The findings suggested that officers enacting the community profiling role changed their conception of police work, increased non-law-enforcement contact with community residents, and developed a more positive attitude toward police and community relations. The project did not measure the effect of this style of policing on crime or residents' fear of crime.

Houston

A companion project to the Newark 2 program, the Houston fear-reduction program was conducted between 1983 and 1984 (Brown and Wycoff, 1987). The program was designed to test the effects of five community policing and fear reduction strategies: (1) a victim recontact program assuring victims of police interest in their cases, (2) a community newsletter program to increase citizen crime prevention activities and crime risk knowledge, (3) a citizen contact patrol program to increase the interaction between the police and the community, (4) a police community station—a storefront office where local residents might have direct access to the police, and (5) a program to organize the community's interest in crime prevention.

Four areas in Houston were selected for participation in the program and a fifth area was designated as the control area. Sites were selected for the existence of disorder, crime, and fear problems, "but none so great that they might not be substantially affected within one year of the life of the program" (p. 79). The evaluation reported the use of experimental procedures for the victim recontact and the neighborhood newsletter programs and a quasi-experimental design for the remaining three programs. Cross-sectional and panel data were collected to facilitate both the area and individual level analyses.

The victim recontact program failed because of the large time lag (about two months) between victimization and police recontact. The newsletter program did not produce the desired results either: No significant distinctions between those receiving and those not receiving additional crime information were detected.[14]

Cross-sectional results included significant decreases in perceptions of social disorder, fear of personal victimization, and the level of personal and property crime. These results were attributed primarily to citizen contact patrol and the police community station. Increased satisfaction with the area was also associated with contact patrol. Community organizing was associated with improvements in the evaluation of the police in the cross-sectional analysis.

The results of the panel analysis partially confirm those reported for the cross-sectional analysis, although there are some important differences. The effects associated with the police community station and the contact patrol programs in the cross-sectional analysis were not as demonstrative in the panel analysis. Specifically, panel respondents were not affected in their perceptions of social disorder or the level of area crime. In the cross-sectional analysis, these two variables were said to have declined.

Boston

In 1983 the Boston Police Department implemented a major plan for reorganizing patrol services. This plan changed the method of patrol in Boston by allocating some 300 police officers to foot patrol throughout the city (Bowers and Hirsch, 1986). In a city that had historically deployed about 80 percent of its patrol officers to two-officer motorized patrol units, the reallocation plan made foot patrol the dominant form of policing (34 percent of all patrol units), while also increasing the use of one-officer motorized patrol units.

In addition to altering the form of patrol, the Boston program shifted police work load responsibilities such that foot patrol officers and one-officer motorized patrol units were made responsible for less serious crime and noncrime service calls. This shift in method of patrol (foot versus motorized), as well as police services to be provided (serious offenses versus less serious and order maintenance) reflects some of the basic ideas about neighborhood policing.

The evaluators examined 105 beats, containing about one-third of the city's reporting areas, classified on the basis of the degree of foot patrol changes represented—high, medium, low, unstaffed, and no change. The study examined changes in calls-for-service among police beats by priority (serious crime, less serious crime, and non-crime related) from 1981 through 1984. Of critical concern was change in the annual percent share of these calls for service within beats.

Overall, the study found no statistically significant association between changes in the level of foot-patrol service provided and either crime control or order maintenance outcomes. That is, "neither the total number of calls for service nor calls at any of the three priority levels rose with increased foot patrol staffing" (p. 27). Violent crimes, such as aggravated or simple assault, were unaffected by changes in foot patrol staffing, while street robbery dropped but commercial robbery rose in the foot patrol beats with added staffing. Property offenses actually increased in the foot patrol beats where additional officers had been added, suggesting some reporting effects, although burglary produced little change. Disturbance behaviors, those most closely associated with the order maintenance activities of the police, fluctuated across the high staffing beats but in inconsistent directions; minor disturbances increased, gang calls increased, and noisy parties dropped.

Collectively, the evaluation of this natural experiment in Boston suggests that in relation to citizen demand for police services, this "citywide patrol reallocation strategy did not produce consistent or systematic changes in the number of kinds of incidents police deal with . . . or, by implications, in the underlying problems that such calls reflect" (p. 38).

Baltimore County

Project COPE, Citizen Oriented Police Enforcement, began in 1981 with the creation of the COPE unit, employing 45 veteran police officers. The prime function of the COPE program was to reduce citizen fear of crime (Cordner, 1985; Taft, 1986).

The COPE project in Baltimore County embraced a relatively new concept in community policing—problem-oriented policing. COPE also stressed a patrol strategy that emphasized the ends of policing—solving community problems that lead to crime, fear and disorder—rather than the means—any particular style of patrol (Goldstein, 1977, 1979). The COPE program had several components. Initially, the program emphasized community surveying and some form of saturation patrol. The second stage of the program replaced saturation patrol with crime prevention, and the final stage emphasized community problem identification and problem solving. When fully developed, the COPE program emphasized several of the features of the Wilson and Kelling model: a concern with community order maintenance problems, an expanded role for the police, and greater interaction between the police and community residents.

The COPE program evaluation used a pre/post research design, without a control or comparison group. The evaluation measured citizen fear of crime, awareness of COPE officer presence in the neighborhood, and satisfaction with police service. Door-to-door surveys were conducted by evaluation staff and COPE police officers in 24 COPE targeted neighborhoods. An independent assessment of changes in reported crime was also undertaken.

Results of the COPE program suggested that residents' awareness of the COPE program steadily increased over the life of the program. Citizen satisfaction with police services generally declined from stage one to stage two of the program (directed patrol to crime prevention), and then increased during stage three (problem-solving). Nonetheless, citizen satisfaction with police services was found to be high during all three stages of the program.

Fear of crime, a central issue in this program, declined modestly through each stage of the project; however, given that fear of crime was "relatively low in most areas of the county also makes it difficult for COPE to show marked decreases in fear following its efforts" (Cordner, 1985:24). Citizens also reported that they were somewhat less likely to stay at home because of fear of crime.

An analysis of reported crime and calls for service suggested that reported crime initially increased, attesting to reporting effects associated with the COPE program. After the program had become established, crime reporting decreased by 12 percent. Calls for service decreased very slightly (1 percent) initially, and more dramatically (10 percent) during stage three of the project. Because the number of neighborhoods was small (N = 24), no tests for statistical significance were reported.

Consistent Findings?

Although there have been eight studies examining community policing and foot patrol, there is not much consistency in findings across studies. With regard to fear of crime, Newark 1 observed a reduction; Newark 2 also observed a reduction in fear of victimization in the panel analysis (individual level), but not in the cross-sectional analysis (area level). Interestingly, in the Houston study, a reduction in fear of victimization occurred in the cross-sectional study but not in the panel study—in precise opposition to the Newark 2 findings. In Flint, resident perceptions of the seriousness of crime problems increased over the three years as did perceptions that fear of crime affected behavior. In San Diego, Oakland, and Boston, fear of crime was not assessed. Finally, in Baltimore the relatively low levels of citizen fear of crime declined modestly. Based on the problems associated with the evaluations of each of these programs, there is at present no consistent evidence that foot patrol reduces fear of crime.

Findings with regard to crime are also inconsistent. The only study to demonstrate a drop in crime was the Oakland evaluation, based on crime reports. This finding, however, was not subjected to statistical tests. In Boston, by contrast, no association between changes in the level of foot patrol and crime or disorder were discernible. Newark 1 reported no impact of foot patrolling on victimization rates, whereas Newark 2 reported an *increase* of victimization among those in the program area (Pate et al., 1985). In Flint and Baltimore, the absence of comparison groups and statistical analysis precludes the interpretation that crime declined in community policing or foot patrol areas. In San Diego the effect of community profiling on crime was not assessed, and in Houston the actual crime effects of citizen contact patrol were not evaluated. Clearly, these studies do not point to decreases in crime or disorder as a consequence of community policing or foot patrol.

Given these inconsistencies, is it appropriate to conclude that community policing and foot patrolling don't work? It would be premature to draw such a conclusion before considering more closely the characteristics of the empirical studies. Several of them share similar shortcomings. These deficiencies preclude drawing any solid conclusions (either pro or con) with regard to this policing innovation.

Major Deficiencies

Numerous shortcomings of the various community policing studies could be mentioned. However, instead of providing a laundry list of design and analytical flaws, it may be more helpful to focus on the most salient deficiencies, particularly those that reflect a vagary of the theory on which the approach is based, or that indicate a slippage between the theory as articulated and the research. We indicate below six features of the studies to date where there is considerable room for improvement.

Inadequate operationalization of "community." As we have noted earlier, the theoretical rationale behind community policing dealt inadequately with the concept of community. Thus it is no surprise to see that studies reflected this confusion. In the various studies, the units selected for treatment have ranged from patrol beats, to agglomerations of beats, to portions of census tracts. Moreover, *in none of the studies has there been an attempt to use ecologically valid neighborhood units.*[15] The practical consequences of this feature of the studies are several. First, officers on foot may have been touring several different communities within the one treatment area, instead of just one. This would make it more difficult for them to learn the particular norms operating in the various communities, and to make reliable distinctions between insiders and outsiders, both of these being a key part, according to Wilson and Kelling, of the maintenance of order. In other words, it would make it much more difficult for the officers to "mobilize," activate, or support the community fabric. Second, inasmuch as treatment areas crosscut extant neighborhood or community boundaries, it is likely that the random heterogeneity of respondents and areas was increased. This can result in increased error variance, therefore making it more difficult to "find" significant results (Cook and Campbell, 1979:44).

Confusion about the appropriate level of analysis. The underlying rationale for community policing explicitly addresses neighborhood- or community-level dynamics. Given that the theory is couched at this level, the appropriate analyses would be those that used neighborhoods or communities as the unit of analysis. But this has not been done. Even though, for example, Pate et al. (1985, 1986) carry out what they call an "area" analysis, it is in fact nothing of the sort. It is an individual-level, pre- versus posttest analysis. Since analyses of data at one level can yield results very different from the analyses of the same data at another level (Thorndike, 1939; Robinson, 1950), these individual-level analyses provide us with no information about what is happening at the community level. Thus, from the viewpoint of the driving theory, they are not useful.

Areal analyses could be carried out in one of two possible ways. First, interrupted time series analyses of one measure in a treatment area could be carried out. Such time series analyses require approximately 50 data points to yield stable results (Cook and Campbell, 1979:225). Unfortunately, none of the studies to date have collected a sufficient amount of data to provide stable analytical results.

A second approach to areal analysis would be to use neighborhoods or communities as the units of analyses to compare treatment to control neighborhoods. For an acceptable level of statistical power for such comparisons (e.g., about 80 percent), for moderate effect sizes, approximately 50-60 treatment and control areas would be needed. Studies to date include nowhere near that number of areas, rendering such areal analyses virtually pointless.[16]

Design. A third problem, which has been more of a problem in some studies than in others, is *weak quasi-experimental designs*. For example, the prepost design of the Oakland evaluation is considered a generally noninterpretable design (Cook and Campbell, 1979:99-103). Several studies have lacked control groups; in addition to Oakland, the Flint and Baltimore studies lacked control groups.

Implementation. A fourth problem in several of the studies appears to have been weak implementation of the treatment. For example, in Newark 2, only 30 percent of the panel respondents could recall being exposed to foot patrol (Pate et al., 1985).[17] In the Flint study, to take another example, respondents complained that they did not see their foot patrol officer enough (Trojanowicz, n.d.:55). In the Houston study, community contact policing was said to have had less of an effect on renters, possibly calling attention to implementation concerns. It seems likely that in many of these studies, the community patrol officers were spread very thinly indeed. In this respect these studies may not be so much studies of community patrolling as of the effects of very minimal levels of community patrolling. This is observed given the relatively small numbers of police officers involved in these community policing programs in contrast to the rather large numbers associated with households, population, or beat area affected.

Defining the treatment. A fifth and important problem in the community policing and foot patrol literature is in the specification of the patrol treatment. What the officers do, not whether they walk or ride, has major implications for this police intervention. Community policing and foot patrol have many definitions; in Newark 2, this treatment included bus riding, car stops, radar enforcement, and the enforcement of order maintenance laws. In Newark 1, foot patrol was defined as "walking and talking." In Flint, foot patrol officers were to be social catalysts so as to include any intervention; and in Houston, citizen contact patrol referred to officers approaching citizens and engaging them in conversations about community order. In Boston, no definition of foot patrol was offered, while in Oakland, the foot patrol intervention was complicated by several other programs (mounted patrol, RID program, and so on) also occurring. The intervention in San Diego was perhaps the most specific in that officers had a charge to profile their beats. Since the police are expected to support the informal norms of the community, then how they do that becomes very important. Future studies of community policing would benefit from specifying the police intervention involved.

Outcome specification. A final problem has to do with outcome specification. Again, this is an instance where vagueness in the underlying theoretical rationale has been reflected in the studies, at least in the case of fear. As mentioned earlier, there are several types of affective, behavioral, and cognitive responses to crime: fear of personal safety, perceived risk of victimization, perceived crime in neighborhoods, or behavioral restriction to mention just some. Studies have taken a scatter-gun approach to assessing fear, including all of the above dimensions of response and more. They have defined fear of crime very broadly; so broadly that it includes not only affective concern about personal safety, recognized by DuBow et al. (1979) as the central fear construct, but other measures as well. The Flint study is a good case in point. Outcomes assessed included matters such as perceived changes in the crime rate of the city as a whole and in the local neighborhood, as well as changes in fear.

Further, when we turn to crime as an outcome, a different difficulty has appeared. Here the empirical studies have failed to reflect accurately the outcome described in the theoretical rationale. According to Wilson and Kelling (1982, crime in an area will go down if foot patrolling or some form of community policing is implemented because there will be less of a chance of criminal invasion. Offenders from outside the neighborhood will go to alternative sites. Given this line of reasoning, the appropriate outcome measure in a community policing study is not the crime rate. Rather, the appropriate measure is the rate at which offenses in the neighborhood are committed by outsiders. According to the theory, the extent to which the area draws outside offenders should decrease under effective community policing. This will not necessarily mean a decrease in the crime rate if offenders living within the neighborhood at the same time increase in number, or increase their rate of offending. So no studies to date have examined the theoretically expected effect of community policing on crime.

Given the numerous and critical weaknesses in several of the community policing and foot patrolling studies to date, coupled with the contradictory findings emerging across the studies themselves, no conclusions can be reached regarding whether or not this style of policing has beneficial or detrimental impacts on fear and crime in urban communities. In fact, the theoretical rationale underlying the proposed benefits of community policing has not yet been tested.

SOME RECOMMENDATIONS

In this penultimate section, we offer some directions in which theory and research in this area could be improved. The suggestions offered are by no means exhaustive and, in fact, we may omit some that others may view as crucial. Nonetheless, we hope that the points offered here may serve to generate debate, theoretical elaboration, and better studies.

Theoretical Improvements

It may be more fruitful to focus attention on the ends of policing rather than the means; to focus on problem-solving patrol rather than foot or some other patrol strategy. Two examples of the problem-centered approach are the Baltimore COPE project, previously discussed (Cordner, 1985; Taft, 1986), and the problem-focused policing project in Newport News, Virginia (Eck and Spelman, 1987a). Both of these projects developed and implemented a problem-focused approach to resolving community conflict through various styles of patrol coupled with an active problem identification strategy. In Baltimore County, police officers used several types of patrol (from saturation to surveillance). As the mission of the project was to reduce crime and fear by solving community problems, this project was primarily concerned with the ends of policing—resolving problems, not maintaining one particular means—such as foot patrol. The project in Newport News is similar in design, stressing a change in the role of the police rather than a style of patrol.

A related issue is with what constitutes the treatment. In many of the community policing programs to date, the treatment is a different form of police presence—most often foot patrol. What the police do, as opposed to how they do it, should be the major concern in establishing a community policing treatment.

Second, the theoretical rationale behind the revision of the police role, whether that be via community policing or some other means, can be adequately articulated only if the approach recognizes and interfaces with extant theories of fear of crime (Taylor and Hale, 1986), informal social control (Greenberg and Rohe, 1986), and community (Heller et al., 1984). Unless such integration is achieved, the desired ends of more effective policing will not be attained.

Third, the theory needs to take into account and be sensitive to community context. Although policy makers are, generally speaking, in favor of policies that are equally effective in all manner of different locations, in reality, programs usually work better in some locations than in others for reasons related to the fabric of the community in which the programs operate (Taylor and Hale, 1986). The rationale behind more effective policing needs to incorporate contextual considerations explicitly and move toward an understanding of the joint impacts of policing and locale on fear and crime.

Empirical Improvements

Better quasi-experimental designs should be used in studies of alternative forms of policing. A broad range of interpretable and robust quasi-experimental designs are available, none of which require random assignment of areas to treatment. At a minimum, the designs used should incorporate matched control groups and implementations of varying treatment strength. Researchers should eschew noninterpretable designs such as simple pre- versus posttests.

Second, only ecologically valid neighborhoods or communities should be used as the treatment areas. Police reporting areas are not coterminous with ecological neighborhoods and communities. The use of ecologically valid communities will have several benefits, including an easier link-up between police and local organizations, and a reduction in the random heterogeneity of respondents.

Finally, neighborhoods should be used as the only unit of analysis. Neighborhood-level analyses necessitate including a large number of neighborhoods in a study (50-60), but unless such analyses are carried out, we will never know if the hypothesized community-level dynamics have any empirical validity.

CONCLUDING NOTE

There is strong and widespread concern with the failure of bureaucratic policing. As an alternative, closer contact of patrol officers with citizens on the street has been proposed. In such contacts, Wilson and Kelling (1982) have recommended that community-oriented foot patrolling police officers can enforce the local, informal norms regarding acceptable public behavior, thereby reducing fear of crime and crime by outsiders. Such an accomplishment, although perhaps feasible, will require a more extensive consideration of local community dynamics and structures than has been yet carried out. Studies to date of community policing programs have yielded inconsistent results and, upon inspection, do not qualify as adequate tests of the proposed theoretical rationale for this new police innovation. So, for both the theory and the research in this important policing area, there is considerable room for improvement.

ACKNOWLEDGMENT

The original draft of this chapter was presented by Jack Greene at the annual meetings of the Society for the Study of Social Problems, Washington, D.C., August 1985. Both authors would like to thank Drs. Ronald V. Clarke, Rutgers University, Gary W. Cordner, Eastern Kentucky University, and Scott H. Decker, University of Missouri-St. Louis for their helpful comments in reviewing the manuscript.

NOTES

1. An easy, quick way to make insider/outsider distinctions is to use race as a criterion. Obviously, the use of such shortcuts may result in considerable discrimination in the patrol officer's application of sanctions to enforce norms.

2. Furthermore, in applying incomplete definitions of who belongs and who does not, the police create "symbolic assailants" (Skolnick, 1966), or selective representations of danger and threats to the community order. These untested

assumptions about community and individual behavior, if acted upon, can have severe negative consequences, including the further deterioration of police and community relations.

3. As far as we know, this list is exhaustive and covers all evaluations of community policing and foot patrolling in large urban cities that have been published in one form or another. At the time of this writing, information about the results achieved in the New York City CPO program were not available. We are also aware that a major foot patrol program is under way in Baltimore with one planned for Philadelphia, neither of which has sufficient information available for our present consideration.

4. No evaluations to date have considered statistical power levels in designing their studies. In many of them, the probability levels of Type II error, even for large effect sizes, must be close to or above 50 percent.

5. There is a rather large discrepancy in the reporting of the number and selection of methods used to determine treatment and control groups in two accounts of this project. One (Pate et al., 1985) indicates that two areas—one treatment, the other control—were selected from five matched candidate areas. In Williams and Pate (1987) three treatment and one control group neighborhoods are identified.

6. This was not specified in either report as a neighborhood.

7. Here, too, there is some discrepancy in the reporting of the evaluation designs and the treatments assessed in this analysis. One account (Pate et al., 1985) reports resident and local business person surveys were conducted in the program and control areas prior to and subsequent to the program implementation. This account did not report a survey sampling design or procedure, although response rates were said to have ranged from 56 to 86 percent, depending upon the survey in question. This version of the program makes no mention of the newsletter campaign. The second account (Williams and Pate, 1987) makes no mention of a business person sample and introduces the idea that a newsletter experimental program was part of the treatment.

8. Fourteen outcome measures were reported in the earlier account of this evaluation.

9. Five were reported in the earlier study.

10. The actual statistics are not reported; rather, a check is placed under the outcome measure if statistical significance was reached.

11. In the earlier version of this report (Pate et al., 1985), post- as compared to preprogram respondents in the treatment area reported increased victimization levels. No changes in fear were observed. In the comparison area, fear decreased over the interval. With the nonresidential samples, a significant change on one out of twelve outcomes was observed; post- as compared to preprogram respondents reported higher levels of concern about crime among employees and patrons.

12. In the prior analysis (Pate et al., 1985), significant changes were observed on two of the fourteen outcome measures. One change was counter to the hypothesized effect: panel respondents reported higher levels of perceived physical problems in the area after the program. In accord with the hypothesized impacts, respondents reported more household crime prevention efforts after the program. Internal analyses of panel respondents who could recall exposure to foot patrolling in their area (32 percent of panel sample) indicated that those who recalled exposure were more likely to have reduced their fear than those panel respondents who could not recall exposure.

13. The evolution of the terms used for this concept is revealing. Hunter (1978) originally used the term "incivilities." Wilson and Kelling (1982) call it "untended behavior." Pate et al. (1985) refer to the "signs of crime." And Reiss (1985a) used the term "soft crime." The shift in terms reflects a progressively more intimate perceived connection to the social and physical incivilities and serious crime. Yet there is little evidence of a unique linkage between these two concepts.

14. Statistical data are not reported in the study.

15. The evaluation currently under way in Baltimore may not fall victim to this flaw; the evaluators of that foot patrolling program have expressed an interest in using such units.

16. Since statistical power is so low, there is little chance of finding an effect, even if it really existed out there.

17. The authors do not report the proportion recalling exposure in the full sample. Since the panel sample probably represents a more stable portion of the full sample, the proportion recalling exposure may have been even smaller for the full sample.

12

COMMUNITY POLICING: A REPORT FROM THE DEVIL'S ADVOCATE

DAVID H. BAYLEY

INTRODUCTION

Community policing is the new philosophy of professional law enforcement in the world's industrial democracies. From London to Perth, Detroit to Singapore, police managers are talking about it. It represents progress and innovation. Wherever change is occurring, community policing is the watchword. According to proponents, community policing enhances public security and lowers crime rates, reduces the fear of crime and makes the public feel less helpless, reconnects the police with alienated publics, raises police morale, and makes the police more accountable. Community policing has emerged as the major strategic alternative to traditional practices that are now widely regarded as having failed (Skolnick and Bayley, 1986: Ch.8).

Despite the benefits claimed for community policing, programmatic implementation of it has been very uneven. Although widely, almost universally, said to be important, it means different things to different people—public relations campaigns, shopfront and mini-police stations, rescaled patrol beats, liaison with ethnic groups, permission for rank-and-file to speak to the press, Neighborhood Watch, foot patrols, patrol-detective teams, and door-to-door visits by police officers. Community policing on the ground often seems less a program than a set of aspirations wrapped in a slogan. This explains why older officers often remark that community policing is nothing new, that its core ideas of prevention, concern, and cooperation have been practiced all along.

It is probably fair to say that community policing in 1988 is more rhetoric than reality. It is a trendy phrase spread thinly over customary reality. Unless this state of affairs changes, the most likely future for community policing is that it will be remembered as another attempt to put old wine into new bottles. While some small changes may be made, enthusiasm will gradually wane. Its failure to live up to its pretensions may deepen cynicism among police and the attentive public about the possibilities for major reform in contemporary policing. Perhaps, unhappily, rhetorical oversell is necessary even for incremental change.

Fortunately, this is not the whole story of community policing at the present time. The reality of it is both more promising and more troublesome. In several places in the world, community policing has taken on solid programmatic form. Courageous police executives, bucking tradition, have used it to change the way police responsibilities are carried out. The practice of community policing is developing and, as a result, an operational definition of it is emerging. Specifically, when community policing rhetoric has been translated into novel programs, four elements tend to be associated: (1) community-based crime prevention, (2) proactive servicing as opposed to emergency response, (3) public participation in the planning and supervision of police operations, and (4) shifting of command responsibility to lower rank levels (Bayley, 1984, 1986; Skolnick and Bayley, 1987). Such changes can be seen in some places in Australia, France, Great Britain, and the United States. Policing in Japan has been based entirely on these principles since World War II; and Singapore is in the process of shifting from a traditional reactive police model, derived from the British, to a Japanese-inspired community model.

These four elements constitute a profound change in customary policing, which is why they are not easy to bring about (Skolnick and Bayley, 1987). But precisely because ambitious rhetoric is now occasionally becoming reality, it is fair to ask whether community policing is really worthwhile as its proponents think. If community policing was a flash in the pan, one need not worry. But if community policing truly becomes the wave of the future, what sort of problems might it engender that should be anticipated? Progress is never entirely unmixed, and the police have been reformed before. From the perspective of 1998, ten years hence, what sort of problems might it have been well to foresee? What might be the unanticipated consequences of community policing? Drawing upon growing experience with community policing in Europe, Asia, and North America, I shall discuss 12 problems that might be anticipated.

PROBLEMS WITH COMMUNITY POLICING

One: Public safety may decline. Community policing is based on the notion that the police cannot protect the public by their own unaided efforts. Successful crime prevention requires public participation as watchdogs and as less-vulnerable victims; successful apprehension and prosecution of criminals requires identification of suspects by the public and willing testimony. Yet the efficacy of the public as co-producers of public safety is untested. So far there is no convincing evidence that community policing strategies are even as effective as traditional ones. New questions are even being raised about Neighborhood Watch, the centerpiece of community crime prevention around the world. After reviewing all the U.S. studies, Dennis Rosenbaum (1987) argues that benefits are equivocal and that both the implementation and the theory of Neighborhood Watch may be flawed. The only solid bits of evidence that community policing may work come from Singapore, where analysis shows that a pilot program establishing five "Neighborhood Police Posts" in 1983-84 reduced street crime and raised public perceptions of safety (Quah and Jon, 1987). By and large, then, community policing is being adopted as a crime-reducing strategy on the strength of a priori arguments rather than evidence.

Most predictions about crime trends are that rates will continue to rise through the end of the century, though perhaps more slowly. Since community policing has not yet demonstrated its crime prevention or crime apprehension efficacy, criminality will probably continue to be perceived as a serious social problem. It is even possible that crime rates could rise disproportionately where it has been established. Former police commissioner Patrick V. Murphy's wry observation may be wrong that whatever police managers do will not make the situation worse. Nor is it justified to argue that going forward with untested strategies is no worse than what has been done traditionally. In such a situation, careful experimentation is preferable to wholesale implementation.

Two: The police may lose the will, and perhaps the capacity, to maintain public order. Community policing emphasizes the development of close relations with the public. The achievement of this goal, which is likely to be determined impressionistically, may undermine the determination of the police to take strong enforcement action when it is needed. Minority businessmen in Handsworth and Broadwater Farm Estate in Great Britain leveled just this charge against the police after fierce rioting and looting recently. The police, they said, had been "soft" on hoodlum elements because the police feared that forceful action would anger the community and jeopardize the gains from community policing. This same scenario could be replayed elsewhere with respect to street gangs intimidating passersby, small-time vice operators willing to help the police in narcotics investigations, unscrupulous employers who become pillars of commercial crime-prevention associations, and corrupt minority politicians who are active in police-community development.

Community policing may even weaken the capacity of the police to enforce the law forcibly. Remember how woefully unprepared U.S. police officers were in the 1960s for crowd-control operations? If community policing changes the operational style and training of a substantial portion of police personnel, where will officers be found who are competent to handle riots and demonstrations? Can the police put on a velvet glove and keep their iron hand in shape?

Three: Community policing provides a new and less demanding rationale for the police at the very moment when the traditional justification is failing. Massive research on the efficacy of the police undertaken during the past 20 years has been singularly unsuccessful in demonstrating any connection between public safety and the numbers of police, budgetary expenditures, or dominant strategies such as random mobile patrolling, rapid emergency response, or specialized criminal investigation (Bayley, 1985; Skolnick and Bayley, 1986). The accumulating evidence has reinforced the finding of criminologists that neither the police nor the larger criminal justice system has much leverage over criminal offending. Most of the variation in crime rates can be explained in terms of structural factors in society having nothing to do with criminal justice processes, such as unemployment, education, age distribution, and ethnic heterogeneity (Radzinowicz and King, 1977). Gradually the implication has been dawning on people that if the police can do little to improve public safety, perhaps a reduction in their activity, which is very costly, would not put society more greatly at risk.

Community policing, however, creates a new role for police with new criteria for performance. If police can not reduce crime and apprehend more offenders, they can at least decrease fear of crime, make the public feel less powerless, lessen distrust between minority groups and the police, mediate quarrels, overcome the isolation of marginal groups, organize social services, and generally assist in developing "community." These are certainly worthwhile objectives. But are they what the police should be doing? They are a far cry from what police were originally created to do. Should this agenda be allowed to eclipse the traditional one of protecting the public? Unless community policing is held to the traditional criteria of effectiveness, policing may become increasingly irrelevant to public safety, while at the same time diverting intellectual and material resources from the construction of other crime-reduction policies.

Community policing is a superb defensive strategy for the police. Whatever happens to public safety, they cannot lose. If community policing fails to protect, police can argue that it was a bad idea and more resources are needed for customary strategies. If community policing succeeds, police can argue that at last they are on the right track and additional funds for it are required. Either way, the result is that the police remain at the center of society's strategy for crime reduction.

Four: Community policing makes the public an interest group for the police. A key feature of community policing is the redeployment of police personnel so as to encourage regular, routine, nonemergency interaction with the public. This is done through foot patrols, park-and-walk patrols, and fixed police posts—variously called koban (Japan), community police stations (Santa Ana), ministations (Detroit), shopfronts (Melbourne), and neighborhood police posts (Singapore). In these ways, the police become a more noticeable, less anonymous presence. They become better acquainted with the community so that they can anticipate and possibly prevent crime and order problems from arising. They assist in organizing crime prevention programs like Neighborhood Watch, develop dependable sources of local information, and encourage cooperation in crime solving. The police also meet a more diverse cross-section of the populace, especially respectable, noncriminal people who welcome and support the police uncritically. Finally, the new modes of deployment encourage people to solicit assistance from the police for problems that are important but not necessarily criminal or urgent. This dramatizes the fact that the police are at the disposal of the public rather than being a spasmodically forceful presence intruding according to an invisible agenda. Community policing seeks to transform the police from what has been described as "an army of occupation" into an accepted, unremarkable, and individually responsive part of the community.

As a public-relations strategy, community policing is exceedingly clever. Studies have repeatedly shown that police are already very popular, even in their traditional reactive deployment (J. Q. Wilson, 1975: Ch.6; Garofalo, 1977). People want a greater police patrol presence and complain loudly when police stations are closed. Community policing will intensify this connection by personalizing police service, making it available to ordinary people who are not victims of crime. By freeing some police from the tyranny of the reactive radio-dispatch system, community policing makes a virtue of the "servicing" that police do so much of anyhow. Detroit's ministations, for example, have become popular even in depressed, disadvantaged neighborhoods. Despite the carping of traditional operational personnel, they are increasing from 52 to almost 100. Every neighborhood in Singapore wants a Neighborhood Police Post and every neighborhood in Japan wants a koban. Police in Australia have more requests for Neighborhood Watch than they can handle. Commercial associations clamor for more "shopfronts" like Melbourne's Broadmeadows.

Community policing provides a rationale for the systematic organization of communities at the grass roots in favor of the police. If police budgets tended to be untouchable in the past due to the public's fear of crime, they may become much more so in the future as community policing transforms communities into police interest groups.

Five: Community policing will increase the power of the police relatively among government agencies. This will occur in two ways. First, crime prevention, unlike crime response, is opened-ended. For example, if the police develop their capacity to diagnose circumstances that lead to crime, as fire departments have done with respect to fires, the police will have a consultative role in planning educational programs, public health, building design, street layout, public housing, municipal services, and welfare and employment policies. Crime prevention gives the police an almost unbounded watching brief over community affairs and government services. Second, community policing places officers in a position to act as advocates for the public vis-à-vis other government agencies. Already Detroit's ministation officers have helped communities obtain the quality of municipal services they are entitled to, such as improved street lighting, garbage removal, and repair of streets. Police in other cities have joined communities in getting abandoned buildings razed, truancy programs tightened up, and school facilities opened for teen recreation. Such interventions are bound to grow in community policing, not just because they serve the interests of public safety, but because the police need to be seen as sympathetic government friends.

Despite the documented importance of noncriminal servicing in police work, the role of the police has become more specialized in the Western world during the last century (Bayley, 1985). Slowly, the police have given up a host of regulatory functions such as inspecting buildings, checking weights and measures, ensuring food supplies, feeding and housing the indigent, guaranteeing cattle, and issuing many permits and licenses. They now concentrate more exclusively on investigating and deterring crime. The diversity of today's police work comes from the nature of the calls that individuals make to the police, not from governmental design. Community policing may reverse this trend as police consciously develop their capacity to assist neighborhoods as minicenters of government service, all in the name of convenience, crime prevention, and community development. Community policing, then, embeds the police not only in communities, but at the heart of government.

Six: Community policing legitimates the penetration of communities by forceful enforcement agents of government. The whole purpose of community policing is to bridge the gap between the populace and the law's enforcers. In order to accomplish this, police in Detroit and Houston have called at individual residences offering to make security inspections and asking about neighborhood crime problems. In Singapore and Japan, such visits are routinely made to every residence twice a year. Officers fill out a short information form on the inhabitants, their relationships, ownership of a motor vehicle, and anything else they think pertinent. So far, such records are not collated or centrally stored. They are available to investigators, however, if the need arises. Computer storage would be a comparatively easy step to take, turning innocuous visits into a tool of systematic government surveillance.

Police in Melbourne and Detroit volunteer to serve on executive committees of local institutions that have security problems—hospitals, mental health homes, shelters for battered women, schools, and industries that employ large numbers of commuting women. Police appoint liaison officers to work with troublesome groups, such as gays and ethnics, to avoid confrontations and smooth relations. Police officers in Darwin and Adelaide, Australia, have been assigned to high schools where they work in uniform to help with discipline, counsel hard-core delinquents, build rapport with students, lecture on crime prevention, and generally show that the police can be friends. Although all these purposes are laudable, the bottom line is that police officers are now being assigned and welcomed to watch, probe, and penetrate social processes and institutions that have previously been out of bounds.

Traditionally the police deterred, arrested, constrained, warned, and did so almost exclusively in public places. Now they advise, mediate, lecture, organize, participate, cooperate, communicate, reach out, solicit, and encourage as much in private places as public. In many countries, the police are being viewed explicitly as agents of community development, responsible for molding and shaping social processes that enhance harmony and order. This is a far cry from the minimalist philosophy of creating an environment in which social processes may safely occur. Just as the public's need for social welfare impelled the state into becoming more than a referee in the economic marketplace, so the public's fear of crime may impel the police to play an interventionist role in social life.

Western political theory as well as practice has tried, increasingly vainly, to separate public from private domains. Community policing seeks to make that division indistinguishable. It tries to enlist the public in the state's maintenance of order just as it tries to insinuate police officers into private spheres of activity. Overcoming distrust of the police may improve public safety, but at what cost? Perhaps suspicion of the police is essential to our freedom?

Seven: Community policing may weaken the rule of law in the sense of equal protection and evenhanded enforcement. An axiom of community policing is that police operations should adapt to local circumstances. Taking advantage of diverse new sources of information as well as public participation in planning of police activities, local commanders are being given the responsibility to develop their own schemes for policing. Command devolves upon lower ranks and geographic decentralization is strengthened (Skolnick and Bayley, 1986). James Q. Wilson and George L. Kelling (1982) have gone further and argued that successful maintenance of civility and order in public places, which is crucial to crime control, requires that police consider local norms. While they do not suggest that innocent people should not be protected, the clear implication is that if standards of public behavior are to be raised, police must work with, rather than against, local inhabitants. As the police well know, what is acceptable on the waterfront may not be acceptable in a shopping mall.

Community policing makes a virtue of command discretion with respect to priorities and operations and hopes to make it responsible. The problem is that enforcement of law is rarely altogether popular. Community policing can easily be read as bending the law so as not to offend. Local commanders may begin to think it is more important not to alienate loud voices than to protect quiet ones. Moreover, communities are complex. Whose interests, priorities, and values are the police to consider? And have they the capacity, indeed the wisdom, to manufacture a consensus? Perhaps it is better in the long run to say that the law should be equally enforced—even though that is often unrealistic—than to say that the law should be used by the police to maintain order acceptable to local communities?

In the late 1960s, minority communities in the United States agitated for the police to decentralize in order to become more responsive and understanding. Police were universally hostile to the idea, arguing that it would mean the collapse of the rule of law. As a result, the initiatives were beaten back, often after bitter election campaigns. Ironically, a decade and a half later the very same notion is being pushed, only this time by the police. Perhaps the police do not recognize that community policing is "neighborhood policing" reborn. Whether they do or not, their reservations of a decade and a half ago may still be valid. Decentralization under police control may seem less political than decentralization by community demand, but the possibility of decay in the rule of law is only slightly reduced.

Eight: Community policing may lessen the protection afforded by law to unpopular persons. It may even encourage vigilantism. Community policing mobilizes the populace for crime prevention, including systematic surveillance and informing. In many U.S. cities, for example, mobile civilian-band radio patrols have been informed. In Japan, neighborhood foot patrols, often targeted on teenagers and runaways, are common. Members of Neighborhood Watch are encouraged to report suspicious persons and activity. Under community policing, local commanders are judged by their ability to develop such activities. In these circumstances, the line between community protection and harassment may become blurred. Neighborhood Watch meetings in Detroit, for instance, have been held outdoors across the street from suspected "drug houses," with uniformed police prominently in attendance. The message was loud and clear, and in several instances drug operations have shifted. But what happens if crime prevention attention shifts from suspected drug dealers to porn shop operators, prostitutes, members of the Nazi party, homosexuals, nonresident minorities, atheists, "lenient" judges, and civil libertarians? Would local police sympathetically investigate complaints of citizen spying, intimidation, and denial of services? Under community policing, would they be more or less bound by local community sentiment?

In "outback" police stations in Australia where one or two officers often work a hundred miles from "backup," police officers dwell on how dependent they are on the support of locals for order maintenance, especially when out-of-towners are involved. Among an evening's drinking crowd at a local pub, officers take pride in pointing out the "blokes" they can count on in a fight. The feeling is strongly reciprocated, only the "blokes" may speak quietly about the need to keep unruly, drunken Aboriginals from overrunning the town. While drunkenness and fighting are indeed chronic problems of the Australian Aborigine, it is not hard to imagine that outback towns must seem cold and indifferent if not actively hostile to Aborigines faced with a tacit alliance between white townie and white police officer (P. R. Wilson, 1982). If push comes to shove, it would be an imprudent officer who chose an Aborigine over a white resident unless the situation was crystal clear. Unless great care is taken to evaluate the quality of protection produced by community policing, the public order that is generated may favor people who belong to majorities more than people who belong to minorities.

Nine: Community policing may exacerbate a growing dualism in the structure of policing in modern industrial societies. Police officers report greater difficulty in organizing crime prevention efforts, eliciting responsible community feedback, and obtaining reliable information among people who are poor and uneducated than people who are affluent and professional. Evaluations of Neighborhood Watch show greater success in ethnically homogeneous, relatively affluent, middle-class communities (Rosenbaum, 1987). This suggests that the vitality of community policing may depend on social structure. Community policing over a period of years may become unevenly distributed socially and hence geographically. It could become the mode for the affluent, educated middle class, while traditional reactive policing remained the mode for the poor and uneducated underclass.

Such a split in policing modalities already exists to some extent due to the rise of private security operations. Private security is characterized as Stenning and Shearing (1979) have shown by the very qualities community policing hopes to develop: prevention, mobilization, intrusiveness, and substantive due process. Accountability is obtained through contact as private police do what the client wishes. Operationally, private security is community policing obtained through the marketplace. It is free enterprise's anticipation of community policing. Conversely, community policing can be seen as the public sector's attempt to emulating what private security does for the well-to-do.

However, unless strenuous efforts are made to implant community policing among the poor, community policing may not equalize the quality of security protection but may reenforce the market's dualism in mode and effectiveness of policing. If social structure affects the implementation of community policing, policing for the rich under both public and private auspices may increasingly conform to a preventive, penetrating, consensual model, while policing for the poor will increasingly reflect a reactive, restricted, procedural due-process model.

Ten: Community policing makes supervision within police organizations ends, rather than means, based. The traditional management system has emphasized avoiding errors, violating rules, and stepping out of line. The rule book was king. Recognizing that this system stifled initiative, undermined the taking of responsibility, and generally lowered morale, modern police executives have tried a much more positive approach where officers are judged according to their ability to achieve general objectives rather than simply avoiding the violation of rules. This is called "management by objective," and it permeates the practice of community policing. Middle- and lower-ranking supervisors are encouraged to adapt resources to circumstances. They are urged to formulate plans for policing that fit the peculiar needs of their jurisdictions. Consequently, under community policing, work schedules become more flexible, paperwork less detailed, dress more casual, contacts with citizens more offhand, supervision more collegial, and working behavior less rule-oriented. In the words of one Detroit ministation officer, community policing is "creative customized police work" (Skolnick and Bayley, 1986:65).

To the extent that community policing magnifies command responsibility at all subordinate levels, encourages initiative and adaptation, and stresses the achievement of objectives over adherence to formal rules, community policing requires more successful internalization of norms of conduct. The training of community police officers must be done with unusual care and thoroughness. If this new sort of police officer is not created, community policing may lead to increased slackness, time-wasting, inattention, and mismanagement.

Eleven: Police organizations may be less accountable for the character of operations because community police officers will have greater freedom of action. Not only can subordinate commanders say that they know best what particular communities need, they will have the political basis to ensure that their plans prevail. Officers in charge of neighborhood police stations speak proudly of their ability to mobilize resources from their communities, such as funds for crime prevention programs, appearances of political VIPs at police functions, coverage by radio and television, and supportive services by area businesses. More quietly, they mention that their support networks can be used to gain independence from the command hierarchy. Although this may seem like a desirable loosening of bureaucratic rigidity in favor of community adaptation, the result is that community police officers can become independent of effective supervision. The community's police officer is less the department's police officer. Community policing may close the gap between police and public, but it may open a gap between subordinate ranks and the police organization.

As long as the conduct of community police officers is exemplary, their independent power base is not a cause for concern. But if they should mismanage funds, take bribes, abuse authority, or wink at violations of the law, they may be able to defy disciplinary action. In New York City recently, for example, the commissioner of police ordered police officers to be reassigned to other precincts every three years in order to lessen the familiarity that he thought bred corruption. The police union protested vainly. If a substantial proportion of New York City police had been assigned to neighborhood police posts rather than large precincts, the commissioner might have faced a public outcry as well because communities would realize that they would periodically lose "their police officer." Proponents of community policing must not forget that command centralization in U.S. cities occurred early in the twentieth century in direct reaction to the corruption and in-discipline engendered by cozy relations between precinct commanders and local power structures (Richardson, 1974; Fogelson, 1977; Walker, 1977; Carte and Carte, 1975).

Twelve: Community policing may undermine professionalism. Community policing is negotiated policing. To some extent, it substitutes responsiveness to community opinion for adherence to exogenous standards, whether of the rule-of-law or as the queen's police officer. Police are prepared to exchange command control for public support. Although this is done in order to achieve higher levels of security, the fact remains that both the ends and the means of policing are now open for discussion rather than being a matter for professional judgment. Community policing is indeed democratic policing. Strategic choices by departments as well as activities of individual officers are worked out under community policing in a consensual manner with a responsible public.

Should this be so? For 75 years, police managers in the United States have argued that fairness and effectiveness in law enforcement could best be achieved by a highly trained, dispassionate, and disciplined cadre of officers operating under authority of law rather than under operational direction by the public. They believed that the judgments police officers make, whether organizational or individual, are too complex and momentous for uninformed, impressionable citizens to make.

Community policing, however, rests on the assumption that law enforcement and the maintenance of order are not so complex or "scientific" that the public cannot play a major role both intellectually and physically. Policing is not a profession with principles of operation understandable only by trained practitioners and supervision best accomplished by peers.

The problem with this view is that while the scientific pretensions of police professionalism have probably been overdone, community policing may forfeit the distance necessary for taking unpopular actions. Policing may not be like the practice of medicine, but it may be like the practice of public health. Concern for the wishes of the patient must be combined with authority to require compliance. Public health, unlike private medical treatment, cannot be refused. Like public health, policing cannot always be popular and must always be equitable.

CONCLUSION

The problems I anticipate arising out of community policing are not yet social fact. They are implications of the theory of community policing supported by scattered observations on the ground where community policing is currently being practiced. Community policing is not yet so well entrenched that is is a problem in itself. It would be unfortunate, therefore, if criticism at this stage discouraged further rethinking of police practices and retarded deserved change. Evidence about the shortcomings of customary policing is much greater than evidence about community policing's failings. I certainly do not believe that community policing should be abandoned. Its goals are worthwhile and its practice responsive to defects in current police performance.

However, because the problems enumerated touch profound questions of morality and politics, responsible policy making should take them into account before they arise. Community policing does not represent a small, technical shift in policing; it is a paradigmatic change in the way police operate. It is the most fundamental change in policing since the rise of police professionalism early in this century. Because community policing is serious and fateful, we must be open minded about its potential infirmities as well as its promise. Specifically, I believe that if community policing is to avoid the problems discussed, it must be accompanied by four additional developments. These are requirements for the responsible implementation of community policing.

First, the effectiveness of community policing as a crime-control strategy must be monitored systematically. On-going evaluation by government, if necessary, out of police budgets is essential in order to render the new policing accountable in performance. Because police effectiveness has not been so evaluated in the past is no excuse for not doing so in the future. Without evidence about effectiveness, crime control policy making will remain the captive of an entrenched, high-priced police bureaucracy with a license to cultivate its own grass-roots support. Society can keep its crime control options open only if it knows what its designated agents are or are not achieving.

Second, an institution outside the police must be given the authority and capacity to determine whether community police operations conform to the rule of law. Are rights protected, laws administered fairly, and power not abused? Local accountability *does not* substitute for professional, independent oversight. Quite the contrary, it makes it more necessary. Americans especially have been naive about this, believing that rectitude was assured by local control. Responsiveness may be achieved in this way, but not propriety under law.

Third, the selection of police officers must be more careful and their training more demanding under community policing. It is not technical capacity that must be stressed, but the moral requirements of policing. Emphasis upon initiative and autonomous decision-making must be accompanied by the development of vocational commitment. Policing must cease to be viewed as a job anyone can do, if only they follow the rules. Police professionalism must grow, not decline nor ever stand still, under community policing; but it must be the professionalism of duty as well as of skills. Policing must become a calling to which only the dedicated can aspire. We cannot trust the police as close to us as community policing entails—sheathed with power and supervised loosely—unless they are restrained by an explicit moral code. This will not be easy to achieve or inexpensive; but it can be done, as the Japanese have convincingly demonstrated.

Fourth, democratic industrial societies must develop the capacity to formulate and implement general policies of policing, calling on all resources both public and private, so as to provide effective and equal protection to all segments of the population. The fruits of police innovation must be evenly distributed. Community policing must not be abandoned too quickly when social circumstances make implementation difficult. But if community policing does not work everywhere, other modes must be found to compensate. Commitment to one kind of innovation must not blind us to the need for several.

Community policing is an attractive movement in contemporary policing, but we must not expect that it will surmount as if by magic familiar problems of effectiveness, fairness, and abuse of authority. The four policies suggested are minimal conditions for ensuring the promise of community policing. Without them, community policing may be seen from the perspective of the future as another well-intention but disappointing attempt at police reform. With them, community policing might truly produce a qualitative transformation in the enterprise of public security.

13

THE RHETORIC OF COMMUNITY POLICING

CARL B. KLOCKARS

> The police are a mechanism for the distribution of non-negotiably coercive force employed in accord with an intuitive grasp of situational exigencies.
>
> The proposed definition of the role of the police entails a difficult moral problem. How can we arrive at a favorable or even accepting judgment about an activity which is, in its very conception, opposed to the ethos of the polity that authorizes it? Is it not well nigh inevitable that this mandate be concealed in circumlocution?
>
> Egon Bittner (1970)

In *The Functions of Police in Modern Society,* Egon Bittner (1970) posed the problem of the relationship between police and the people they police in an extremely general but remarkably provocative form. Bittner advanced the argument that for nearly two centuries the core culture goal of Western society has been the establishment of peace, both international and domestic, as a condition to everyday life. Our failures to achieve peace between nations are no secret, but each one of these failures, be it either of two world wars, Korea, or Viet Nam, seems to have strengthened both our cultural commitments to the virtue of peace, as well as our resolve that such destructive failures to secure it should not occur again. While diplomacy, treaties, trade, and aid are pursued as alternatives to forceful conflict on the international level, bureaucracy, democracy, education, and a host of social services are promoted as the proper, noncoercive terms of the relationship between the state and citizens domestically. In both domestic and international relations, it is not merely that peace has become a nearly universal cultural goal, but that it is believed to be a goal that can *only* be successfully secured through the development and application of peaceful means to its achievement.

In ways wholly consistent with this aspiration to achieve peace through peaceful means as a condition of everyday domestic life, Western societies have sought to circumscribe to the greatest degree possible the legitimacy of the use of force by its citizens. Save for occasions of self-defense from criminal attack and intrafamily discipline of children by their parents, Western states have all but eliminated the rights of its citizens to use coercive force. The historical trade-off for this elimination of citizen rights to employ coercive force is, of course, the allocation of an exclusive right to it to police. After repeated failures of attempts to do so otherwise, a major component in the move toward the elimination of violence as a condition of everyday domestic life in every modern Western society has been to seek to extend a virtual monopoly on the legitimate right to use coercive force to police.

While no one whom it would be safe to have home to dinner argues that modern society could be without police, this situation places police in a most uneasy relationship with both the society and the state that authorize it. In their aspiration to eliminate violence as an acceptable means of conducting human affairs, both are forced to accept the creation of a core institution whose special competence and defining characteristic is its monopoly on a general right to use coercive force. Understood in this light, the police are not only fundamentally and irreconcilably offensive in their means to the core cultural aspiration of modern society, but an ever present reminder that all of these noble institutions, which should make it possible for citizens to live in nonviolent relations with one another and with the state, often come up very short.

It is this truth that Bittner argues must be "concealed in circumlocution." That is, in order to reconcile itself with an institution whose means are irreconcilably offensive to it, society must wrap that institution in signs, symbols, and images that effectively conceal, mystify, and legitimate police actions. In *Functions,* Bittner attends to three of these circumlocutions, the legalization, the militarization, and the professionalization of police in considerable detail.

The thesis of this chapter is that the modern movement toward what is currently called "community policing" is best understood as the latest in a fairly long tradition of circumlocutions whose purpose is to conceal, mystify, and legitimate police distribution of nonnegotiably coercive force. However, before we look directly at the cluster of circumlocutions that constitute the community policing movement, it will be helpful to follow some of Bittner's leads in analysis of legalization, militarization, and professionalization.

LEGALIZATION

As late as 1900 when Chicago's police department numbered 3,225 men, there was no organized training. New policemen heard a brief speech from a high ranking officer, received a hickory stick, a whistle, and a key to the call box, and were sent out to work with an experienced officer. Not only were policeman untrained in law, but they operated within a criminal justice system that generally placed little emphasis on legal procedure. Most of those arrested by police were tried before local justices who rarely had legal training. Those arrested seldom had attorneys so that no legal defense was made. Thus, there were few mechanisms for introducing legal norms into street experience and crime control activities of police (Haller, 1976:303).

Although the quote above from Mark Haller's "Historical Roots of Police Behavior, Chicago, 1890-1925" describes Chicago police at the turn of the century, the situation was not very different in any major U.S. city at that time. At the turn of the century, the newly formed U.S. police were under no illusions that they were a "law enforcement" agency nor that their mandate or principal activity was to enforce law. While there is no question but what they understood that they were engaged in law enforcement in some formal sense, "the law" for U.S. police in their early years was but one of many tools they might be called upon to use in their work. By no means was it as crucial to that work as their whistle, call box key, or hickory stick.

Things are, of course, very different today, and Haller's observations on big city policing at the turn of the century provide an ideal vantage point from which to lay a perspective on those changes. Although, in fact, contemporary police may not mobilize the law with any greater frequency than their turn-of-the-century predecessors, modern police view themselves, at least publicly, as "law enforcement agencies" and are widely understood to be fairly closely governed in their work by the courts through the procedural and evidentiary requirements of the criminal law. Historically, this process of the progressive legalization of the enterprise of policing is widely appreciated to have begun at the federal level in 1914 with the *Weeks* decision, a decision whose exclusionary rule principles were extended to all jurisdictions in 1961 by *Mapp*. Since *Mapp,* literally dozens of fourth, fifth, eighth, and fourteenth amendment decisions have promoted this view of the intimate and binding relationship between the police, the courts, and the law.

In light of these and other developments in laws that bear upon police behavior, it is probably fair to say that no other police anywhere in the world are as thoroughly "legalized" as the U.S. police. How then can we, following Bittner, speak of their "legalization" as a "circumlocution?" To do so requires the appreciation of three major points, one of which is analytical and the other two of which are empirical. The analytical point is offered by Bittner (1970:25): "Our courts have no control over police work, never claimed to have such control, and it is exceedingly unlikely that they will claim such powers in the foreseeable future, all things being equal." Bittner's point hinges on the meaning of "control." He argues that the relationship between the courts, the law, and police is rather like that between independent consumers and suppliers of services. What the courts offer to police is the opportunity, if they wish to take advantage of it, to seek the state's capacity to punish. In effect, the courts say to the police that if they wish to make use of that capacity, they must demonstrate to the courts that they have followed certain procedures in order to do so. Thus it is Bittner's point that only on those occasions that the police wish to employ the state's capacity to punish do the two institutions have any relationship of any kind. Despite the enormous growth in police law in the past quarter century, the courts have no more "control" over the police than local supermarkets have over the diets of those who shop there.

Even that analogy, however, may give more substance to the relationship between the police and the courts than is actually warranted in fact. Empirically, it is probably the case that the cost and kind of products supermarkets offer do influence the diets of the people who shop there. It is likewise the case with police that it is almost inevitable that they will seek to secure the state's capacities to punish in certain instances. For example, in cases of reported homicides, police behave on the assumption that the case may well end up in court. On these occasions, procedural requirements certainly influence how police behave (and what they choose to report to the courts on their behavior).

Empirically, however, we know two major things about the terms of this relationship between the police, the law, and the courts. The first is that the felony arrest rate for patrol officers is very, very low even in areas in which felony offense rates are very high. For example, a recent study by Walsh (1986) found that 40 percent of the 156 patrol officers assigned to a very high crime area in New York City did not make a single felony arrest during the entire year under study, and that 68.6 percent of these officers made no more than three felony arrests.

The second empirical fact we know about police behavior has to do with the frequency with which police choose not to arrest when they have every legal right and all the evidence necessary to do so, or, alternatively, choose to make arrests when they have no legal grounds to do so whatsoever. For example, in his well-known study of 299 cases of dispute settlements by police, Black (1980:183) found that in 52 cases in which there was ample evidence that a violent felony had occurred, police made arrests in only 27 percent of those cases. In cases of violent misdemeanor offenses, the arrest rate dropped to 17 percent. Black also found that in 78 cases in which police had no grounds for legal action of any kind, they nevertheless made arrests in 17 percent of those cases as well. Similar results are reported in many other studies. Collectively, they constitute the major empirical discovery of police research of the past two decades: the discovery of selective enforcement and the enormous influence on police discretion of such things as suspect demeanor, complainant preferences, and a host of other factors that have nothing to do with "the law."

MILITARIZATION

While legalization is probably the most powerful circumlocution currently mystifying the institution and functions of police in modern society, the militarization of police runs a close and complicating second. Begun as a reform movement in the history of U.S. police, an effort to establish discipline within police ranks and to extricate police from the stink of municipal machine politics, militarization drew upon a powerful and abiding analogy (Fogelson, 1977, especially Ch. 2, "The Military Analogy":40-67). The analogy held that police were, in effect, a domestic army engaged in a "war" on crime.

The analogy drew upon three compelling themes. First, by associating police with the heroes and victories of the military rather than the back rooms of city politics, the military analogy sought to confer some honor and respect on the occupation of policing. Second, the idea of a war on crime struck a note of emergency that gave the movement to militarize the U.S. police a moral urgency and a rhetorical tone that was difficult to resist. To fail to support the police in their war on crime, to stand in their way, or to be stingy with the resources they would need to fight it was siding with the enemy and metaphorically tantamount to treason. Third and finally, the military analogy sought to establish a relationship between local politicians and police chiefs that was analogous to the relationship between elected executives at the national level and the general of the U.S. military. The politicians would, of course, retain the right to decide whether or not a given war ought to be fought, but the conduct of the battles and the day-to-day discipline and management of the troops was to be left to the control of the generals. At bottom then, the military analogy was a way of talking about police that sought to wrest from the hands of local politicians and place into the hands of police chiefs the administrative tools—hiring, firing, promotion, demotion, assignment, and discipline— that those chiefs needed to manage the organizations they headed.

To a degree that no turn-of-the-century police chief could have imagined, the military analogy proved a smashing success. The popularity of police and the size of police budgets have grown enormously. While no one would argue that the police are free of political control or influences (and no thoughtful person in a democratic society can argue that they should be), the political "autonomy" of police makes them a major, independent political force in many U.S. cities. The real problem in policing today is more often to find ways of putting politics into policing than it is to find ways of taking it out.

While extricating police from the shabby sides of urban politics and establishing discipline within the ranks were no small achievements in the history of U.S. police, the military metaphor that made those achievements possible brought with it some mighty long-term costs. Administratively, it left U.S. police with a quasi-military administrative structure that is wholly inappropriate as a device for managing the highly discretionary activity of police work. Almost wholly punitive in its approach to controlling employee behavior, it stifles innovation, imagination, experimentation, and creativity. It is no accident that the CYA (cover-your-ass) syndrome is endemic in U.S. police agencies, supported as it is by the absolute organizational truth that the department administration is preoccupied with punishment.

Equally important as a long-term cost of the militarization of the U.S. police is the dramatization of the police role in fighting crime that the military metaphor required. The fact is that the "war on crime" is a war police not only cannot win, but cannot in any real sense fight. They cannot win it because it is simply not within their power to change those things—such as unemployment, the age distribution of the population, moral education, freedom, civil liberties, ambitions, and the social and economic opportunities to realize them—that influence the amount of crime in any society. Moreover, any kind of real war on crime is something no democratic society would be prepared to let its police fight. We would simply be unwilling to tolerate the kind of abuses to the civil liberties of innocent citizens—to us—that fighting any kind of a real war on crime would inevitably involve.

These absolute limitations on the police capacity to influence crime notwithstanding, the expectation that police should be able to do so remain and are routinely reinforced by police themselves. Police take credit for drops and blames for rises in the crime rate. So strong is the crime-fighting image of the U.S. police, that for the past 50 years virtually every purchase of equipment, every request for additional personnel, and every change in operating procedure has had to be promoted or defended in terms of its role in fighting crime.

The impassioned, crime-fighting rhetoric of militarization is often juxtaposed to the supposedly restraining metaphor of legalization. For example, we find that motif magnified in images suggesting that the courts are "handcuffing" the police. However, in two important ways, both of which mystify police activity and shield it from scrutiny, the rhetorics of militarization and legalization are profoundly complementary. First, both focus exclusively on crime. While the military analogy holds that fighting crime is the *raison d'être* of police, the circumlocution of legalization holds that police are controlled by the courts because they must show compliance with certain procedures on occasions when they petition the courts to punish.

Second, both legalization and militarization tend to discourage police accountability to political authorities. Legalization does so by sponsoring the impression that the courts oversee and control police practice. Insofar as the police function can be understood as simply "law enforcement" and the consequences of law enforcement governed by the judgments of the courts, there is apparently very little room or need for legitimate political accountability of police. The metaphor of militarization makes essentially the same point, only more strongly. It holds that in the war against crime, political involvement is suspect. Only someone interested in aiding the enemy would have reason to interfere with police.

PROFESSIONALIZATION

Like militarization and legalization, the circumlocution that police administrators were to call "professionalization" also sought to distance police from the influence of the political process. And, like militarization, it did so by drawing upon an analogy. The professional analogy held that, like doctors, lawyers, engineers, and other professionals, police possessed a body of special skills and knowledge that were necessary both to do and to understand their work. Hence it would be no more appropriate for a politician to instruct a police officer on how to do his or her work than it would be for a politician to instruct a doctor on how to remove an appendix, or an engineer on how to build a bridge. It followed from this analogy that to do the work of professional policing, police administrators would require not only the highly sophisticated technological tools of professional policing, but also officers of intelligence and education to employ them. Only in a police agency equipped and staffed in this way, and working in an environment free from political interference, could truly professional policing flourish.

Although the professional analogy was effective in getting improved personnel and technical resources for police, in encouraging police research, and in increasing the political autonomy of police, the analogy was not without its difficulties. Even on its own metaphorical terms, it was defective. While it is true that no politician should have a hand on a surgeon's scalpel during an appendectomy or calculate weight displacement factors for an engineer's bridge, political involvement in medicine, engineering, and numerous other professions is thoroughgoing and, by most accounts, needs to be. While politicians do not dictate the depth of a surgeon's cut, they do influence where hospitals are built, what kinds of health insurance programs may be offered in a state, how and in what form health care will be provided for indigent patients, and to what extent the government will support specialized clinics, medical certification, education, and specialization. On a still broader political scale, state agencies review petitions for experimental surgical procedures and supervise in minute detail the development of all new medications. On balance and despite the intended political thrust of the professional analogy, it is probably fair to say that the state plays a much larger and more systematically influential role in the practice of medicine than it does in influencing the practice of policing.

The professional analogy also concealed a second major circumlocution. The fact is that the "professional" police officer, as conceived by the professional police model, was understood to be a very special kind of professional, a kind of professional that taxes the very meaning of the idea. The distinctive characteristic of the work of professionals is the range of discretion accorded them in the performance of their work. By contrast, the police view of professionalism was exactly the opposite. It emphasized centralized control and policy, tight command structure, extensive departmental regulation, strict discipline, and careful oversight. While the professional model wanted intelligent and educated police officers and the technological appearance of modern professionals, it did not want police officers who were granted broad, professional discretion. It wanted obedient bureaucrats.

Of course, it never really got them. The reason it did not is that the shape and variety of tasks and situations police encountered in their day-to-day work were too complex to be covered by the crude provisions of general bureaucratic regulations. Understanding this, the professional model focused its regulatory apparatus not on what police do with citizens, but on the behavior of police within the department bureaucracy. If one looks at the manuals that most modern police departments publish, some of which are hundreds and even thousands of pages long, one finds that virtually all the rules within them govern how the officer is supposed to behave within the department. With the exception, perhaps, of a policy on when to use deadly force, they are silent on the question of how they should treat the people they police.

It is against this backdrop of the three major circumlocutions in the history of the U.S. police that the emerging circumlocution of community policing must be considered. Although the mystiques of legalization, militarization, and professionalization have been largely demystified in the scholarly literature, they remain a part of the popular consciousness and continue to influence police conceptions of themselves. While they are assuredly myths about policework, they are not myths that can be dismissed. They have hardened into beliefs that govern police management and officer self-conceptions. They are driven deeply into the organizational structure and administrative apparatus of police agencies. Community policing thus must face the twin problems of dealing with the long-term consequences of those circumstances, and of replacing those circumlocutions with others powerful and compelling enough to permit a societal reconciliation with an "activity which is, in its very conception, opposed to the ethos of the polity that authorizes it" (Bittner, 1970).

THE CIRCUMLOCUTIONS OF COMMUNITY POLICING

There are many notions of what community policing is, what it means, and what it can mean (Kelling, 1985; Wilson and Kelling, 1982; Sykes, 1986; Klockars, 1985). Perhaps the most comprehensive attempt to identify the critical elements of the movement is to be found in Jerome Skolnick and David Bayley's *The New Blue Line* (1986). The chief virtue of that book from our perspective is that it is uniformly cheerful about the movement and wholly without critical reservations as to its capacities and limits. Conceding that a more measured advocacy of community policing might provoke a less-revealing analysis of the rhetoric of community policing, we will, nevertheless, focus on what Skolnick and Bayley identify as the four elements of community policing that make it the "wave of the future" (p. 212): (1) police-community reciprocity, (2) areal decentralization of command, (3) reorientation of patrol, and (4) civilianization.

Police-Community Reciprocity

The first and most distinctive element of the community policing movement is what Skolnick and Bayley term "police-community reciprocity." The term as Skolnick and Bayley employ it embodies practical, attitudinal, and organizational dimensions. Practically, it implies that "the police must involve the community . . . in the police mission." Attitudinally, police-community reciprocity "means that police must genuinely feel, and genuinely communicate a feeling that the public they serve has something to contribute to the enterprise of policing" (p. 211). Organizationally, police-community reciprocity implies that "the police and the public are co-producers of crime prevention. If the old professional leaned toward, perhaps exemplified, a 'legalistic' style of policing . . . the new professionalism implies that the police serve, learn from, and are accountable to the community" (p. 212).

Two central circumlocutions mark this vision of the relationship between police and the people they police. They are: (1) the mystification of the concept of community, and (2) the mixed metaphors of reduced rime. Although the two circumlocutions are heavily intertwined, let us begin by considering each of them separately.

The Mystification of the Concept of Community

Sociologically, the concept of community implies a group of people with a common history, common beliefs and understandings, a sense of themselves as "us" and outsiders as "them," and often, but not always, a shared territory. Relationships of community are different from relationships of society. Community relationships are based upon status not contract, manners not morals, norms not laws, understandings not regulations. Nothing, in fact, is more different from community than those relationships that characterize most of modern urban life. The idea of police, an institution of state and societal relations, is itself foreign to relations of community. The modern police are, in a sense, a sign that community norms and controls are unable to manage relations within or between communities, or that communities themselves have become offensive to society. The bottom line of these observations is that genuine communities are probably very rare in modern cities, and where they do exist, have little interest in cultivating relationships of any kind with police. University communities, for example, have often behaved in this way, developed their own security forces and judicial systems, and used them to shield students (and faculty) from the scrutiny of police.

The fact that genuine communities do not exist or are very rare and are largely self-policing entities in modern society raises the question of just why it is that the community policing movement has chosen to police in their name. An hypothesis suggests itself. It is that nonexistent and uninterested communities make perfect partners for police in what Skolnick and Bayley have termed the "co-production of crime prevention." What makes them perfect partners is that while they lend their moral and political authority as communities to what police do in their name, they have no interest in and do not object to anything that might be done.

The flaw in this thesis is that it asks police to behave like good sociologists and use their concepts carefully. Of course, police do not behave in this way and it is probably unfair to ask them to do so. If we admit this flaw and excuse police for using the concept of "community" in far too casual a sense, we are obliged to ask what "police-community reciprocity" implies if it is not policing "communities." One answer is "neighborhoods," "districts," and "precincts," each of which can often be spoken of as having legitimately identifiable characters and characteristics that police rightly and routinely take into account when working there.

There are, however, two major difficulties with substituting real entities like neighborhoods, districts, or interest groups for the concept of community. The first is that doing so misrepresents what working police officers in those places do. Those officers who actually work in those areas see themselves policing people and incidents, perhaps even "corners," "houses," "parks," "streets," or even a "beat." But the concept of a patrol officer policing an entire neighborhood, district, or precinct extends the notion of a police officer's sense of territorial responsibility beyond any reasonable limits.

The only persons in police departments who can be said to police entities as large as entire neighborhoods, districts, or precincts are police administrators. It is police administrators who can be pressured by representatives of groups or associations from those areas. In policing such areas, police captains, inspectors, and police chiefs have rather limited resources and a rather limited range of real things they can do for or offer to such groups. By and large, police administrators at captain rank or above, the only persons in police agencies who can be said to police areas of the size of communities, police those areas with words. Thus the idea of police-community reciprocity becomes a rhetorical device for high-command-rank police officers to speak to organizations or groups in areas that are at once, geographically, too large to be policed and, politically, too large to be ignored.

The second major difficulty with substituting a concept like neighborhood for the too casual police use of community is that such a term tends to belie the character of the entities with which police leaders interact. In speaking to traditional neighborhood groups, police community relations officers have always had their "community-is-the-eyes-and-ears-of-the-police" speeches. But what is distinctive about the community policing movement is that it places the burden of bringing those groups into being and giving them an institutional or organizational reality on police. The typical strategy involves creating some form or organization that can act as a public forum for information exchange. In Santa Ana, California, the model community policing agency in Skolnick and Bayley's study, the department's organizational efforts are described as follows:

Each of the four community areas has 150-250 block captains who may be responsible for thirty or forty neighbors.... Block captains are actively involved as liaisons, communicating with the Police Department. The result is quite extraordinary. The Police Department has not only responded to the community it has, in effect, *created* a community—citywide—where formerly none existed. Neighbors who were strangers now know each other. A sociologist who wants to consider the "positive functions" of the fear of crime need only look at the Santa Ana team policing experience. Consider that up to 10,000 residents annually participate in a "Menudo cook-off and dance" organized by participants in community-oriented policing programs. This sort of community support is obviously important for social adhesion. It is equally significant for the Police Department. Community support is not simply an abstraction. It is also a grass-roots political base, assuring the department a generous portion of the city budget (of which in 1983 it received 30.7 percent) (pp. 28-29).

The city-wide community the Santa Ana police have created is, of course, not in any meaningful sense of the word a community at all. Nor is it a neighborhood, precinct, district, or any other form of indigenous, area-based entity. It is, rather, a grass-roots political action organization, brought into being, given focus, and sustained by the Santa Ana police.

As such, it is a very new form of political organization and one that our review of the history of circumlocutions in U.S. policing has prepared us to understand. Historically, each of those circumlocutions has served to increase the autonomy and independence of police, making them not only less receptive to demands from indigenous neighborhood action and interest groups, but also less tractable to control by elected political leaders. Progressively, these movements eventually left a void in municipal government. For while they increased the autonomy of police, they robbed them of both their popular and political support.

From the police point of view, the type of organization Skolnick and Bayley describe in Santa Ana as a model for community-oriented policing fills the void perfectly. It does so because it creates a political base for police that is not only independent of other municipal political organizations—indeed it deems itself "apolitical" in the case of the Santa Ana organization—but is totally dependent upon, organized by, and controlled by police themselves.

The Mixed Metaphors of Reduced Crime

Despite the fact that for the past 50 years the police have been promoting themselves as crime fighters, devoting enormous resources to the effort, taking credit for drops in the crime rate and criticism for rises in it, the best evidence to date is that no matter what they do they can make only marginal differences in it. The reason is that all of the major factors influencing how much crime there is or is not are factors over which police have no control whatsoever. Police can do nothing about the age, sex, racial, or ethnic distribution of the population. They cannot control economic conditions; poverty, inequality; occupational opportunity; moral, religious, family, or secular education; or dramatic social, cultural, or political change. These are the "big ticket" items in determining the amount and distribution of crime. Compared to them what police do or do not do matters very little.

While all of this is true for police, it is equally true of the kind of political entities the community policing movement calls communities. This reality is not lost on Skolnick and Bayley. Unlike some authors in the community policing movement (Kelling, 1985; Wilson and Kelling, 1982; and Sykes, 1986) and some community action groups, Skolnick and Bayley have chosen poses with respect to the prospect of controlling crime that leave the community policing movement some important outs and may even have diversified sufficiently to withstand the depression that is inevitable when it is realized that they have failed once again.

The Skolnick and Bayley construction of the relationship of community-oriented policing to crime control appears to consist of three images. The first is the image of the police and the people working side by side as coproducers of crime prevention. Describing community-oriented policing as the "new professionalism," Skolnick and Bayley (pp. 212-213) write: "The new professionalism implies that the police serve, learn from, and are accountable to the community. Behind the new professionalism is a governing notion: that the police and the public are co-producers of crime prevention." If ordinary citizens are actually to become crime prevention coproducers, reciprocity is a necessity. Communities cannot be mobilized for crime prevention from the top down. Members of the community have to become motivated to work with and alongside professional law enforcement agents.

Prevention. Historically, the most significant semantic shift in the relationship between police and crime is the shift from promises to reduce it to promises to prevent it. The difference is important because, practically speaking, failures of crime reduction are measurable while failures of crime prevention are not. It is possible, though difficult, to test promises of crime reduction by determining whether there is more or less crime today than last year or the year before. By contrast, the success of crime prevention can only be evaluated against a prediction of what would have happened had the crime prevention effort not been made. Given that such predictions are presently impossible and that prevention efforts of any kind are able to produce at least some anecdotal evidence of occasional successes, the promise of successful prevention is virtually irrefutable. Skolnick and Bayley (p. 48) write of Santa Ana:

Measures of police department effectiveness continue to baffle those inside departments as well as those who try to write about them. One measure is the crime rate. Santa Ana Police Department statistics show crime rising less than had been projected between 1970 and 1982. It is possible, however, that the overall rise in reported crime rates is attributable to citizen willingness to report having been victimized. Another [sic!] indicator of Santa Ana success is the willingness of banks to provide loans on residents where they would not have been so willing a decade earlier.

Skolnick and Bayley do not report how the 12-year predicted rise in crime rates was arrived at, what the actual rise in crime rates was, nor how they arrived at measures of the "not so" willingness of banks to provide loans a decade ago, or of their alleged willingness to do so today.

Coproduction. Even though prevention efforts will invariably be judged successful, a second rhetorical line of defense should prevention somehow be found to be slightly less successful than was hoped is provided by the contention that it is the product of the police and community coproduction. As this coproduction cannot be imposed from the top down, shortcomings in preventive efforts will be attributable to a lack of genuine community support. Although police may then step up their community organizing efforts, the blame for shortcomings will fall on the community.

The Virtue of Crime. Skolnick and Bayley lay atop the notions of prevention and coproduction a third theme to guard against the possibility that community-oriented policing might be judged a failure against some crime control standard. Even though controlling crime is the manifest justification for coproductive prevention efforts, Skolnick and Bayley suggest a line of argument that, if taken seriously, leads to the conclusion that even if such efforts failed completely, coproductive prevention efforts would in and of themselves be sufficient evidence of community-oriented policing's success (1986:214):

> We have spoken freely about "neighborhoods" and "communities." In actuality, these forms of social organization—implying face-to-face interaction and a sense of communal identity may be weak . . . [T]he police may find they have to activate neighborhood and community associations. In our often anomic urban society, the transcendent identity of many city dwellers is that of crime victim. Their neighbors may be the very people they fear. In such circumstances, police departments can facilitate, even create, a sense of community where one did not previously exist or was faintly imprinted. . . .
>
> Could it be that crime, like war and other disasters, might turn out to be America's best antidote to anomie in the United States?

It is with this third theme that Skolnick and Bayley's circumlocution of the idea of community-oriented policing comes full circle. Community-oriented policing is brought into being with the expectation that it will reduce crime. Political action groups are organized by police under that assumption. The assumption itself is converted into an untestable and irrefutable promise of prevention, coupled with an escape clause under which failure to achieve prevention becomes the fault of the "community." Finally, in the face of their failure to reduce crime, the organizations police created for the manifest purpose of reducing it become ends in themselves—success as antidotes to the problems of urban anomie. Indeed, such success would appear to be much like the success of war and other disasters.

Areal Decentralization of Command

After police-community reciprocity, understood as we have outlined it above, the second theme Skolnick and Bayley identify as crucial to community-oriented policing is "areal decentralization of command." It refers to the creation of ministations, substations, storefront stations, and the multiplication of precincts, each of which is given considerable autonomy in deciding how to police the area in which it is located. "The purpose behind all of them," explain Skolnick and Bayley (p. 214) "is to create the possibility of more intensive police-community interaction and heightened identification by police officers with particular areas."

As a symbolic gesture of police focus on a particular area, the ministation concept has considerable surface appeal. But as Skolnick and Bayley themselves admit, such decentralization does not automatically lead to the kind of community-oriented policing they advocate. They merely create conditions under which police assigned to these substations might engage in that type of behavior if they were motivated to do so. For example, Detroit had over 100 ministations before 1980, which were considered a joke by local residents, an administrative nightmare by police administrators, and a rubber-gun assignment by police officers.

The Skolnick and Bayley position on ministations, which is that unless they are genuinely committed to and motivated to do neighborhood organization, they will not promote community-oriented policing, conceals an administrative paradox. The paradox is that the more latitude and autonomy one gives to ministations to decide what is best for their local area, the less capacity one has to insure that those decisions are made in the genuine interest of that local area. Under such conditions, one simply has to trust that ministation crews embrace the community-oriented policing philosophy to a degree that will prevent them from perverting their autonomy for their own ends.

Perhaps the greatest danger in a police administrative structure in which command is radically decentralized to hundreds of ministations is corruption. Skolnick and Bayley (p. 215) are well aware of this problem and in acknowledgment of it they write:

[T]here is a significant potential problem with the delegation of command to relatively small areas. Where a department has an unfortunate history of corruption, decentralization could prove to be a disaster, creating the exact conditions that facilitate further corruption. Where corruption prevails, however, it is unlikely that one would find much genuine interest in the sort of community crime prevention philosophy we have described here.

Their words are not, to say the least, very assuring. Their argument is that only a department with an "unfortunate history" of corruption would be subject to the danger of corruption in their ministations. The fact is that such decentralization of command invites new corruption to develop as surely as it invites old corruption to spread. Their further argument that departments in which corruption prevails would not have much "genuine" interest in developing an operating philosophy that creates the "exact conditions that facilitate further corruption" is even less comforting.

Reorientation of Patrol

The third rhetorical pillar in Skolnick and Bayley's construction of the idea of community policing is what they term the "reorientation of patrol." Practically speaking, the term means two things: increased use of foot patrol, and a reduction in police response to telephone calls for emergency service.

Skolnick and Bayley offer four claims in favor of foot patrol, all of which they report are supported by their observations and other studies. According to Skolnick and Bayley, foot patrol: (1) prevents crime, (2) makes possible "order maintenance" in ways motor patrol does not, (3) generates neighborhood goodwill, and (4) raises officer morale.

While it is not possible to refute Skolnick and Bayley's observational claims for these meritorious effects of foot patrol—except perhaps to say that they were made by observers who were categorically convinced of its virtues before they began their observations—at least some of those observations run directly counter to systematic, empirical evaluations of the effects of foot patrol. It is generally conceded that foot patrol can have some effect in reducing citizen fear of crime and in affecting positively citizen evaluations of the delivery of police service. It is also accepted that in certain very high-density urban areas foot patrol officers can engage in certain types of order maintenance policing that motor patrol officers cannot easily do. However, there is no evidence whatsoever that foot patrol can reduce or prevent crime (Police Foundation, 1981).

Moreover, it is of utmost importance to add to these observations on the effects of foot patrol that all of them are the product not of foot patrol alone, but of foot patrols added to areas already patrolled at normal levels by motor patrol. This fact is especially bothersome in light of the second theme in Skolnick and Bayley's idea of "reorientation of patrol." In *The New Blue Line* (pp. 216-217), they write:

> Police departments are also trying in various ways, though they don't like to admit it, to unplug the 911 emergency dispatch system selectively for patrol officers. By doing so, they free themselves for community development and crime prevention activities of their own devising. In many cities, the 911 system with its promise of emergency response has become a tyrannical burden.... The pressure of 911 calls has become so great that few officers are available for proactive community development. Moreover, patrol personnel can exhaust themselves speeding from one call to another, using up the time needed for understanding the human situations into which they are injected.
>
> ... So, cautiously, [community-oriented police departments] are experimenting with measures that have the effect of reducing 911 pressure. Some departments are directing officers to park patrol cars periodically and patrol on foot; ... others encourage patrol officers to take themselves 'out of service' and simply stop and talk to people; and still others help them to prepare individualized plans for meeting local crime problems, even if it means not responding to calls or going under cover.

We are obliged to point out that not one of the measures Skolnick and Bayley identified above has, as they claim, "the effect of reducing 911 pressure." The pressure remains constant. Only the level of police response to it changes when patrol officers take themselves out of service or otherwise make themselves unavailable to respond.

Civilianization

The fourth and final rhetorical dimension Skolnick and Bayley fashion into the circumlocution of community policing is "civilianization"—the employment of nonsworn employees to do jobs that were formerly done by police officers. "Where civilianization does not prevail—and it does not in most police departments—it is difficult to offer much more than lip service to crime prevention" (p. 219).

Of all the arguments in *The New Blue Line,* the argument linking civilianization to community policing may be the most puzzling. There is, of course, a simple, powerful, and straightforward argument in favor of civilianization. It is that it can be significantly cheaper to have civilian employees do certain types of tasks than to have full-fledged, sworn officers do them. This argument is well accepted in police agencies in the United States, virtually all of which are concerned with findings ways to save money. In fact, it is probably difficult to find a U.S. police department that has not already civilianized at least a portion of its traffic control, motor pool, maintenance, clerical, and communication functions. At present, about 20 percent of the employees of the typical U.S. police agency are civilians. Moreover, it is quite likely that as the costs of police officers' salaries and benefits increase, police agencies will continue to civilianize certain routine tasks and duties that are unlikely to require the use of coercive force.

It is obvious that this economic argument in favor of civilianization is totally salient on the question of community-oriented policing. Its only premise is that police agencies have some interest in saving money and its only promise is that through civilianization they may do so. However, while Skolnick and Bayley accept this economic argument, they find that civilianization leads almost directly to the creation of successful community organization and crime prevention programs. "[O]ur investigations have persuaded us," say Skolnick and Bayley, "that the more a department is civilianized, the greater the likelihood that it will successfully introduce and carry out programs and policies directed toward crime prevention (p. 219)."

Skolnick and Bayley attempt to link the economic argument for civilianization to successful community crime prevention via two different but parallel arguments. The first argument holds that once some portion of their present duties are civilianized, police officers can be made available for crime prevention and community liaison activities. The second argument holds that by civilianizing the community liaison or crime prevention activities in a police officer's role, the officer can be freed to attend to genuine emergency situations.

Both arguments rest upon four highly questionable assumptions. The first assumption is that civilianization will be achieved by adding civilian employees to an agency's payroll rather than replacing sworn employees with civilians. No one is freed for any new forms of work if a department merely replaces retired police officer clerks, evidence technicians, or dispatchers with less costly civilian employees.

The second assumption is that new civilian employees performing tasks formerly assigned to police officers are not hired in lieu of needed additional police officers. If, for example, an agency concludes that it needs ten new police officers in its patrol division, but obtains them by hiring ten civilian employees who, in turn, free ten officers already employed for patrol duty, no one, neither sworn officer nor civilian, is freed for any new form of work.

The third assumption linking the economic argument for civilianization with the conclusion that it leads to community-oriented policing is the belief that any additional funds or personnel resources, police or civilian, gained by civilianization will be devoted to crime prevention and community organization. Needless to say, such additional funds and resources must compete with every other need for funds and resources in a modern police agency and there is no reason to believe that crime prevention will gain or merit first priority.

Fourth and finally, Skolnick and Bayley link civilianization with community-oriented policing with the assumption that civilian employees will be more sensitive, receptive, and responsive to community needs and values than sworn police officers. "If civilians are drawn from within the inner-city communities that are being policed, they are likely to possess special linguistic skills and cultural understandings ... [which can] further contribute to strengthening mobilization efforts to prevent crime" (p. 219). This assumption pales quickly when one begins to examine its credibility in numerous other municipal government agencies. Consider it in light of urban education, transportation, social welfare, public housing, and sanitation, none of which are much appreciated for their sensitivity, receptivity, or responsiveness to the communities they serve, even though all of them are 100 percent civilianized.

WHITHER THE CIRCUMLOCUTION OF COMMUNITY POLICING?

This chapter attempts to point out the errors, in fact, logic, and judgment, that mark the modern movement that goes by the name of community policing. Whatever the merit of the arguments and observations advanced here, they will undoubtedly strike some readers as misdirected and perhaps even mean spirited. Its difficulties, exaggerations, misrepresentations, and shortcomings notwithstanding, some will find it offensive to be critical of a movement that aspires to diminish urban anomie, to prevent crime by enlisting local support for police, and to make police agencies more sensitive to the cultural complexities of the areas they police. This reaction is to be anticipated and its appearance is central to the core argument of the chapter.

The only reason to maintain police in modern society is to make available a group of persons with a virtually unrestricted right to use violent and, when necessary, lethal means to bring certain types of situations under control. That fact is as fundamentally offensive to core values of modern society as it is unchangeable. To reconcile itself to its police, modern society must wrap it in concealments and circumlocutions that sponsor the appearance that the police are either something other than what they are or are principally engaged in doing something else. Historically, the three major reform movements in the history of the U.S. police, their militarization, legalization, and professionalization, were circumlocutions of this type and all sought to accomplish just such concealments. To the extent that these circumlocutions worked, they worked by wrapping police in aspirations and values that are extremely powerful and unquestionably good.

The movement called community policing is precisely this type of concealment and circumlocution. It wraps police in the powerful and unquestionably good images of community, cooperation, and crime prevention. Because it is this type of circumlocution, one cannot take issue with its extremely powerful and unquestionably good aspirations. Who could be against community, cooperation, and crime prevention? To do so would not only be misdirected and mean spirited, it would be perverse.

This chapter is not against any of these aspirations. What it does oppose is the creation of immodest and romantic aspirations that cannot, in fact, be realized in anything but ersatz terms. Police can no more create communities or solve the problems of urban anomie than they can be legalized into agents of the courts or depoliticized into pure professionals. There is no more reason to expect that they can prevent crime than to expect that they can fight or win a war against it.

Be that as it may, the circumlocution of community policing, like the circumlocutions of militarization, legalization, and professionalization before, enjoys a peculiar form of rhetorical immunity that it is likely to sustain in the face of even the most damaging criticism. At the International Conference on Community Policing at which an early draft of this chapter was first presented, Chris Murphy of the Office of Canadian Solicitor General captured the sense of this immunity elegantly by observing that criticizing community policing was "like criticizing the tune selection of the singing dog." It is not that the police dog is singing well that is so remarkable, but that he is in fact singing.

What this chapter attempts to show is that it is not at all remarkable that we should find the new song of community policing being sung by or about police. We have heard the songs of militarization, legalization, and professionalization in the past and we will no doubt continue to hear the tunes of community policing in the future. An echo of the songs that preceded it, this tune also is about some very good things we might gladly wish, but which, sadly, cannot be.

BIBLIOGRAPHY

Alderson, J. 1979. *Policing Freedom*. Plymouth: Macdonald and Evans.

Allen, D. N. 1982. "Police Supervision on the Street: An Analysis of Supervisor/Officer Interaction During the Shifts." *Journal of Criminal Justice* 10:91-109.

Allen, D. N. and M. G. Maxfield. 1983. "Judging Police Performance: Views and Behavior of Patrol Officers." In R. R. Bennett (ed.), *Police at Work: Policy Issues and Analysis*. Beverly Hills, Calif.: Sage Publications, pp. 65-86.

Andrews, K. R. 1971. *The Concept of Corporate Strategy*. Homewood, Ill.: Dow-Jones-Irwin.

Angell, J. E. 1971. "Toward an Alternative to the Classic Police Organizational Arrangements: A Democratic Model." *Criminology*, August/November:185-206.

Baldwin, R. and R. Kinsey. 1982. *Police Powers and Politics*. London: Quartet Books.

Barker, T. and D. L. Carter (eds.). 1986. *Police Deviance*. Cincinnati: Anderson.

Bayley, D. H. 1984. "Community Policing." Working paper. Australian Institute of Criminology.

———. 1985. *Patterns of Policing*. New Brunswick, N.J.: Rutgers University Press.

———. 1986. *Community Policing in Australia*. Adelaide: National Police Research Unit.

Beare, M. 1987. "An Analysis of Police Rhetoric: Policing as Ideological Work." Paper delivered at the annual meeting of the American Society of Criminology, Montreal (November).

Bittner, E. 1970. *The Functions of Police in Modern Society*. Washington, D.C.: National Institute of Mental Health.

———. 1983. "Legality and Workmanship: Introduction to Control in the Police Organization." In M. Punch, (ed.), *Control in the Police Organization*. Cambridge, Mass.: The MIT Press, pp. 1-11.

―――. 1986. "Afterword." *Fighting Fear: The Baltimore County C.O.P.E. Project,* by Philip B. Taft, Jr. Washington, D.C.: Police Executive Research Forum.

Blaber, A. 1979. *The Exeter Community Policing Consultative Group.* London: NACRO.

Black, D. J. 1976. *The Behavior of Law.* New York: Academic Press.

―――. 1980. *Manners and Customs of Police.* New York: Academic Press.

Blagg, H., G. Pearson, A. Sampson, D. Smith, and P. Stubbs. Forthcoming. "Interagency Cooperation: Rhetoric and Reality." In T. Hope and M. Shaw (eds.), *Communities and Crime Reduction.* London: HMSO.

Block, R. 1971. "Fear of Crime and Fear of the Police." *Social Problems* 19(1):91-100.

Bohm, R. M. 1984. "The Politics of Law and Order" (Book Review). *Justice Quarterly* 3(1):449-455.

Bordua, D. and A. J. Reiss, Jr. 1987. "Law Enforcement." In P. Lazarsfeld, W. Sewell, and H. Wilensky (eds.), *The Uses of Sociology.* New York: Basic Books, pp. 275-303.

Bowers, W. J. and J. H. Hirsch. 1986. *The Impact of Foot Patrol Staffing on Crime and Disorder in Boston: An Unmet Promise.* Boston: Center for Applied Social Research, Northeastern University.

Bowman, J. 1987. "Two Cops Broke the Code." *Reader* 17(10), November 27.

Boydstun, J. E. and M. E. Sherry. 1975. *San Diego Community Profile: Final Report.* Washington, D.C.: Police Foundation.

Bradley, D., N. Walter, and R. Wilkie. 1986. *Managing the Police.* Brighton: Wheatsheaf.

Braiden, C. 1986. *Bank Robberies and Stolen Bikes.* Programs Branch User Report 1986-04. Ottawa: Ministry of the Solicitor General.

―――. 1987. *Community Policing: Nothing New Under the Sun.* Edmonton: Edmonton Police Department.

Brent, E. E. and R. E. Sykes. 1983. *Policing: A Behavioristic Perspective.* New Brunswick, N.J.: Rutgers University Press.

Bright, J. A. 1969. *The Beat Patrol Experiment.* Police Research and Development Branch, Report 8/69. London: Home Office.

Brown, D. and S. Iles. 1985. *Community Constables: A Study of a Policing Initiative.* Research and Planning Unit Paper 30. London: Home Office.

Brown, L. P. 1983. *The Plan of Action.* Houston Police Department, (April).

―――. 1985. "Police-Community Power Sharing." In W. A. Geller (ed.), *Police Leadership in America: Crisis and Opportunity.* New York: Praeger.

Brown, L. P. and M. A. Wycoff. 1987. "Policing Houston: Reducing Fear and Improving Service." *Crime and Delinquency* 33(1):71-89.

Brown, M. K. 1981. *Working the Street.* New York: Russell Sage Publications.

Burke, K. 1962. *A Grammar of Motives and a Rhetoric of Motives.* Cleveland: World.

Carte, G. E. and E. H. Carte. 1975. *Police Reform in the United States: The Era of August Vollmer, 1905-1932.* Berkeley: University of California Press.

Chandler, A. 1962. *Strategy and Structure.* Cambridge, Mass.: The MIT Press.

Clarke, R. V. G. and P. Mayhew. 1980. *Designing Out Crime.* London: HMSO.

Cohen, S. 1985. *Visions of Social Control: Crime, Punishment and Classification.* Cambridge: Policy Press.

Commission to Investigate Allegations of Police Corruption and the City's Anti-Corruption Procedures (The Knapp Commission). 1972. *Commission Report*. New York: By the Commission, December 23.

Compton, J. L. and C. W. Lamb. 1986. *Marketing Government and Social Services*. New York: John Wiley.

Comrie, M. D. and E. J. Kings. 1975. *Study of Urban Workloads*. Police Research Services Unit Report No. 11/75. London: Home Office.

Conklin, J. 1975. *Impacts of Crime*. New York: Collier.

Cook, T. D. and D. T. Campbell. 1979. *Quasi-Experimentation*. Boston: Houghton Mifflin.

Cordner, G. W. 1985. *The Baltimore County Citizen Oriented Police Enforcement (COPE) Project: Final Evaluation*. New York: Florence V. Burden Foundation.

_____. 1986. "Fear of Crime and the Police: An Evaluation of a Fear-Reduction Strategy." *Journal of Police Science and Administration* 14(3):223-233.

Crenson, M. A. 1983. *Neighborhood Politics*. Cambridge, Mass.: Harvard University Press.

DePew, R. 1986. *Native Policing in Canada: A Review of Current Issues*. Programs Branch User Report 1986-46. Ottawa: Ministry of the Solicitor General.

Durkheim, E. 1933. *The Division of Labor*. Trans. by G. Simpson. London: Macmillan.

_____. 1961. *The Elementary Forms of Religious Life*. New York: Collier.

DuBow, F. E., E. McCabe, and G. Kaplan. 1979. *Reactions to Crime: A Critical Review of the Literature*. Washington, D.C.: National Institute of Law Enforcement and Criminal Justice.

Eck, J. E. 1983. *Solving Crimes: The Investigation of Burglary and Robbery*. Washington, D.C.: Police Executive Research Forum, National Institute of Justice.

Eck, J. E. and W. Spelman. 1987a. *Solving Problems: Problem-Oriented Policing in Newport News*. Washington, D.C.: Police Executive Research Forum.

_____. 1987b. "Who Ya Gonna Call? The Police as Problem-Busters." *Crime and Delinquency* 33(1):31-52.

Ekblom, P. and K. Heal. 1982. *The Police Response to Calls from the Public*. Research and Planning Unit Paper 9. London: Home Office.

Ericson, R. V. 1982. *Reproducing Order. A Study of Police Patrol Work*. Toronto: University of Toronto Press.

Ericson, R. V., P. Baranek, and J. Chan. 1987. *Visualizing Deviance*. Toronto: University of Toronto Press.

Ericson, R. V. and C. Shearing. 1986. "The Scientification of Police Work." In G. Bohme and N. Stehr (eds.), *The Knowledge Society*. Dordrecht: D. Reidel, pp. 129-156.

Fogelson, R. M. 1977. *Big-City Police*. Cambridge, Mass.: Harvard University Press.

Fowler, F. J. and T. W. Mangione. 1982. *Neighborhood Crime, Fear and Social Control: A Second Look at the Hartford Program*. Washington, D.C.: U.S. Department of Justice.

_____. 1986. "A Three-Pronged Effect to Reduce Crime and Fear of Crime: The Hartford Experiment." In D. P. Rosenbaum (ed.), *Community Crime Prevention: Does It Work?* Beverly Hills, Calif.: Sage Publications, pp. 87-108.

Gardner, J. R., R. Rachlin, and H. W. Allen. (eds). 1986. *Handbook of Strategic Planning.* New York: John Wiley.

Garofalo, J. 1977. *The Police and Public Opinion.* Washington, D.C.: U.S. Government Printing Office.

―――. 1981. "The Fear of Crime: Causes and Consequences." *The Journal of Criminal Law and Criminology* 72(2):839-857.

Geller, W. A. 1983. "Deadly Force: What We Know." In C. B. Klockars (ed.), *Thinking About Police: Contemporary Readings.* New York: McGraw-Hill, pp. 313-331.

Gladstone, F. J. 1980. *Coordinating Crime Prevention Efforts.* Home Office Research Study 62. London: HMSO.

Gluck, F. W. 1986. "Strategic Management: An Overview." In J. F. Gardner, R. Rachlin, and H. W. A. Sweeney (eds.), *Handbook of Strategic Planning.* New York: John Wiley.

Goffman, E. 1959. *The Presentation of Self in Everyday Life.* Garden City, N.Y.: Doubleday.

Goldstein, H. 1977. *Policing a Free Society.* Cambridge, Mass.: Ballinger.

―――. 1979. "Improving Policing: A Problem-Oriented Approach." *Crime and Delinquency* 25(April):236-258.

―――. 1987. "Toward Community-Oriented Policing: Potential, Basic Requirements and Threshold Questions." *Crime and Delinquency* 33(1):6-30.

Gouldner, A. W. 1954. *Patterns of Industrial Bureaucracy.* Glencoe, Ill.: The Free Press.

Greenberg, S. W. and W. M. Rohe. 1986. "Informal Social Control and Crime Prevention in Modern Urban Neighborhoods." In R. B. Taylor (ed.), *Urban Neighborhoods: Research and Policy.* New York: Praeger, pp. 79-118.

Greene, J. R. 1981. "Changes in the Conception of Police Work: Crime Control Versus Collective Goods." In K. Wright (ed.), *Crime and Criminal Justice in a Declining Economy.* Boston: Oeleschlager, Gunn and Hain, pp. 233-256.

―――. 1985. "Religiosity and Crime Control: A Look at Foot Patrol and Community Based Policing." Paper presented at the Society for the Study of Social Problems, Washington, D.C. (August).

―――. 1987. "Police-Community Relations and Officer Job Satisfaction: An Evaluation." Paper presented to the Academy of Criminal Justice Sciences, St. Louis (March).

Greenwood, P. W., J. M. Chaiken and J. Petersilia. 1977. *The Criminal Investigation Process.* Lexington, Mass.: D.C. Heath.

Gusfield, J. 1981. *The Culture of Public Problems.* Chicago: The University of Chicago Press.

Hagan, J. and J. Leon. 1981. "The Philosophy and Sociology of Crime Control, Canadian American Comparisons." In H. M. Johnson (ed.), *Social System and Legal Process.* San Francisco: Jossey-Bass.

Hall, E. 1966. *The Hidden Dimension.* New York: Doubleday.

Haller, M. H. 1976. "Historical Roots of Police Behavior: Chicago, 1890-1925." *Law and Society Review* 10(2):303-323.

Hayeslip, D. W., Jr. and G. W. Cordner. 1987. "The Effects of Community-Oriented Patrol on Police Officer Attitudes." *American Journal of Police* 4(1):95-119.

Heller, K., R. P. Price, S. Reinharz, S. Riger, and A. Wandersman. 1984. *Psychology and Community Change: Challenges of the Future.* Homewood, Ill.: Dorsey.

Hillery G. 1955. "Definitions of Community: Some Areas of Agreement." *Rural Sociology* 20:111-123.

Home Office. 1965. *Report of the Committee on the Prevention and Detection of Crime.* London: Cornish Committee.

_____. 1967. *Police Manpower, Equipment and Efficiency. Reports of Three Working Parties.* London: HMSO.

Home Office. Crime Prevention Unit. 1985. *Crime Prevention Initiatives in England and Wales.* London: Home Office.

Home Office. Standing Conference on Crime Prevention. 1985. *Report of the Working Group on Revised Guidelines for Crime Prevention Panels.* London: Home Office.

_____. 1986. *Report of the Working Group Guidelines Revised for Crime Prevention Panels. Explanatory Notes and Specimen Constitution.* London: Home Office.

Hope. T. 1985. *Implementing Crime Prevention Measures.* Home Office Research Study 88. London: HMSO.

Hope, T. and D. J. I. Murphy. 1983. "Problems of Implementing Crime Prevention: The Experience of a Demonstration Project." *The Howard Journal* 22:38-50.

Horowitz, R. 1984. *Honor and the American Dream: Culture and Identity in A Chicago Community.* New Brunswick, N.J.: Rutgers University Press.

Houston Police Department. 1987. *General Order 100-6.* Houston Police Department (February).

Hughes, E. C. 1958. *Men and Their Work.* Glencoe, Ill.: The Free Press.

Hunter, A. 1974. *Symbolic Communities.* Chicago: The University of Chicago Press.

_____. 1978. "Symbols of Incivility." Paper presented at the annual meeting of the American Society of Criminology, Dallas (November).

Jacobs, J. 1961. *The Death and Life of the Great American City.* New York: Vintage.

Jermeir, J. and L. Berkes. 1979. "Leader Behavior in a Command Bureaucracy." *ASQ* 24 (March):1-23.

Jones, J. M., K. R. Williams, J. F. Nicholson, J. J. Allinson, and D. B. Jenkins. 1987. *Community-Oriented Policing: A Report by the 24th Senior Command Course.* Bramshill: The Police Staff College.

Jordan, K. E. 1972. *Ideology and the Coming of the Professional: American Urban Policing in the 1920s and 1930s.* Ann Arbor, Mich.: University Microfilms International.

Kelling, G. L. 1978. "Police Patrol Services: The Presumed Effect of a Capacity." *Crime and Delinquency,* April:173-184.

_____. 1981. "Conclusions." In *The New York Foot Patrol Experiment.* Washington, D.C.: Police Foundation.

_____. 1984. "The Reform of Boston's Police." Unpublished manuscript. Cambridge, Mass.: Kennedy School, Harvard University. 1987.

_____. 1985. "Order Maintenance, the Quality of Urban Life, and Police: A Line of Argument." In W. A. Geller (ed.), *Police Leadership in America: Crisis and Opportunity.* New York: Praeger, pp. 296-308.

_____. 1986a. "From Thin Blue Line to Linebacker. The Changing Organizational Strategy of Police." Unpublished. Executive Session on Community Policing, Harvard University (November).

_____. 1986b. "Neighborhood Crime Control and the Police: A View of the American Experience." In K. Heal and G. Laycock (eds.), *Situational Crime Prevention: From Theory into Practice.* London: HMSO.

_____. 1987a. "Acquiring a Taste for Order: The Community and Police." *Crime and Delinquency* 33 (1):90-102.

_____. 1987b. "Juvenile and Police: The End of the Nightstick." in F. X. Hartmann (ed.), *From Children to Citizens,* Vol. 2: *The Role of the Juvenile Court.* New York: Springer-Verlag.

Kelling, G. L., A. Pate, D. Dieckman, and C. E. Brown. 1974. *The Kansas City Preventive Patrol Experiment: A Summary Report.* Washington, D.C.: Police Foundation.

Kinsey, R., J. Lea, and J. Young. 1986. *Losing the Fight Against Crime.* Oxford: Basil Blackwell.

Klockars, C. B. 1985. "Order Maintenance, the Quality of Urban Life, and Police: A Different Line of Argument." In W. A. Geller (ed.), *Police Leadership in America: Crisis and Opportunity.* New York: Praeger, pp. 309-321.

_____. 1986. "Street Justice: Some Micro-Moral Reservations: Comments on Sykes." *Justice Quarterly* 3(4):513-516.

Lavrakas, P. J. 1986. "Evaluating Police-Community Anticrime Newsletters: The Evanston, Houston, and Newark Field Studies." In D. P. Rosenbaum (ed.), *Community Crime Prevention: Does It Work?* Beverly Hills, Calif.: Sage Publications, pp. 269-291.

Lindsay, B. and D. McGillis. 1986. "Citywide Community Crime Prevention: An Assessment of the Seattle Program." In D. P. Rosenbaum (ed.), *Community Crime Prevention: Does It Work?* Beverly Hills, Calif.: Sage Publications, pp. 46-67.

Lipset, S. 1986. "Historical Traditions and National Characteristics: A Comparative Analysis of Canada and the United States." *Canadian Journal of Sociology* 11(2) (June).

Manning, P. K. 1977. *Police Work: The Social Organization of Policing.* Cambridge, Mass.: The MIT Press.

_____. 1980. *The Narcs' Game.* Cambridge, Mass.: The MIT Press.

_____. 1982. "Organizational Work. ... " *British Journal of Sociology,* March:118-139.

_____. 1984. "Community Policing." *American Journal of Police* 3(2):205-227.

_____. Forthcoming. *Symbolic Communications: Signifying Calls and the Police Response.* Cambridge, Mass.: The MIT Press.

Mapp v. Ohio. 1961 81 Sup. Ct. 1684.

Mastrofski, S. D. 1984. "Police Revitalization in its Second Decade, A Reflection on the Direction of Research Based Reform." Paper presented at the annual meeting of the American Society of Criminology (November).

_____. 1987. "The Prospects of Change in Police Patrol Work: A Decade in Review." Paper presented at the annual meeting of the American Society of Criminology, Montreal (November), pp. 11-14.

_____. forthcoming. "Varieties of Police Governance in Metropolitan America." *Journal of Politics and Policy.*

McCoy, C. 1986. "The Cop's World: Modern Policing and the Difficulty of Legitimizing the Use of Force." *Human Rights Quarterly* 8:270-293.

Menke, B. A., M. F. White, and W. L. Carey. 1982. "Police Professionalism: Pursuit of Excellence or Political Power?" In J. R. Greene (ed.), *Managing Police Work*. Beverly Hills, Calif.: Sage Publications, pp. 75-106.

Merelman, R. 1984. *Making Something of Ourselves*. Berkeley: University of California Press.

Miller, W. 1977. *Cops and Bobbies*. Chicago: The University of Chicago Press.

Monkkonen, E. H. 1981. *Police in Urban America, 1860-1920*. New York: Cambridge University Press.

Moore, C. and J. Brown. 1981. *Community Versus Crime*. London: Bedford Square Press.

Moore, M. H. and G. L. Kelling. 1983. "To Serve and Protect: Learning from Police History." *The Public Interest* 70 (Winter):49-65.

Morgan, R. 1987. "The Local Determinants of Policing Policy." In P. Willmont (ed.), *Policing and the Community*. London: Policing Studies Institute.

Morgan, R. and C. Maggs. 1984. *Following Scarman? A Survey of Formal Police/ Community Consultation Arrangements in Provincial Police Authorities in England and Wales*. University of Bath: Bath Social Policy Papers.

_____. 1985. *Setting the PACE: Police/Community Consultative Arrangements in England and Wales*. University of Bath: Bath Social Policy Papers.

Mott, Charles Stewart Foundation. 1987a. *Annual Report*. Flint, Mich.: Charles Stewart Mott Foundation.

_____. 1987b. *Community Policing: Making the Case for Citizen Involvement*. Flint, Mich.: Charles Stewart Mott Foundation.

Muir, W. K., Jr. 1977. *Police: Streetcorner Politicians*. Chicago: The University of Chicago Press.

Murphy, C. 1985. "The Social and Formal Organization of Small Town Policing: A Comparative Analysis of RCMP and Municipal Policing." Ph.D. dissertation, University of Toronto.

Murphy, C. and D. Loree (eds.). 1987. "Community Policing in the 1980's: Conference Proceedings." Canadian Police College and Programs Branch. Ottawa: Ministry of the Solicitor General.

Murphy, C. and G. Muir. 1984. "Community-based Policing. A Review of the Critical Issues." Technical Report TRS No.6, Programs Branch. Ottawa: Ministry of the Solicitor General.

_____. 1985. *Community-Based Policing: A Review of the Critical Issues. Executive Summary*. Ottawa: Office of the Solicitor General Canada.

Murphy, C. and J. de Verteuil. 1986. "Metropolitan Toronto Community Policing Survey." Working Paper No. 1, Ottawa: Office of the Solicitor General of Canada.

Newman, O. 1979. *Community of Interest*. New York: Doubleday.

Oettmeier, T. N. and W. H. Bieck. 1987. *Developing a Policing Style for Neighborhood Oriented Policing: Executive Session #1*. Houston Police Department (February:9).

Ostrom, E., R. Parks, and G. Whitaker. 1973. *Community Organization and Police Services*. Newbury Park, Calif.: Sage Publications.

Pate, A. M. 1986. "Experimenting with Foot Patrol: The Newark Experience." In D. P. Rosenbaum (ed.), *Community Crime Prevention: Does It Work?* Beverly Hills, Calif.: Sage Publications, pp. 137-156.

Pate, A. M., R. A. Bowers, and R. Parks. 1976. *Three Approaches to Criminal Apprehension in Kansas City: An Evaluation Report*. Washington, D.C.: Police Foundation.

Pate, A. M., W. G. Skogan, M. A. Wycoff, and L. W. Sherman. 1985. *Reducing the 'Signs of Crime': The Newark Experience—Executive Summary*. Washington, D.C.: Police Foundation.

———. 1986. *Reducing Fear of Crime in Houston and Newark. A Summary Report*. Washington, D.C.: Police Foundation.

Peters, T. J. and R. H. Waterman, Jr. 1983. *In Search of Excellence: Lessons from America's Best Run Companies*. New York: Warner Books.

Pierce, G., et al. 1987. *The Character of Police Work and Technology: Tactical and Strategic Implications*. Report to the National Institute of Justice. Washington, D.C.: National Institute of Justice.

Police Foundation. 1981. *The Newark Foot Patrol Experiment*. Washington, D.C.: Police Foundation.

———. 1983. *Experiments in Fear Reduction: Houston and Newark Program and Evaluation Plans*. Proposal submitted to the National Institute of Justice. Washington, D.C.

Quah, S. and S. T. Jon. 1987. *Community Policing*. Singapore: Oxford University Press.

Radzinowicz, L. and J. King. 1977. *The Growth of Crime: The International Experience*. New York: Basic Books.

Reiss, A. J., Jr. 1985a. *Policing a City's Central District: The Oakland Story*. Washington, D.C.: National Institute of Justice.

———. 1985b. "Shaping and Serving the Community: The Role of the Police Chief Executive." In W. A. Geller (ed.), *Police Leadership in America: Crisis and Opportunity*. New York: Praeger.

Reith, C. 1938. *The Idea of the Police*. Oxford: Oxford University Press.

Reppetto, T. 1978. *The Blue Parade*. New York: The Free Press.

Rich, R. C. 1986. "Neighborhood-Based Participation in the Planning Process: Promise and Reality." In R. B. Taylor (ed.), *Urban Neighborhoods: Research and Policy*. New York: Praeger, pp. 41-73.

Richardson, J. F. 1974. *Urban Police in the United States*. Port Washington, N.Y.: Kennikat Press.

Rieder, J. 1985. *Canarsie: The Jews and Italians of Brooklyn Against Liberalism*. Cambridge, Mass.: Harvard University Press.

Robinson, W. S. 1950. "Ecological Correlations and the Behavior of Individuals." *American Sociological Review* 15:351-357.

Rosenbaum, D. P. 1987. "The Theory and Research Behind Neighborhood Watch: Is It a Sound Fear- and Crime-Reduction Strategy?" *Crime and Delinquency* 33(1):103-134.

Rosenbaum, D. P., D. A. Lewis and J. A. Grant. 1986. "Neighborhood-Based Crime Prevention: Assessing the Efficacy of Community Organizing in Chicago." In D. P. Rosenbaum (ed.), *Community Crime Prevention: Does It Work?* Beverly Hills, Calif.: Sage Publications, pp. 109-133.

Royal Commission on the Police. 1962. *Final Report*. London: HMSO.

Rubinstein, J. 1973. *City Police*. New York: Farrar, Straus and Giroux.

Scarman, Lord. 1981. *Report of an Inquiry into the Brixton Disorders 10-12 April 1981*. London: HMSO.

Scheingold, S. A. 1984. *The Politics of Law and Order: Street Crime and Public Policy*. New York: Longman.

Schneider, A. L. 1986. "Neighborhood-Based Antiburglary Strategies: An Analysis of Public and Private Benefits from the Portland Program." In D. P. Rosenbaum (ed.), *Community Crime Prevention: Does It Work?* Beverly Hills, Calif.: Sage Publications, pp. 68-86.

Schwartz, A. I. and S. N. Clarren. 1977. *The Cincinnati Team Policing Experiment: A Summary Report*. Washington, D.C.: The Urban Institute and Police Foundation.

Selznick, P. 1952. *The Organizational Weapon*. New York: McGraw-Hill.

Shapland, J. and J. Vagg. 1987. "Policing by the Public and Policing by the Police." In P. Willmont (ed.), *Policing and the Community*. London: Policy Studies Institute.

Shearing, C. (ed.). 1981. *Organizational Police Deviance: Its Structure and Control*. Scarborough: Butterworths.

Sherman, L. W. (ed.). 1974. *Police Corruption: A Sociological Perspective*. New York: Anchor Books.

_____. 1980. "Causes of Police Behavior: The Current State of Quantitative Research." *Journal of Research in Crime and Delinquency* (January):69-100.

_____. 1986a. "Policing Communities: What Really Works? In A. J. Reiss, Jr. and M. Tonry (eds.), *Community and Crime*. Chicago: The University of Chicago Press, pp. 343-386.

_____. 1986b. "Research Strategies and Experimentation in Community Policing." Paper presented at Community Policing in the 1980's Conference, Ottawa (March).

Sherman, L. W., C. H. Milton, and T. V. Kelly. 1973. *Team Policing-Seven Case Studies*. Washington, D.C.: Police Foundation.

Sherman, L. W. et al. 1987. *Repeat Calls to the Police in Minneapolis*. Washington, D.C.: Crime Control Institute (February).

Short, C. 1983. "Community Policing—Beyond Slogans." In T. Bennett (ed.), *The Future of Policing*. Cambridge: Institute of Criminology.

Skogan, W. G. 1986. "Fear of Crime and Neighborhood Change." In A. J. Reiss, Jr. and M. Tonry (eds.), *Communities and Crime*. Chicago: The University of Chicago Press, p. 203-230.

_____. 1987. "The Impact of Victimization on Fear." *Crime and Delinquency* 33(1):135-154.

Skogan, W. G. and M. Maxfield. 1981. *Coping with Crime*. Beverly Hills, Calif.: Sage Publications.

Skogan, W. and A. M. Pate. 1987. "Reducing the Signs of Crime: Two Experiments in Controlling Public Disorder." Paper presented at the annual meeting of the American Political Science Association, Chicago.

Skogan, W. and M. A. Wycoff. 1986. "Storefront Police Officers: The Houston Field Test." In D. P. Rosenbaum (ed.), *Community Crime Prevention: Does It Work?* Beverly Hills, Calif.: Sage Publications, pp. 179-199.

Skolnick, J. H. 1966. *Justice Without Trial: Law Enforcement in a Democratic Society*. New York: John Wiley.

Skolnick, J. H. and D. H. Bayley. 1986. *The New Blue Line: Police Innovation in Six American Cities*. New York: The Free Press.

_____. 1987. "Theme and Variation in Community Policing." *Crime and Justice.* Washington, D.C.: National Institute of Justice.

Slovak, J. 1987. "Police Organization and Policing Environment: Case Study of a Disjuncture." *Sociological Focus* 20 (January):77-94.

Snelson, J. W. and T. N. Oettmeier. 1987. *Operational Plan for the Westside Command Station.* Houston Police Department (February):5-6.

Snow, C. C. and R. E. Miles. 1978. *Organizational Strategy, Structure and Process.* New York: McGraw-Hill.

Spelman, W. and D. K. Brown. 1981. *Calling the Police.* Washington, D.C.: Police Foundation.

Spelman, W. and J. E. Eck. 1987. *Problem-Oriented Policing.* Washington, D.C.: National Institute of Justice.

Statistics Canada. 1986. *Policing in Canada, Canadian Centre for Justice Statistics.* Ottawa: Ministry of Supply and Services.

Stead, J. (ed.) 1977. *Pioneers of Policing.* Montclair, N.J.: Patterson Smith.

Stenning, P. C. 1981. "The Role of Police Boards and Commissions as Institutions of Municipal Government in Organizational Police Deviance." In C. Shearing (ed.), *Organizational Police Deviance, Its Structure and Control.* Scarborough: Butterworths.

Stenning, P. C. and C. D. Shearing. 1979. *Modern Private Security—Its Principal Characteristics and Role: Some General Legal Implications.* Ottawa: Law Reform Commission of Canada, Ministry of Supply and Services.

Stinchcombe, A. 1964. "Institutions of Privacy. . . . " *AJS* 69 (September):150-160.

Stonich, P. J. 1982. *Implementing Strategy: Making Strategy Happen.* Cambridge, Mass.: Ballinger.

Suttles, G. D. 1968. *The Social Order of the Slum.* Chicago: The University of Chicago Press.

_____. 1972. *The Social Construction of Communities.* Chicago: The University of Chicago Press.

Sykes, G. 1986. "Street Justice: A Moral Defense of Order Maintenance." *Justice Quarterly* 3 (4).

Taft, P. B., Jr. 1986. *Fighting Fear: The Baltimore County C.O.P.E. Project.* Washington, D.C.: Police Executive Research Forum.

Taub, R., G. Taylor, and J. Dunham. 1981. *Path of Neighborhood Change.* Final Report to the National Institute of Justice.

_____. 1984. *Paths of Neighborhood Change.* Chicago: The University of Chicago Press.

Taylor, I. 1983. *Crime, Capitalism and Community.* Toronto: Butterworths.

Taylor, R. B. 1982. "Neighborhood Physical Environment and Stress. In G. W. Evens (ed.), *Environmental Stress.* New York: Cambridge University Press.

Taylor, R. B., S. Gottfredson, and S. Schumaker. 1984a. *Neighborhood Responses to Disorder.* Final report. Center for Metropolitan Planning and Research, Johns Hopkins University, Baltimore.

_____. 1984b. "The Roots of Fear." Paper presented at the annual meeting of the American Society of Criminology, Ohio (November).

Taylor, R. B., S. Schumaker, and S. Gottfredson. 1985. "Neighborhood-level Linkages between Physical Features and Local Sentiments: Deterioration, Fear of Crime, and Confidence. *Journal of Architectural Planning and Research* 2:261-275.

Taylor, R. B. and M. M. Hale. 1986. "Testing Alternative Models of Fear of Crime." *Journal of Criminal Law and Criminology* 77:151-189.

Thompson, J. 1967. *Organizations in Action*. New York: McGraw-Hill.

Thorndike, G. L. 1939. "On the Fallacy of Imputing the Correlations Found for Groups to the Individuals in Smaller Groups Composing Them." *American Journal of Psychology* 52:122-124.

Trojanowicz, R. n.d. *An Evaluation of the Neighborhood Foot Patrol in Flint, Michigan*. East Lansing: Michigan State University.

_____. 1983. "An Evaluation of a Neighborhood Foot Patrol Program." *Journal of Police Science and Administration* 11, 4:410-419.

_____. 1986. "Evaluating a Neighborhood Foot Patrol Program: The Flint, Michigan Project." In Dennis P. Rosenbaum (ed.), *Community Crime Prevention: Does It Work?* Beverly Hills, Calif.: Sage Publications.

_____. 1987. "The Fear of Crime." Unpublished paper. East Lansing: School of Criminal Justice, Michigan State University.

Trojanowicz, R. C. and D. W. Banas. 1985a. *Job Satisfaction: A Comparison of Foot Patrol Versus Motor Patrol Officers*. East Lansing: The National Neighborhood Foot Patrol Center.

_____. 1985b. *Perceptions of Safety: A Comparison of Foot Patrol versus Motor Patrol Officers*. East Lansing: Michigan State University, National Neighborhood Foot Patrol Center.

Trojanowicz, R. and J. Belknap. 1986. *Community Policing: Training Issues*. East Lansing: Michigan State University, National Neighborhood Foot Patrol Center.

Trojanowicz, R., R. Gleason, B. Pollard, and D. Sinclair. 1987. *Community Policing: Community Input Into Police Policymaking*. East Lansing: Michigan State University, National Neighborhood Foot Patrol Center.

Trojanowicz, R., B. Pollard, F. Colgan, and H. Harden. 1986. *Community Policing Programs. A Twenty-year Review*. East Lansing: Michigan State University, National Neighborhood Foot Patrol Center.

Van Maanen, J. 1974. "Working the Street: A Developmental View of Police Behavior." In H. Jacob (ed.), *The Potential for Reform of Criminal Justice*. Beverly Hills, Calif.: Sage Publications, pp. 83-130.

_____. 1983. "The Boss: First-Line Supervision in an American Police Agency." In M. Punch (ed.), *Control in the Police Organization*. Cambridge, Mass.: The MIT Press, pp. 227-250.

Waegel, W. 1981. "Case Routinization in Investigative Police Work." *Social Problems* 28:263-275.

Wagner-Pacifici, R. 1986. *The Moro Morality Play*. Chicago: The University of Chicago Press.

Walker, S. 1977. *A Critical History of Police Reform*. Lexington, Mass.: D. C. Heath.

_____. 1984. "Broken Windows and Fractured History: The Use and Misuse of Police History in Recent Police Patrol Analysis." *Justice Quarterly* 1:75-90.

Walsh, W. F. 1986. "Patrol Officer Arrest Rates: A Study of the Social Organization of Police Work." *Justice Quarterly* 2(3):271-290.

Wasson, D. K. 1977. *Community-based Preventive Policing: A Review*. Ottawa: Solicitor General of Canada.

Weatheritt, M. (ed.). forthcoming. *Police Innovation*. Farnborough: Gower.
_____. 1986. *Innovations in Policing*. Beckenham: Croom Helm.
_____. 1987. "Community Policing Now." In P. Willmott (ed.), *Policing and the Community*. London: Policing Studies Institute.
Weeks v. United States. 1914. 222 U.S. 383.
Weisburd, D., J. McElroy, and P. L. Hardyman. n.d. "Challenges to Supervision in Community Policing: Observations on a Pilot Project." Paper. New Brunswick, N.J.: Rutgers University.
Weitzer, R. 1985. "Policing a Divided Society: Obstacles to Normalization in Northern Ireland." *Social Problems* 33(1):41-55.
Williams, H. and A. M. Pate. 1987. "Returning to First Principles: Reducing the Fear of Crime in Newark." *Crime and Delinquency* 33 (1)(January):53-70.
Willmott, P. (ed.). 1987. *Policing and the Community*. London: Policing Studies Institute.
Wilson, J. Q. 1968. *Varieties of Police Behavior*. Cambridge, Mass.: Harvard University Press.
_____. 1975. *Thinking About Crime,* rev. ed. New York: Vintage Books.
_____. 1986. "Forword." *Reducing Fear of Crime in Houston and Newark. Summary Report.* Washington, D.C.: Police Foundation.
Wilson, J. Q. and G. L. Kelling. 1982. "The Police and Neighborhood Safety: Broken Windows." *Atlantic Monthly* 127 (March):29-38.
Wilson, P. R. 1982. *Black Death, White Hands*. Sydney: George Allen and Unwin.
Wycoff, M. A. 1982. "The Role of Municipal Police." Washington, D.C.: Police Foundation. Mimeographed.
Wycoff, M. A., W. Skogan, A. Pate, and L. W. Sherman. 1985. *Citizen Contact Patrol: Executive Summary*. Washington, D.C.: Police Foundation.
Wycoff, M. A. and W. G. Skogan. 1985a. *Citizen Contact Patrol: The Houston Field Test. Technical Report*. Washington, D.C.: Police Foundation.
_____. 1985b. *Police Community Stations: The Houston Field Test. Technical Report*. Washington, D.C.: Police Foundation.
Yin, R. K. 1986. "Community Crime Prevention: A Synthesis of Eleven Evaluations." In D. P. Rosenbaum (ed.), *Community Crime Prevention: Does It Work?* Beverly Hills, Calif.: Sage Publications, pp. 294-308.

INDEX

ABOUT THE EDITORS AND CONTRIBUTORS

JACK R. GREENE is an Associate Professor of Criminal Justice at Temple University. He has served on the faculties of Michigan State University and the University of Wisconsin at Milwaukee. He received his Ph.D. in Social Science, specializing in organizational and public policy analysis and has written widely on police organizational issues, including the implementation of police programs, personnel administration and human resource management, police role enactment, and strategic and tactical decision making. He edited *Managing Police Work* (1982) and has conducted numerous evaluation studies. Most recently he has served as a consultant to the Philadelphia Police Department in its efforts to implement a city-wide community police program and in the improvement of police training.

STEPHEN D. MASTROFSKI is Assistant Professor of Administration of Justice at Pennsylvania State University. He has written on police behavior, agency performance, and contemporary reform efforts. His publications include *Basic Issues in Police Performance* (1982, coauthored), articles and book chapters evaluating neighborhood policing strategies, police agency accreditation, and the role of elected officials in governing police. He holds a Ph.D. in political science.

DAVID H. BAYLEY, a Professor in the School of Criminal Justice at SUNY Albany, is internationally known for his comparative research in law enforcement. Dr. Bayley has written several books, including *Minorities and the Police* (1969), *The Police and Political Development in India* (1969), *Forces of Order: Police Behavior in Japan and the United States* (1976), and *Patterns in Policing* (1985). Two recent books, *The New Blue Line* (1986) and *Community Policing in Australia: An Assessment* (1986), examine the large-scale changes in community policing in several U.S. cities and in Australia. Dr. Bayley has also conducted numerous research projects on the effectiveness of police practices, and is a regular consultant to several U.S. and international police organizations.

LEE P. BROWN is Chief of Police, Houston, Texas. Formerly the Director of Public Safety in Atlanta, Georgia, and in Multnomah County, Oregon, he has been a long-standing advocate of innovative management in police organizations, and is widely recognized as a leader in improving police and community relations. He holds an M.S. in sociology and a master's and a doctorate in criminology. He has written widely on matters of police administration and on improving police and community interaction, including, as coauthor *The Police and Society: An Environment for Collaboration and Confrontation* (1981).

GARY W. CORDNER is an Associate Professor in the Department of Police Studies at Eastern Kentucky University. Prior to joining the Eastern Kentucky faculty, he spent three years as the Chief of Police in St. Michaels, Maryland. He has also served on the faculties of Washington State University and the University of Baltimore. Dr. Cordner has conducted evaluation research on a number of police interventions, including the Baltimore County Citizen Oriented Police Enforcement Project, the Baltimore County Repeat Offender Experiment, and the Pontiac, Michigan Integrated Criminal Apprehension Project. He has coauthored two textbooks, *Planning in Criminal Justice Organizations and Systems* (1983) and *Introduction to Police Administration* (1988, 2nd ed.), and is currently the editor of the *American Journal of Police.*

MICHAEL J. FARRELL is an Associate Director of the Vera Institute of Justice, in charge of Police Planning operations. He is the principal architect of the New York City Police Department's Community Patrol Officer Program and continues to provide technical assistance to the NYPD during its expansion. He is a former Inspector in the NYPD, where he headed the Criminal Justice Bureau. He has worked with the Vera Institute for more than 20 years and has played a major role in the design, implementation, and evaluation of criminal justice action programs. Mr. Farrell holds an M.A. and is currently pursuing a Ph.D. in criminal justice.

GEORGE L. KELLING is Professor of Criminal Justice at Northeastern University and Research Associate at the Kennedy School of Government, Harvard University. Professor Kelling is widely known among criminal justice scholars as the principal investigator and coauthor of *The Kansas City Preventive Patrol Experiment* (1974). He is also coauthor (with James Q. Wilson) of the provocative and widely cited *Atlantic Monthly* article, "The Police and Neighborhood Safety: Broken Windows" (1982). He has authored numerous articles, book chapters, and monographs on policing and law enforcement policy in *The Public Interest, Crime and Delinquency,* and *Police Leadership in America: Crisis and Opportunity* (1986). He is also coauthor (with Mary Ann Wycoff) of *The Dallas Experience: Human Resource Development* (1978).

CARL B. KLOCKARS is Professor of Criminal Justice at the University of Delaware. His research and writing have focused on professional crime, policing, values, and ethics in law enforcement, criminal investigations, criminological theory, and research ethics. His books include *The Professional Fence* (1974), *Deviance and Decency: The Ethics of Research with Human Subjects* (1979, coedited), *Thinking About Police: Contemporary Readings* (1983), and *The Idea of Police* (1985). He received B.A., M.A., and Ph.D. in sociology.

PETER K. MANNING is Professor of Sociology and Psychiatry at Michigan State University. Professor Manning holds a Ph.D. in Sociology and is an internationally recognized scholar on policing matters. Dr. Manning has authored numerous books, book chapters, and journal articles on law enforcement issues, including *Police Work: The Social Organization of Policing* (1977), *Policing: A View from the Street* (1978, coedited with John Van Maanen), and *Narc's Game: Organizational and Informational Constraints on Drug Enforcement* (1979). Dr. Manning's research on the police has also appeared in *Sociology and Social Research, Contemporary Sociology, American Behavioral Scientist,* and *The Annals of the American Academy of Political and Social Sciences.* Dr. Manning has also conducted several cross-cultural studies of the police in Britain and the United States.

JEROME E. McELROY is Associate Director of the Vera Institute of Justice in New York City, with management responsibility for the Institute's research department. He is currently directing Vera's expanded study of New York City's Community Patrol Officer Program. Since coming to Vera several years ago, he has directed research projects concerned with such subjects as police civilian complaint review procedures; the effects upon dispositional outcomes of a case preparation process used by detectives in preparing felony arrests for presentation to the prosecutor; the relationships between employment status and experience and criminal behavior patterns among various high-risk populations; and the comparative effects of alternative detoxificaition treatments for public inebriates.

MARK H. MOORE is the Guggenheim Professor of Criminal Justice Policy and Management at Harvard University's John F. Kennedy School of Government, where he also chairs the Executive Training Programs, which are conducted in conjunction with the Police Executive Research Forum, and are designed for senior-level managers in police organizations. He has written widely on public-sector organizations and law enforcement policy development, and has conducted several management studies of major police agencies.

CHRIS MURPHY has a Ph.D. in sociology. He is currently a Senior Researcher in the Ministry of the Solicitor General, Federal Government of Canada, where he is responsible for managing research and development on community-based policing programs. He has written a number of reports and articles on policing issues in Canada and is coauthor of a major study on community policing, "Community Based Policing: A Review of the Critical Issues." He is also teaching courses on police and society at Carleton University, the University of Ottawa, and the Canadian Police College.

TIMOTHY N. OETTMEIER is a Lieutenant in the Houston Police Department. He has been directly involved in the implementation of the Houston Executive Sessions program, a project designed to improve the planning and analytic capabilities of the organization. He has also authored several reports on implementing community policing programs in Houston.

RALPH B. TAYLOR holds a Ph.D. in social psychology. By training a social psychologist, by temperament an environmental psychologist, and by practice a criminologist and urban researcher, Dr. Taylor has held positions at Virginia Tech (Psychology) and Johns Hopkins (Psychology, Center for Metropolitan Planning and Research). He is currently Associate Professor of Criminal Justice at Temple University. His books include *Urban Neighborhoods, Human Territorial Functioning,* and *The Baltimore Fact Book: 1970 & 1980.*

MOLLIE WEATHERITT is Deputy Director of the British Police Foundation, where she has worked since 1981. She has worked for the Home Office where she undertook studies on aspects of criminal justice, including bail, sentencing, and parole. Between 1978 and 1981 she directed the research program of the Royal Commission on Criminal Procedure. Ms. Weatheritt has written and spoken widely on community policing. Her review of community policing practice in England and Wales was published in 1986.

DAVID WEISBURD is Assistant Professor in the School of Criminal Justice at Rutgers University. He is also a Senior Research Associate at the Vera Institute of Justice. He has conducted research on vigilantism and antigovernment violence in Israel, and currently he is coprincipal investigator for two studies—"Policing the Hot Spots of Crime," and "The Effects of Sanctions on Recidivism"—both supported by the National Institute of Justice. Recent publications include *Deviance on Social Reaction: A Study of Jewish Settler Violence in the Land of Israel,* "Vigilantism as Community Social Control" (*The Journal of Quantitative Criminology*), and "White Collar Crime and Criminals" (with colleagues, *The American Criminal Law Review*).

MARY ANN WYCOFF joined the Police Foundation in 1972 and has since directed research on organizational change, the crime effectiveness of police, the police role, police supervision, police reduction of community fear, and the implementation of community-based policing. She is completing her Ph.D. dissertation in sociology. Her areas of interest include socialization, supervision, organizational change, service delivery, and the measurement of attitudes and performance.